A Western Horseman Book

ARABIAN LEGENDS

Outstanding Arabian Stallions and Mares

By Marian K. Carpenter

Edited by Pat Close

D1119578

ARABIAN LEGENDS

Published by
Western Horseman magazine

3850 North Nevada Ave.
Box 7980
Colorado Springs, CO 80933-7980

www.westernhorseman.com

Design, Typography, and Production
Western Horseman
Colorado Springs, Colorado

Cover painting by
Dwayne Brech

Printing
Publisher's Printing, Inc.
Salt Lake City, Utah

©1999 by Western Horseman
a registered trademark of
Morris Communications Corporation
725 Broadway
Augusta, GA 30901
All rights reserved
Manufactured in the United States of America

Fourth Printing: August 2002

ISBN 0-911647-48-1

DEDICATION

To those who planted the seeds:
my grandfather, Carlyle Willette; his daughter, my Aunt Christine;
my Uncle Bill and Aunt Virginia Orthel; and my husband,
Gary Carpenter, who understands.
Thank you all.

ACKNOWLEDGEMENTS

This book would not have been possible without the
hard work of all those writers, editors, photographers, and Arabian horse
lovers who have come before, and those who work hard today,
just because they love these horses. In particular:

Arlene Magid, copy editor and researcher extraordinaire,
Mary Jane Parkinson, writer, researcher, and sounding board,
Linda White, writer, cheerleader, and pal, and
Leslie Goncharoff, my best friend.

I also am deeply grateful to the many people who
agreed to be interviewed and who shared their stories and
materials for this book. Your generosity is inspiring.

MARIAN KAYE STUDER CARPENTER

INTRODUCTION

LEGEND TELLS of the Prophet Mohammed and his decision to test the obedience and courage of his Arabian mares. One hundred of the finest were penned, without water, for several days.

Freed at last, they galloped toward a nearby stream. Just as they were about to reach it, Mohammed raised the war bugle to his lips and blew the call to battle.

Only five mares stopped. Wheeling about, they ran to their master. Mohammed chose those five to mother the breed.

One may or may not believe the old story of the Al Khamsa ("The Five") mares, yet the tale bears dramatic witness to the Arabian horse's powerful bond with man. So valuable and beloved were these creatures, that mares and foals often shared the tents of their nomadic Bedouin owners and their families. Often, they were not for sale at any price.

Arabian horses were first and foremost war horses. Their courage, stamina, speed, and strength could determine whether a battle was won or lost, whether their riders lived or died. Loyalty and bravery

*The mare *Nedjme was the first horse recorded in the Arabian Horse Registry of America Studbook. Foaled in Syria, she is pictured here in 1893 at the Chicago World's Fair.*
Photo courtesy Arabian Horse Trust

were imperative.

In these pages, you will find similar stories of courage, stamina, power, and faith concerning 24 modern-day Arabian horses. This book begins and ends with the two most popular and influential Arabian stallions of the 20th century: *Bask and Khemosabi.

Between them stand 22 others, including two mares, who, either through deed or story (and often both), have significantly influenced the Arabian horse breed in America in some special way. We do not claim to include all those horses who have done so. After all, there are at least as many opinions on Arabian horses as there are Arabian horse lovers.

In addition, only those horses who have lived in North America and were or are registered with the Arabian Horse Registry are included. This leaves out such vitally important horses as Nazeer and Skowronek, as well as many others, who have had a tremendous influence on the breed.

When possible, we have included information on other important horses within the chapters covering their offspring or other relatives. Still, it was pure agony to whittle down our original list of 56 "must do's" to the 24 presented here.

We hope they are a fair representation of the various types within the breed, the various influential foreign bloodline groups, and the various human personalities so entwined in the lives and histories of these horses.

A Brief History

The origin of the Arabian horse is lost in the mists of time. We do know that he probably was first domesticated somewhere in the Middle East and has been recognized as a separate breed, even a sub-species, for at least 3,500 years.

Horses who look exactly like modern-day Arabians appeared etched in stone Egyptian hieroglyphics, pulling the Pharoah's chariots, about 1500 B.C. Ancient writings, including the *Bible* and the *Koran,* are filled with references to beautiful, fleet-footed, courageous animals who most certainly were the ancestors of the Arabian horses we know today.

The "hot-blooded" horses of the East were ideal for the nomadic desert peoples of Northern Africa, and the Arabian peninsula and surrounding areas. The harsh environment allowed only the strongest and most intelligent to survive, and molded the characteristics for which Arabians are still noted.

For example: Their circulatory systems, with arteries and veins lying close to the thin-skinned surface, high-carried tails, and dark skin were defenses against the burning sun and allowed heat to more easily dissipate. Large lungs and a heart hidden beneath well-sprung ribs, with a deep girth, and bones and hooves like steel, gave the Arabian horse incredible endurance and strength over long distances.

It was to the desert-dwelling people that the Prophet Mohammed spoke. Followers of Islam, passionately determined to spread the Prophet's message, rode Arabians as they conquered countries from Spain to China and points in between during the years after 600 A.D.

During the Holy Land Crusades of the Middle Ages, heavily armored Christian knights mounted on large, ponderous European horses were no match for the fierce Muslims on their swift, little Arabians. The knights trudged home defeated, but word spread about the speedy, nimble horses who helped their riders triumph.

Soon, Arabian stallions were imported to Europe and England and crossed with native animals, resulting in impressive individuals, and eventually forming new breeds.

In fact, all Thoroughbred racehorses today descend from three Arabians: the Darley Arabian (who appears in about 90 percent of racehorse pedigrees), the Byerly Turk, and the Godolphin Arabian. In the late 1600s and early 1700s, these three were imported into England and crossed with the heavier stock there, resulting in the fastest horses in the world.

Indeed, it is partially through this Thoroughbred influence that the Arabian horse is today considered to be the "father" of nearly all light breeds: Thoroughbreds, Quarter Horses, Saddlebreds, Standardbreds, Mustangs, Appaloosas, Tennessee Walkers, Morgans, Lipizzans, Hackneys, etc. Even the Percheron draft horse and the Welsh Mountain Pony have some Arabian blood.

During the 1800s, Arabian stud farms were established, especially by royalty, in Poland, Germany, Hungary, and several other European countries. Toward the end of that century, Sir Wilfrid and Lady Anne Blunt founded the world-famous Crabbet Arabian Stud in England with imports from Egypt and other Middle Eastern countries.

Crabbet horses became the seedstock for significant breeding programs in Russia, Poland, South America, Australia, and eventually the United States and Canada. The Blunts' only child, Lady Wentworth, continued their Arabian horse breeding tradition well into the 20th century. (Crabbet Park is now a business facility.)

The first Arabian horse in America to have some impact was a stallion imported in 1725 by Nathan Harrison of Virginia, who bred about 300 foals from various grade mares. These offspring were dispersed throughout the Colonies and were used in various capacities and breeding programs.

George Washington even rode an Arabian during the Revolutionary War, but did not breed them.

In 1853 and 1856, A. Keene Richard brought in desert horses and started a breeding herd. However, the Civil War ended his venture.

A Turkish sultan in 1873 presented to General Ulysses S. Grant two Arabian stallions, Leopard and Linden Tree. Leopard eventually was part of Randolph Huntington's breeding program in New England.

The Registry

The few purebred Arabians in America during the 1800s were recorded along with Thoroughbreds in The Jockey Club stud books. Not until 1908 was there a separate recording entity for them: the Arabian Horse Registry of America. Its first president was Albert Harris, a businessman from Chicago who set up its offices there.

Registered as #1 was the little gray mare *Nedjme. She was bred by Hedje Memmed of Damascus, Syria, and was foaled on December 1, 1887. *Nedjme was imported along with some other "Eastern" horses by the Hamidie Society for an exhibition of Arabian horses at the 1893 Chicago World's Fair. Her stablemate, the stallion Obeyran, was given the number 2.

Other major early Arabian importations were made by Harris, Spencer Borden, W.R. Brown, W.K. Kellogg, Roger Selby, Joseph Draper, J.M. Dickinson, and Henry Babson, and the breed slowly began to grow in the United States. Nevertheless, it took 65 years to hit the 100,000 mark.

To date, the Registry has duly recorded more than half a million purebred Arabian horses in the United States, Canada, and Mexico. Lucky number 500,000 was the bay mare Krystal Lily, by La Khemo (a Khemosabi son) and out of Maarjis Dafadil. She was bred and is owned by Lewis Huffstutter of Bakersfield, California. The Registry

Albert W. Harris, first president of the Arabian Horse Registry of America, on his stallion Khalil.

also handles all ownership transfers.

The Arabian Jockey Club promotes Arabian horse racing and keeps its computerized race records with those of the Registry's. Its offices are located with the Registry's at the Arabian Horse Center in Westminster, Colorado.

Strains & Bloodlines

The Bedouins and other early breeders carefully kept detailed oral pedigrees on their horses. They were acutely aware of specific characteristics carried by some horses and not by others, and the manner in which such things as color and conformation were passed on.

Judith Forbis in her book *The Classic Arabian Horse* lists at least 22 strains of Arabians noted in the desert and elsewhere. From these, five seem to be most dominant, leading many devotees back to the orginal five "Al Khamsa" mares from the famous story, although there may not be any connection.

While this is an infinitely complex area, some mention here of the major strains is helpful. Through widely-varied sources, it becomes apparent that the five major strains (and this is up for discussion) are Kuhaylan, Saklawi, Dahman Shahwan, Hadban Enzahi, and Abeyan. (Keep in mind that the Arabic alphabet does not easily translate into ours, and that all names are spelled phonetically. Therefore, expect to see different spellings throughout Arabian horse literature.) Of these, two are most often mentioned: the Kuhay-lan and the Saklawi.

Arabians with Kuhaylan (Kehailan, Kuhailan, etc.) type are usually described in a masculine manner; that is, they are often bay (but not always), tall and strong with large muscles, a straighter facial profile, and a more upright carriage. The Polish stallion Ofir is an excellent example of this type, and in this book *Bask and *Witez II would be considered good examples.

The Saklawi (Saklawiyah, Saqlawi, Seklavi, etc.) strain is more feminine. Many are gray or chestnut (but again, not always) and are noted for their refined conformation, "dry" faces with large eyes, and unusual courage, "like a lion." Famous names here are Crabbet Stud's Mesaoud, and *Morafic and *Serafix in this book.

Because the Arabian as a breed was not developed here in America, horses were and still are imported. From these importations, horses have been tagged as being "pure Polish" or "straight Egyptian" and so on. Some breeders remain fiercely loyal to particular foreign bloodlines. Indeed, some are more noted for certain attributes than others—such as the strong emphasis the Poles place on racing, which has given their horses an edge in this area.

Those most often referred to include:

- Crabbet or English horses,
- Russian, from the Tersk stud, located in the Caucasus Mountains,
- Polish, mainly from three government-run stud farms,
- Spanish, from private farms,
- Egyptian, in particular those from El Zahraa near Cairo, which is managed by the Egyptian Agricultural Organization.

Breeder associations, such as The Pyramid Society for the Egyptian horses,

Skowronek
Ibrahim — Jaskótka

have grown up to promote these blood-line groups.

The Abbreviations

In the pedigrees for the horses featured in this book, many names are followed by abbreviations, such as GSB and PASB. Those initials refer to the studbooks in which the horses were registered. Here are those initials, and what they stand for:

AAS, Austrian Arabian Studbook
AHSB, Arabian Horse Society of United Kingdom
ASBB, Babolna State Stud (Hungary)
EAO, Egyptian Agricultural Organization
GSB, General Studbook (England)
IOHB, Inchass Original Herd Book (Egypt)
NSB, Netherlands Studbook
PASB, Polish Arabian Studbook
RAS, Royal Egyptian Society
RASB, Russian Arabian Studbook
SAHR, Swedish Arabian Studbook
SBWM, Studbook for Wurttemburg Marbach (Germany)

INTRODUCTION

IAHA

In 1950, the International Arabian Horse Association was founded to promote the Arabian horse and organize horse shows and other exhibitions. Its offices are in Aurora, Colorado.

IAHA also registers Half-Arabian and Anglo-Arabian horses, but leaves the purebreds to the Registry and, for the most part, is strictly considered to be the promotional arm of the industry. (Anglo-Arabians are part Arabian and part Thoroughbred.)

Its first president, from 1950 to 1954, was Earle Hurlbutt, owner of *Witez II. His wife, Frances, was the secretary.

Today, IAHA coordinates and approves Arabian horse shows, events and award programs, with 18 regions across the United States and Canada, each offering an annual regional show. Other major shows sponsored include the Youth National Championships, the U.S. National Championships, Canadian National Championships, U.S. Futurity/Maturity Championships, and national championships in competitive trail and endurance riding. Its largest approved horse show is the Scottsdale Arabian Show, held each February in Arizona, with more than 2,000 entries.

Young people can participate in the International Arabian Horse Youth Association, with programs ranging from judging contests to scholarship opportunities.

Awards

As Arabians are shown, they accumulate points toward IAHA Achievement Awards. Throughout the book, you will see references to a horse being a Legion of Merit winner, for example, and that title is earned through these points. An award-winning horse is ever after allowed to use after his/her name a symbol of the achievement, such as a "+" sign for Legion of Honor, a "++" for Legion of Merit, and so on. (However, these symbols were not used in this book.)

Points must be won in four or more shows or rides and under four or more judges. They may be won in halter, performance classes, dressage, combined training, racing, competitive trail, or endurance rides. The number of points awarded per event varies with the number of horses entered in that particular event.

Legion of Honor Champion - "+" - 75 points

Legion of Supreme Honor Champion - "+/" - 150 points

Legion of Excellence Champion "+//" - 375 points - must also have 2 regional wins or 1 national win

Legion of Merit Champion - "++" - 75 points, of which at least 30 are from halter classes and 30 from performance classes or events, such as endurance

Legion of Supreme Merit Champion - "+++" - 150 points, of which at least 75 are won in halter and 75 in performance classes or events, such as endurance

Legion of Masters Champion - "++++" - 225 points, of which at least 105 are from halter classes and at least 105 from performance classes or events, such as endurance; and at least one win is at the national level, with a total of at least two wins, the other may be at the regional level.

The Trust

Also housed in the Arabian Horse Center in Colorado is the library and museum dedicated to the Arabian horse and managed by the Arabian Horse Trust, a 501(c)3 charitable organization. It has a wealth of artifacts and rare books invaluable to Arabian horse devotees and researchers.

Climate-controlled vaults under the building ensure that these treasures remain safe and available to future generations. It is open to the public.

The Trust is dedicated to preserving the history of the Arabian horse and to education involving the breed. Each year it sponsors a gala art auction and stallion breeding auction to raise money for its many worthwhile programs.

Arabians Today

The Arabian horse in America today enjoys a reputation of both beauty and versatility. He continues to attract horse lovers entranced by his fire and vitality, yet tempered with an intelligence and gentleness difficult to put into words but thrilling to experience.

Just as in the day of the Bedouin, Arabians often become part of the family; indeed, people often remark on the breed's ability to closely relate to humans.

Arabian horses allow us to dream. Their beauty somehow touches our souls and inspires us to reach higher and be better than we ever before could imagine.

Here are the stories of some of the best. Welcome to the magic.

Marian K. Carpenter

THE BREED STANDARD

THE BREED standard, as described for judges by the American Horse Shows Association, lists the following characteristics of a good Arabian horse (summarized):

The head in profile is preferred to be slightly concave below the eyes; small muzzle; large nostrils; large, round, dark eyes; short from eye to muzzle; wide between the eyes; deep jowls; and small, thin ears with tips curved inward, almost to touching

The neck is long and arched, set high on a long, sloping shoulders; high withers; deep chest with well-sprung ribs; short back; strong loins; relatively level croup with high-set-on tail, carried naturally high (Note: the Arabian does not have one less rib or vertebrae, as is sometimes stated)

Legs have short cannons, long forearms, large joints, good muscles, flat bone and sloping pasterns; feet are round and proportionate to size

Average size is 14.1 to 15.1 hands

Skin is always dark; solid colors of bay, chestnut, gray, black, roan; white markings if present are preferred to be on face, lower legs

Also note balance, cadenced gaits, smoothness, agility, stamina

Nature is vital, animated, sensitive, intelligent, kind.

Yet, for all of our modern definitions, this old Arabic poem, written in 1860 by Salim Abdulla Haj for the ruler of Bahrain, perhaps best describes the ideal Arabian horse. It was translated by Judith Forbis and Hasan bin Salah al Ruwa'y. From *The Arabian Horse Through History* by Judith Forbis and Dr. Eugene LaCroix (available from the Arabian Horse Trust):

Know ye there exists a mare
Swift
With highborne silken tail
Broad and level of croup
With rounded hip and short back
The length of thumb and forefinger;
Her stride swallows the distance
Yet her canter becomes a soft cushion.
She stands high over the earth,
Deep of girth and
Lean of flank as the bounding saluki.
Long is her neck which joins a delicate throat.
Sparse is her head and lean her head, and
Lean her ears pricked close together.
Her forelock is a net, her forehead a lamp lighted,
Illumining the tribe
. . . long black lashes
Fringe her great eyes . . .
Her nostrils flare when she gathers the wind to her.
Her chest is power;
The grace and strength of her shoulders
Astonishes the eye.
Allah! like a gazelle
Alert
She leaps from danger's path.
Her round jet-hued hooves
Ravish the earth
Yet the desert takes delight
Wheresoever she treads.
Behold her short pasterns
Span but four fingers;
Indeed Allah has fashioned
Her forelimbs
In His perfect way.
She stands high from earth to hock
to hip
And broad are her buttocks.
Her shapeliness bears testimony to
Allah's enduring blessing . . .
She exemplifies that which is called beautiful.

CONTENTS

1   *BASK

As a sire, he was incomparable.

IN THE MIDDLE of Poland's worst winter in 100 years, on January 25, 1963, 15 purebred Arabian horses were carefully loaded into wooden crates aboard a ship bound for New York City.

Ignacy Jaworowski, who would one day be the director of Poland's famous Michalow Stud Farm, was responsible for the precious cargo. He was anxious to get underway, as weather delays and a dockworkers' strike in America had postponed the departure for weeks.

Jaworowski knew he guarded some of his country's finest Arabians. And he knew their new American owners were just as concerned for their safety as he was. As the freighter churned through the frigid harbor and out into open water, he checked the hay supply. Then he walked among the stalls and mentally tallied his charges: the mares *Gwozdawa, *Gwadiana, and *Wiganda, and the stallions

Bask, a striking bay stallion, was the most influential sire of the 20th century.

Photo by
Johnny Johnston

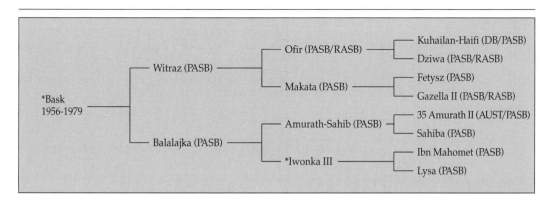

*Bajram, *Naborr, and *Bask among them. Jaworowski smiled. All would soon be safe in their new homes.

The ship's captain decided to pick up more cargo and spent another week stopping at various European ports. Jaworowski prudently purchased a bit more hay in Le Havre, and the vessel finally sailed westward.

All was well for the first few days. Then, with little warning, a terrible storm hit. For 10 days no forward progress was made. The ship tossed violently in mountainous waves. The crew and horses became sick. It was impossible to eat or drink. *Wiganda aborted her foal. *Bask, usually so animated, stood stoically in his crate. As the trip lengthened, hay supplies ran low.

Finally, 44 days after departure, the nightmare was over. The weary band arrived in New York on March 9, 1963.

They were a sorry lot. All had lost weight. *Bajram's skin was raw and the hair gone from his chest where it had for days rubbed against the crate. *Naborr fared somewhat better, but *Wiganda died just 5 days later from stress and foaling complications.

*Bask was a pitiful sight. He had colicked, lost more than 100 pounds, and his body had taken quite a beating. For the rest of his life—whether in national championship spotlights or the most illustrious breeding shed in the world—*Bask would bear witness to that horrible journey with a thin white scar running along one side of his body. The horse who would so transform the Arabian horse industry in America had almost been lost at sea.

*Bask was, quite simply, the most influential and widely recognized Arabian horse of the 20th century. As an individual, he was quite impressive. But as a sire, he was incomparable.

Halter and Performance Record: Legion of Merit (++); 1964 United States National Champion Stallion; 1965 United States National Park Champion.

Progeny Record:

Purebred Foal Crops: 17
Purebred Foals Registered: 1,050
U.S./Canadian National Winners: 196
Class A Champions: 495
IAHA Legion of Honor Award Winners: 41
IAHA Legion of Supreme Honor Award Winners: 21
IAHA Legion of Excellence Award Winners: 1
IAHA Legion of Merit Award Winners: 49
IAHA Legion of Supreme Honor/Merit Award Winners: 4
IAHA Legion of Supreme Merit Award Winners: 7
Race Starters: 5
Race Money Earned: $26,353

*Dr. Eugene LaCroix and *Bask shared a long, close relationship.*

Photo by Jerry Sparagowski

15

*Here's Kathy LaCroix presenting *Bask to the audience at the Lasma III Sale in Scottsdale, February 1977. Note Hollywood producer/ director Mike Nichols in the background. Nichols helped the LaCroixes produce their spectacular sales.*

Photo by
Jerry Sparagowski

His offspring became the models by which most Arabian horses were judged—both in halter and performance competition. The chances are slim, at best, that any other stallion will ever even come close to threatening his solid gold sire records. *Bask, as a sire, reigned supreme.

But even the best seldom make it alone. In *Bask's case, the story was shared by Dr. Eugene LaCroix, D.O., and his family— wife Mary Jean, sons Gene and Raymond, and daughter Kathy. They were responsible for *Bask's importation from Poland, his campaign to national championships, and similar campaigns for many of his offspring. Furthermore, the LaCroixes developed innovative marketing strategies the

likes of which had never before been seen in the Arabian business, and in some cases, in the entire horse industry.

To begin, it is important to understand the climate in America when *Bask appeared. By the early 1960s, the Arabian horse industry in general had reached a point of relative inertia. With the exception of a handful of exotic Egyptian, Spanish, and Polish imports about that time, the majority of purebred Arabian horses in North America were bred and cross-bred from the same seed stock: mainly Crabbet lines, sprinkled with some Davenport and other assorted old desert pedigrees.

Many horsemen looked on Arabians as rare, cute, little, hot-tempered animals best suited as occasional riding horses or as pretty pasture ornaments for eccentric breeders.

Prices had remained about the same for decades, and the demand for Arabian horses was to some extent limited to fellow

16

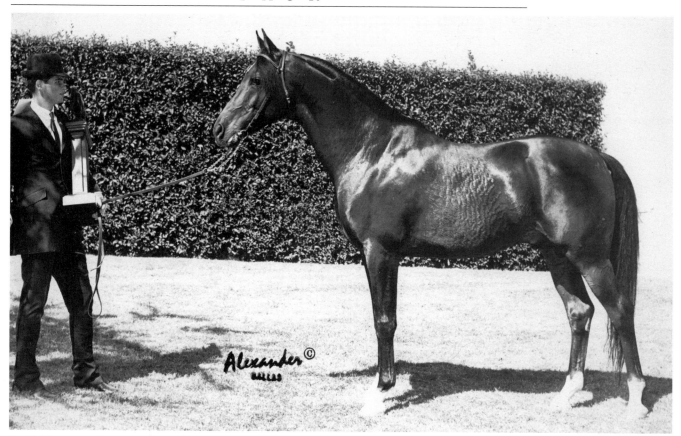

*In 1964, young Gene LaCroix showed *Bask to the U.S. National Stallion Championship. The national championship classes were held that year in Dallas during the Texas Fall Arabian Show.*   Photo by Alexander

breeders and the slow trickle of newcomers. There were a few, such as Bazy Tankersley at Al-Marah Arabians in Maryland, Daniel C. Gainey in Minnesota, Frank McCoy and the Tones in California, and a handful of others, who managed to breed some lovely horses, turn a profit, and successfully promote the breed to others. But that was not the case for the majority.

*Bask was like a catalyst that—when combined with previously inert substances—creates a fiery chemical reaction. Temperatures climb until, seemingly all at once, the mixture explodes with an array of fireworks breathtaking to behold.

Suddenly, or so it seemed, Arabian horses came into their own as beautiful, showy, powerful athletes. As pedigree expert and author Gladys Brown Edwards wrote in 1985 of *Bask's contributions: "The result was real riding-horse conformation with a high-carried elegant neck, a willingness to learn and do, and especially a free and high way of going in classes where action is paramount."

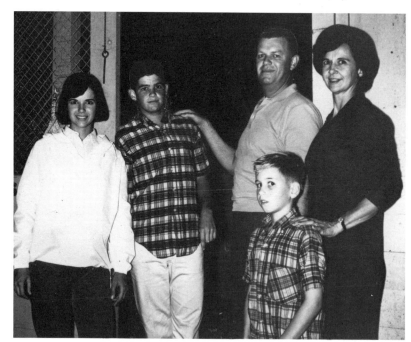

This snapshot of the LaCroix family was taken in 1964 at the Texas Fall Arabian Show. Left to right are Kathy, Gene Jr., Gene Sr., Raymond, and Mary Jean.   Photo by Pat Close

As of this writing, Zodiac Matador is *Bask's top-siring son in terms of national winners, with 37 to his credit. During his show career, this handsome chestnut was three times a national park champion in the United States and Canada. Ray LaCroix is aboard in this photo.

Photo by Jerry Sparagowski

In other words, as writer Lucille Shuler first pointed out, "*Bask horses set new standards by which other Arabians were judged." Registrations and prices rose. By the late 1970s, America was falling head over heels in love with the "new" Arabian horse.

Could another stallion have done the same? Perhaps. Did other stallions and breeders contribute to this phenomenon? Yes, definitely.

Ultimately, however, if only one may claim the title, then The Sire of the 20th Century was *Bask.

Polish Heritage

*Bask was foaled on February 9, 1956, at Albigowa Stud Farm in Poland. Roman Pankiewicz, former director of that farm and highly respected within the Polish Arabian horse breeding community, recalled *Bask's sire, Witraz, and dam, Balalajka, for an article run in the May 1980 issue of *Arabian Horse World:*

"Of all the mares I found on my arrival at Albigowa, I considered Bask's dam, Balalajka, the most valuable," he wrote. "Balalajka was a very well-conformed mare of excellent lines and great beauty, combined with feminine looks and gentleness. . . . however, at that time nothing could foretell her future career."

Balalajka's dam, *Iwonka III, was among those Polish horses taken to the United States after World War II as "spoils of war." She left behind her in Poland only one other foal, Cellist, a 1942 colt by Trypolis who was used mainly to sire Anglo-Arabs in Poland. *Iwonka III does have several lines descending from her in North America, however.

Balalajka's sire, Amurath Sahib, was an outstanding sire of broodmares and is well-represented in the pedigrees of many of today's U.S. and Canadian champions. Wrote Pankiewicz, "He passed on his clean lines, size, beauty, and type. Every daughter used in breeding left a lasting record."

About *Bask's sire, Witraz, Pankiewicz said: "Balalajka produced her best foals with Witraz, who had a difficult temper and often passed it on to his get. He was the most handsome of contemporary sires, but, unfortunately, he wasn't too popular with our breeders due to his character. But great people are also sometimes a little crazy, aren't they? Witraz, *Bask's sire, was by all means a great horse."

Witraz is often compared to another great Polish stallion of his era, Wielki Szlem. Both were Ofir sons, and both shared a common granddam, Gazella II. Witraz was out of the mare Makata (by Fetysz), who produced only the colts Teheran and Witraz before World War II, when most Polish breeding efforts came to a halt.

Wielki Szlem, on the other hand, was out of Elegantka (by Bakszysz), Poland's most esteemed broodmare prior to the war. He was, according to Pankiewicz, "a small,

"... I considered
*Bask's dam,
Balalajka, the
most valuable...."

handsome athlete of very good conformation, general soundness, and substance.

"Witraz was more of a dandy, who, because of his charm and beauty, was forgiven some minor incorrectness of conformation. When you looked at him, you didn't have that impression of substance—that's the way it was.

"Wielki Szlem sired many good and very good horses, whereas Witraz sired a number of less impressive horses but also not a few great ones."

Pankiewicz explained that several Wielki Szlem sons were used to extend the Kuhailan Haifi line, but only two of Witraz's sons, Como and Banio, were used and only in a limited manner. Only later was a third son, Celebes, used more often.

Ariston, by *Bask and out of *Amfibia (a park champion and U.S. Top Ten Mare), was a National Top Ten Stallion in both the United States and Canada. He has sired numerous regional and national winners and is managed by his biggest fan, Denise Borg of Paso Robles, California.

**Photo by
Jerry Sparagowski**

"Having the great Ofir in mind, our breeders put more trust in Wielki Szlem, who was more like his father," wrote Pankiewicz. "At Janow (Podlaski Stud Farm), Czort (by Wielki Szlem) was decided to be sufficient representation of the Ofir line and was kept to do the job. For these reasons, the great *Bask was sold and never used in Polish breeding."

The LaCroixes

Enter the LaCroixes of Lasma Arabians in Scottsdale, Arizona. Dr. Eugene LaCroix is a brilliant man long respected as an exceptional Arabian horse breeder and revered as a pedigree expert.

He was raised with and grew to love horses while still a Kansas farm boy. There he heard stories about rare Arabian horses and hoped to someday see one.

While serving his medical internship in Los Angeles in 1940, he fulfilled that dream when he first saw Arabians at the Kellogg Ranch and at Alice Payne's. He was determined to someday own one, and in 1944 purchased his first. An astute scholar, Dr. LaCroix practically memorized General Dickinson's *Traveler's Rest Catalog of Arabian Horses* and other publications in an effort to

*This gray son of
*Bask, Gdansk, was
a wonderful perfor-
mance show horse
and then a top sire,
with at least 20
national winners to
his credit. He was out
of *Gdynia.*

Photo by
Jerry Sparagowski

learn as much as possible about the breed.

By the late 1950s, Dr. LaCroix and his family owned a nice herd of Crabbet-bred horses, including the fine California-bred stallions Rabab, by Rabiyas and out of Mutrabba; Ga'Zi, by Abu Farwa (see his chapter) and out of Ghazna; and Aarief, by *Raffles and out of Aarah.

Dr. LaCroix and his three children enjoyed showing and, with trainer Jerry Smola, often won their classes. Soon, however, Dr. LaCroix felt the need to find a classic out-cross stallion for his mares.

"It hit me when I saw *Ardahan and *Muzulmanin (two Polish stallions imported by Charles Doner of Elsinore, Calif.,) out in the ring in 1961, winning. It really didn't hit me 'til then—that, after all, the leading sires had come from Poland originally," Dr. LaCroix explained in an interview with Lucille Shuler and Gladys Brown Edwards published in the May 1980 issue of *Arabian Horse World*.

"Ferseyn, *Raseyn, and *Raffles all went back to Skowronek, and Skowronek was bred in Poland. I thought, if you could buy horses in Poland such as I was seeing in the ring—of that extreme quality and elegance, a whole new pattern from what we'd been looking at—by George, I better get over there and find out what they had."

Traveling to Poland in the early 1960s was no easy trip. The Cold War with communism was at its height and the red tape was thick. Not since Gen. Dickinson and Henry Babson purchased some Polish Arabians there in the 1930s had Americans bought Arabians directly from that source. All importations from Poland in the late 1950s and early 1960s were arranged through Englishwoman Patricia Lindsay, based solely on photographs and her descriptions.

*The *Bask son MS Santana, out of the *Sambor daughter SW Saruchna, won the 1986 U.S. National Stallion Championship with handler Ray LaCroix. He had won the same title in Canada in 1983, and both times was the unanimous choice of all three judges. That's Patricia Dempsey on the right, presenting the awards.*

Photo by Rob Hess

Nevertheless, Dr. LaCroix, his teenage son, Gene, and Dr. Howard Kale and his son, Howard Jr., set off to go behind the Iron Curtain. Their first stop was in England where the Kales purchased the wonderful stallion *Silver Drift, who would so influence their breeding program in Washington state.

A few days later, on a beautiful, crisp autumn day in 1962, the men were standing in a pasture near the stallion barn at Janow Podlaski Stud in Poland. The Poles began to parade their best and brightest. *Bask was the fifth horse to appear.

In the book *Lasma In Retrospect,* Dr. LaCroix recalled his first look at the dynamic bay stallion who would change so many lives. "*Bask was the best horse of all. When we saw him, he was just 2 months off the track. He was in racing

shape and felt great . . . couldn't keep his feet on the ground. He jumped 4 feet straight in the air. *Bask jumped that way, and then I jumped that way. I tried to act unconcerned, and I think Gene did, too, but we knew we had found what we were looking for; we had to have him."

Dr. LaCroix later said to writer Mary Jane Parkinson, "I had the feeling of being hit with a ton of bricks or a bolt of lightning. Or both. Gene and I looked at each other, and that was it."

Attempting to remain casual and unconcerned, the LaCroixes offered the Poles options on 20 horses. They placed *Bask eighteenth on the list. An import package was put together that included horses for other American buyers as well. The deal was done and the money was paid. Prices were not negotiated, as Dr. LaCroix felt the listed prices were fair.

When *Bask finally arrived at the LaCroixes' Lasma Arabians in Scottsdale, it took more than 3 months to get the stal-

The *Bask daughter FF Summer Storm (out of Zarahba) was the 1980 U.S. National English Pleasure Champion, ridden by Gene LaCroix.

Photo by Scott Trees

lion back in shape from the effects of his traumatic ocean voyage. Curious friends and breeders came to see the new Polish imports, and Dr. LaCroix recalled one exchange with amusement.

"Leland Mekeel and Wayne Van Vleet and another person came over to inspect the horses for the Registry," he told *Arabian Horse World*. " After they had looked and looked and looked and were just about to leave, I asked Leland what he thought of *Bask. He said, 'Well, you know, Gene, he's different.' I told him I was glad he said that because I knew darn well he was different. Leland is very cautious and quiet and I asked him again, 'Well what do you *really* think?' And he said, 'Gene, I think he's *really* different.'"

Mekeel and his family, as well as Van Vleet, eventually used *Bask in their own breeding programs.

*Bask literally lived in the LaCroixes' backyard, just like a member of the family. Mrs. LaCroix fed him carrots and cooked him hot Polish mashes of vitamins, flaxseed, and oats. Dr. LaCroix fed him sugar cubes daily, calling out, "Basko, are you here?" as he approached his stall.

Often friendly and affectionate, *Bask was usually a gentleman but was never "cute." He has been described as a true "horseman's horse."

For many years, *Bask's greatest friend was the bay Polish stallion *El Mudir (Wielki Szlem x Munira), who was stabled next to him. They never fought, and spent many a lazy afternoon in quiet "conversation," nose to nose, heads hanging out of their stall windows.

Almost everybody rode *Bask at one time or another: Gene, Kathy, Ray and wife Kris, trainers Jerry Smola and Bonnie Lestikow (Bradbury), and even Dr. LaCroix. And *Bask dumped them all too!

Fame was the first *Bask daughter to be named a U.S. National Champion Mare. That was in 1969. Out of Wirdah Jameel, she also won national Top Tens in both the United States and Canada in English and western pleasure. She was a Legion of Merit winner and an excellent broodmare for her owner, Lasma Arabians.

Photo by Johnny Johnston

In 1970, Dancing Flame became the second *Bask daughter to be named a U.S. National Champion Mare. She was also the 1969 Canadian National Champion Mare and the 1969 U.S. National English Pleasure Champion. Out of the Legion of Merit winner Habina, Dancing Flame was also a top broodmare for Lasma Arabians.

Photo by Johnny Johnston

*Bask was smart, talented, and full of himself. With his strong back and beautifully shaped neck, he was wonderfully collected under saddle and moved with power, grace, and animation. At the trot, his four matching white socks moved in perfect cadence, his muscles rippled under a satin coat. *Bask's large, expressive eyes missed nothing, and seemed to drink in the world around him. He was the king, and he knew it.

Show Career

The royal monarch's show ring career was launched in 1964. In February, with 16-year-old Gene leading him, *Bask was named Scottsdale Champion Stallion. Hours later, Jerry Smola rode him to the park championship over 26 entries. He was an instant hit.

The LaCroixes decided not to show him again until the U.S. Nationals in Dallas later in the year. There, with Gene again leading him, *Bask was named U.S. National Champion Stallion. Smola rode him to a Top Ten win in park.

In 1965, the Nationals were in Springfield, Ill., and *Bask dominated 39 competitors to win the park championship.

"*Bask was always a pleasant, agreeable horse to be around; always tried to get along. But get him in the show ring, and he'd get all blown up and ready for everything and anything," recalled trainer Jerry Smola in *Arabian Horse World*. "He had the fire and the brilliance—and a tremendous way of going—that made a real show horse.

"When he got all fired up, like he wanted to in a park class, why, he was a hard horse to ride. He liked to set up and go! When he won the national championship, I had a stirrup hanger break, and the ringmaster said, 'Why don't you just ride him around a time or two without it. The class is almost over.' I couldn't have done it. I had to switch saddles. I would not have tried to ride him around that ring with only one stirrup."

*Bask was now the first Arabian national champion stallion ever to win a national championship under saddle. He also became the first Arabian to achieve his Legion of Merit title in only four shows.

24

*Here is Gene LaCroix riding Ambra, a wonderful performance mare who was by *Bask and out of *Ambara. Ambra was the 1979 Canadian National Park Champion.*

Photo by
Jerry Sparagowski

*Bask was now the first Arabian national champion stallion ever to win a national championship under saddle.

An article soon after in *Arabian Horse World* described his action as being as light and precise as a ballet dancer's. The free, high-stepping, athletic movement he demonstrated at that show became the legacy he passed to his descendants.

In 1966, *Bask was again Scottsdale Park Champion, this time with young Gene aboard. He then was put into harness and at the 1967 national show in Albuquerque was named U.S. Reserve National Champion in both formal driving and formal combination. With that, *Bask was retired in glory to the breeding shed.

His proven reputation as a beautiful athlete with a bright, trainable mind, all of which was consistently passed on, would bring the best mares in the country to his door. As early as 1964, the top breeders in the country were lined up, including Dan Gainey, Dr. Blake Gammell, R.B. Field, and Leland Mekeel. From the earliest foal crops came future significant sires such as Baske-Tu, Gai-Robert, and Tornado, and the lovely mares Basquina, Spring Baskette, Gali-Croix, and Dancing Flame.

From then on, through his final year as a breeding stallion in 1979, nearly everyone in the industry dreamed of or vied for a chance to bring a mare to the court of *Bask. He first stood for $500, which was quite high for the time. By the late 1970s, his stud fee had climbed to $10,000.

Offspring

In all, *Bask sired 1,050 registered Arabians, from which came 196 national winners, 495 Class A champions, and numerous race winners, including National Champion Racehorse Bask-O-Zel.

Furthermore, 292 of his offspring

Baske-Tu, by *Bask and out of Nafta, sired at least 15 national winners.
Photo by Judith

went on to produce or sire national winners themselves.

He sired only one Half-Arabian, Bask's Warlock, who won three national championships by his fourth birthday. He was out of the Saddlebred mare Strega, herself a national champion.

Space does not permit an in-depth study of *Bask's national-winning offspring. Suffice to say that what makes the list so incredible, in addition to sheer numbers, is that virtually every division offered is represented, from halter and driving to park, English and western pleasure, and working western events.

Overall, his greatest influence has proven to be in the halter and English/park divisions. It can safely be said that, on average since 1980, at least 30 percent of the national halter winners and more than 50 percent of the national English division winners are direct descendants of *Bask. His influence is amazingly strong into the second, third, and even fourth generations.

A partial list of some of the better-known *Bask offspring who were U.S. or Canadian national champions or reserve champions (and only some of their wins!) is included here by division. Many won in more than one division, such as in halter and park.

Park: Mieczych, Ambra, Promotion, Red Tape, Reign On, The Judge, Zodiac Matador, Pro-Fire, EW Natal, First Class, Scarlett Lace, Hallelujah Bask, Cognac, Ibn Prowizja.

English pleasure: Basquina, Basquelle, La Basque, LeBask, TC Expression, FF Summer Storm, Taask, Lite My Fire, Anitaa, Fyre Water, Cease Fire, Sprint, Mark IV Coronation, Raya Royale, Dark Eyes, Genuine, MHR Sterling, Bask De Espana, Hask, Fire Devil, Taask, Basks Last Love.

Hunter pleasure: Crown Royale.

Driving: Promotion, TC Expression, Scarlet Lace, Task, Serinask, Pro-Fire, FF Summer Storm, Cease Fire, Red Tape, Mark IV Coronation, Abaskus, Diamond Bask.

Western/working western: Jask, Cinco Grande, Talabask, Fielon, Famest, Bask Image, Chaz.

Halter stallions/colts: GG Jabask, La Basque, MS Santana, Tornado, Amurath Baikal, Baske-Tu.

Halter mares/fillies: Amurath Bandeira, Bask Melody, Basquina, Basquelle, Dancing Flame, Fame, Fire Music, Mi Fire Dream, Alove Note.

Among *Bask's many sons who are top sires are: Gdansk (x *Gdynia), Cognac (x *Gdynia), Tornado (x *Silwara), Wisdom (x Wizteria), Serinask (x Serinne), GG Jabask (x Jalana), Fire Wind (x Lakshmi), Cal O Bask (x Susecion), Negatraz (x *Negotka), Ariston (x *Amfibia), Baske-Tu (x Nafta), Mi Tosk (x Toi), Mon Ta Basko (x *Bint Ambara), The Chief Justice (x Sey Cherie), Port Bask (x *Portulaka), Safire (x Caridina), Le Fire (x Susecion), Zodiac Matador (RO Fanciray), Bask Flame (x Mudira), Pro-Fire (x *Prowizja), and Promotion (x *Prowizja).

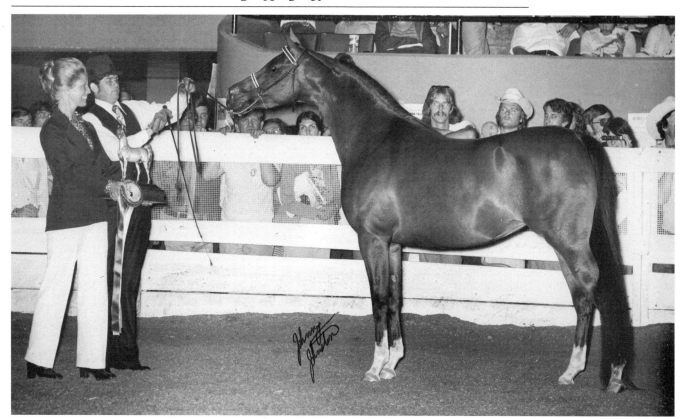

Statistically, as of this writing, U.S. National Park Champion Zodiac Matador is *Bask's top-siring son of national winners, with 37. GG Jabask, a U.S. Reserve National Champion Stallion, is his top-siring son of Class A or better champions, with 118.

Sadly, two stallions near the top of the list, Wisdom and The Chief Justice, died in a tragic fire on January 31, 1996, while still active breeding stallions. Had they had full careers, they might have become *Bask's best-siring sons, based on their early records.

Determining *Bask's best daughters as broodmares is more difficult, since females naturally have far fewer offspring than males. Furthermore, subjectivity plays more of a role. For example, one mare might have several offspring who are all Class A winners while another has two national-winning offspring and a few "no-shows" out of several foals. Now, who is to objectively say which is the better broodmare?

With that in mind, some of *Bask's best-producing daughters include: Spring Baskette (x Narteza), Autumn Fire (x Sparkling Burgundy), Scarlet Oharra (x Gai Ferzona), Alove Song (x *Elkana), Balalinka (x *Bachantka), Basks Maria (x Judith-B), HAR Nahra (x *Portulaka), MHR Princess Bask (x Hayley), Baskera (x *Bandera), Dancing Flame (x Habina),

Masquerade (x Faseyna), Gwyndalyn (x *Gwyn), MS Baqueta (x Bandy), Sha Baska (x Shalem), New Fashion (x *Boltonka), TC Charm (x Khemogina), Shooting Star (x Lasma Star), Spinning Song (x Moska), Raya Royale (x Alouma), Star of Ofir (x Llana), and Wizteria (x *Cosmosa).

Autumn Fire is the best-producing *Bask daughter, with nine championship-winning offspring, of which seven are national winners. More importantly, she is the all-time leading dam of national winners in the entire breed.

Gwyndalyn, another leading *Bask daughter, produced eight champions, four of whom are national winners, including U.S. National Champion Stallion Strike (by *Aladdinn).

Marketing Magic

*Bask offspring not only made their mark in the horse show ring and as breeding stock, but they also dominated sales arenas as well.

The LaCroixes were among the first in the Arabian industry to realize the marketing potential of public auctions produced on a lavish, grand scale.

The *Bask daughter Bask Melody was the 1976 U.S. National Champion Mare and was shown by Gene LaCroix. Bask Melody was out of the esteemed broodmare Susecion.

Photo by Johnny Johnston

The gifted Ibn Prowija was by *Bask and out of *Prowizja. At the 1975 Arabian Horse Fair, he won both the Formal Driving and Park Horse stakes, and was shown by Ray LaCroix. His owner at the time: Tejas Arabians of Houston.

Photo by
Johnny Johnston

Their first, the 1971 Lasma Sale, saw the *Bask daughter Silhoulette, out of *Silwara, top the sale at $56,000. Four other *Bask offspring sold, attaining an average of $29,300—excellent by that day's standards.

By the time the Lasma Sale III rolled around in 1977, the business had a new sales center on Scottsdale's Bell Road. The LaCroixes, especially young Gene, believed that all components—from music and decorations to lighting and dramatic staging—were important to the sale's success. The theory paid off as 14 *Bask offspring brought $1,231,000, for an average of $87,928.

Over the 15-plus years they were held in conjunction with the huge Scottsdale Horse Show each February, Lasma's sales became ever more impressive. Advertising was heavy, the sales catalogs were beautiful full-color books, and the horses were trained and groomed to perfection.

The audience never knew what to expect when the massive velvet curtains lifted. Stage settings ranged from stallions charging through rock-n-roll glitter and strobe lights to matronly broodmares standing peacefully in front of an amazing reproduction of a Polish stable as "snow" fell gently upon them.

Attendees were treated to entertainers such as Bob Hope, Sammy Davis Jr., Dottie West, Glen Campbell, the Pointer Sisters, the Four Tops, and more. Food and drink were plentiful, and high-rollers dressed in sequined gowns and black-tie poured in from across the country and around the world. Security became necessary, and horse lovers begged for the exclusive invitations.

Incredibly, at the Lasma Sale V in 1983, the *Bask daughter Scarlet Lace (out of Elsinor Muzuleyna) sold for $1 million, and Gardenia, by *Bask and out of *Gdynia, sold for $1.5 million. In all, 15 *Bask get were sold at three Lasma-managed sales that year, averaging $466,333 each.

*Gene LaCroix and the *Bask daughter Afire won the English Pleasure Stake at the 1975 Arabian Horse Fair in Louisville, Kentucky. Afire was out of *Wirginia, by *Naborr.*

Photo by Johnny Johnston

In 1985, Fyre-Love, by *Bask and out of Dargantka, also hit $1.5 million at the *Bask Classic Sale.

To date, the only Arabian mare to sell for more at public auction than these *Bask daughters is NH Love Potion, a *Bask granddaughter who sold for $2.55 million in 1984 at the Lasma Classic Sale.

In July 1979, *Bask became ill when he was accidentally dewormed with a substance to which he had had a near-fatal reaction 3 years before. Rumors flew as the Canadian Nationals got underway. Gene and Ray were there with the Lasma show string. At about 2 a.m. on July 25, they received the heartbreaking news that *Bask had died a few hours before, on July 24, 1979, from a ruptured intestine. The brothers sat together, until dawn, mourning the great stallion's death at age 23.

Later that day, Gene rode the *Bask daughter Ambra to the Canadian National Park Championship. "It was the most emotional ride I ever had," Gene told Mary Jane Parkinson in 1985. "It was like she and I both wanted to do it for *Bask, and we did."

*Bask's last foal crop, in 1980, totaled 89 registered offspring. His last foal was the aptly named Forever Bask, a chestnut colt foaled on June 5, 1980, to perhaps *Bask's best mate: the superb broodmare Susecion.

*Bask first was buried at Lasma Arabians on Bell Road in Scottsdale. His stall remained empty, its nameplate on the door, for many years. The facility later was torn down for development.

In the early 1990s, *Bask's remains, remarkably well-preserved, were transferred to the Kentucky Horse Park near Lexington. There he is interred near another 20th Century legend, the mighty Thoroughbred Man O' War.

Today, Edwin Bogucki's famous bronze depicting a rearing *Bask guards the doorway to the park's world-renowned Museum of the Horse—just as it should.

29

2 *WITEZ II

He survived World War II and went on to become a very successful sire in the United States.

HIS IS A STORY of which movies are made. Flight across war-torn Europe. Capture by the enemy. Survival under the occupation. Dramatic rescue by the good guys. And, finally, sanctuary in America.

But, wait. There's more.

Enter Californians Frances and Earle Hurlbutt. In America, the couple ensure he achieves success as a champion show horse, and he becomes renowned as a superb breeding stallion, inspires fan clubs and the admiration of children—and lives out his long life surrounded by people who truly love him.

Perhaps his grand destiny was apparent from the day he was foaled—April 1,

1938, at the Janow Podlaski Stud in Poland—for he was named "Witez" (pronounced VEE-tez), an ancient Polish name meaning "chieftain, knight, hero, prince." To keep the studbook records straight, the Roman numeral II was added. Following his importation to the United States, the asterisk was attached. Thus, he was known to the world as *Witez II.

A handsome bay, with a large star on his forehead, a snip on his nose, and neat, white pasterns on all four feet, *Witez II bore a pedigree as regal as his carriage.

His sire, Ofir, was one of the greatest

*A photograph of *Witez II taken in the 1940s at the Kellogg Ranch in California.*

Photo courtesy Arabian Horse Trust

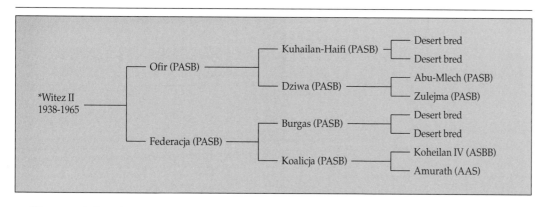

stallions in Poland, a country renowned for breeding strong, athletic, wonderfully-conformed Arabian horses over hundreds of years. Ofir's blood has influenced breeding programs throughout Europe, and many in North America, as well, through his amazing offspring. Three in particular: Witraz (sire of *Bask), Wielki Szlem, and, of course, *Witez II.

Ofir's sire, Kuhailan Haifi, was imported into Poland in 1931 from the deserts of Saudi Arabia by Prince Roman Sanguszko, and proved to be the ideal dose of outcross blood needed in the Polish program. Ofir's dam, Dziwa, a lovely bay with a blaze face and two white hind pasterns, carried Poland's most ancient lines, and was, obviously, a superb match for Kuhailan Haifi.

The dam of *Witez II was the beautiful Federacja. She, too, was by an imported desert-bred stallion—Burgas—and was out of the esteemed Koalicja, a gorgeous white-gray mare with huge dark eyes and a near-classic head and neck.

But there was something else about Federacja that set her apart from the other good mares at the Janow Podlaski Stud in 1938. Her coat was a typical gray, but across her withers a patch of hair remained red-brown. Federacja had a "bloody shoulder," a marking considered mystical by the Bedouin desert tribes, who called it "the mark of Allah." Any horse who bore such a red patch was destined to do great things, the ancient nomadic people believed, and would sire or produce stellar offspring. Federacja would prove this true through her son *Witez II.

The colt grew strong running in the

Halter and Performance Record: 1951 Pacific Coast Champion Stallion.

Progeny Record:

Purebred Foal Crops: 20
Purebred Foals Registered: 223
U.S./Canadian National Winners: 16
Class A Champions: 48
IAHA Legion of Merit Award Winners: 7

Janow pastures with his playmates, and life was good. Then at dawn on September 1, 1939, Hitler's German Nazi Army invaded Poland.

Soon after, the Janow managers—fearing their horses' seizure by the German cavalry or by Russian troops (as its border was less than 5 miles away)—evacuated the farm and dispersed the herd throughout the countryside. Despite the Poles' best efforts, however, many horses were found and returned to Janow.

In the case of *Witez II, who at one point was covered with mud to disguise his quality, his distinctive brand (in the shape of a royal crown) betrayed him to the searching German soldiers.

(Some of the Janow Arabians were

*This famous photo of *Witez II appears on the cover of the fictionalized book of his life,* **And Miles to Go,** *written by Linell Smith. The original photo was taken by Frances Hurlbutt.*

*Ofir, the sire of *Witez II, was known as a progenitor of tremendously athletic and intelligent Arabian horses in Poland. This photo was reproduced from the book,* **And Miles to Go,** *courtesy of the Arabian Horse Trust.*

eventually taken by the Russians, and later used at their Tersk Stud. Refer to the chapters on Bay El Bey and *Muscat for more information.)

In 1940, *Witez II began his life under the Nazi Occupation. In many ways, the days went on as before but with German military men running the Janow Podlaski stables. The young stallion was trained to ride, jump, and drive, and, with some work, as a race horse, although the war prevented his ever starting in a race.

Years later, the Hurlbutts would receive a letter from a woman named Lisolette Tarakus, who was an assistant in the stallion barn at Janow during that time. It read, in part: "Little Witez was my favorite among all the colts. He was the most beautiful and classic among all the colts. He was the most typical and charming purebred Arabian of the Polish breeding after 1939."

*Witez II was bred to several mares

32

Witez II at Calarabia, the Hurlbutts' ranch in California. This photo is reproduced from the book And Miles to Go, *courtesy of the Arabian Horse Trust.*

with good results. In addition, maturity showed him to be a particularly superior individual. In 1943, he was shipped to a stud farm established by the Nazis at Hostau, which lay on the German-Czechoslovakian border. More than 600 of Europe's finest horses—including 100 Arabians—were housed there, with the goal of breeding elite super horses for the elite German "super" race.

By early 1945, Hitler's mad, grand campaign was falling apart and the war was drawing to a close. The German men who ran the Hostau stud farm, several respected veterinarians among them, feared for the safety of the horses—especially from the hungry Russian troops who were advancing from the East. The Americans and their allies were closing in from the West, and seemed the lesser of two evils.

According to U.S. Army records, on April 26, 1945, a German intelligence unit was captured close to Hostau. Its commander pleaded with Colonel Charles Reed of the Second Armored American Cavalry to free the horses at the stud farm, *Witez II and other

*Even when in his 20s, *Witez II still had the look of an eagle.*

Photo courtesy of Lisa Betts Cover

Witezar (x Gezana) was considered to be one of the greatest sons of *Witez II. He was campaigned by Betts Circle 2 Ranch to the title of 1965 AHSA Horse of the Year.

Photo by
Johnny Johnston

Many of Europe's finest Arabian horses were lost or dead, but a handful— including *Witez II— survived.

Arabians among them.

Colonel Reed immediately contacted the legendary Gen. George S. Patton of the U.S. Third Army for permission. Patton, an excellent horseman and cavalry officer himself, instantly ordered their rescue.

One particularly brave German veterinarian, Capt. Rudolph Lessing, crossed enemy lines under cover of darkness and met with the Americans to plan for the safe surrender of Hostau and its horses.

In what must truly have been an awe-inspiring sight, on April 28, 1945, more than 200 horses—Lipizzans, Thoroughbreds, Arabians, and more—were moved across the border into Bavaria. U.S. cavalrymen rode the stallions, and the mares and young horses were shipped in open army trucks, eventually traveling at least 200 miles to safety at Monsbach Stud.

Just days later, on May 9, 1945, Hitler surrendered and the war in Europe was over. The continent lay in ruins, with millions of people dead and its survivors in despair.

Many of Europe's finest Arabian horses were lost or dead, but a handful— including *Witez II—survived.

Across the Atlantic

The Americans selected the best of the Monsbach horses (now considered "spoils of war"), *Witez II among them, and had the animals shipped to the United States for use in the U.S. Army's remount breeding program.

After a rough ocean voyage, *Witez II first saw his new country when he landed at Newport News, Va., in late 1945. He spent the winter at the remount station at Front Royal, Va., and then he and 21 other Arabians were shipped in early 1946 to the Army's Remount Depot at Pomona, California. This was formerly the Kellogg Ranch (see *Raseyn's chapter for more on this famous ranch).

On June 23, 1946, a special showing of these Arabians was given by the U.S. Army for the members of the fledgling Arabian Horse Breeders Society of California, later the Arabian Horse Club of Southern California. In the viewing stands was one of the group's founders, Earle Hurlbutt. It was the first time he saw the horse who would so change his life.

Hurlbutt was a native Californian who had served in World War I and then married budding actress Frances Cosgrave in 1929. The Hurlbutts, like many others in the Los Angeles area, often went to the Kellogg Ranch Sunday Shows, which featured Arabian horses.

Hurlbutt decided Arabians were for him, and bought a 740-acre farm near Calabasas in the San Fernando Valley. He began to buy a few horses and became quite involved with them.

So involved did he become, in fact, that he is considered one of the founders of both the previously mentioned California club in 1944, and, in 1950, the International Arabian Horse Association. He served as that national group's first president from 1950 through 1954. Frances Hurlbutt was its volunteer office secretary.

Hurlbutt recalled the first time he saw *Witez II, at that Army showing, in an interview for a historical video. This video was produced by Gary Carpenter (this author's spouse) with the Arabian Horse Trust, and it was entitled *Calarabia: The Story of the Hurlbutts and *Witez II.* (Note: Frances Hurlbutt passed away in 1991, and Earle in 1993, at age 98.)

Said Hurlbutt in the video: "I was sitting in the stands, and they started out with about 10 stallions going around the ring. I looked at all of them closely and finally the one that ended up the bunch was *Witez II. I thought he was the smartest horse in the whole gang."

At that time, *Witez II was not for sale, so Hurlbutt consoled himself by breeding

*Frances Hurlbutt and trainer Rocky Wright with *Witez II after he was named, at age 15, grand champion stallion and Pacific Coast Champion Stallion at the large 1951 Southern California Arabian Show. This photo was taken by John H. Williamson and appears on the back cover of* And Miles to Go. Photo by Williamson

two of his mares, Rabkhal (Rehal x Rabk) and Ghazawi (Ghazi x Gharifet), to the Polish stallion. They produced two chestnut colts, Zitez (who was *Witez II's first champion offspring) and Ghazitez.

At about the same time, it became apparent that the need for U.S. Army cavalry horses had disappeared in the face of modern warfare mechanization. The remount program transferred ownership of its horses to the U.S. Department of Agriculture, and in

Burrtez (left), with Mona Betts Benson, and Witezar, with Burr Betts, graced the March 1965 cover of **Western Horseman** *magazine. The photo was taken by* **WH** *publisher Dick Spencer III in Colorado's Great Sand Dunes National Monument.*

The
WESTERN HORSEMAN
MARCH 1965 • 50 CENTS

ICD

☆ ARABIANS IN THE SAND

☆ HORSE HANDLING ON KING RANCH

☆ ALL-INDIAN RODEO

☆ AUSTRALIAN MOUNTED POLICE

☆ FLINTRIDGE, HORSEMEN'S PARADISE

The Magazine for Admirers of Stock Horses

• RANCHERS   • CONTESTANTS   • BREEDERS   • RIDING CLUBS

November 1948, *Witez II and many other remount horses were shipped by rail to Fort Reno in Oklahoma.

According to the Arabian Horse Trust video, Hurlbutt in late May of 1949 heard, only by accident, that Fort Reno was about to be closed and its horses, including *Witez II, auctioned off. He immediately went to Oklahoma.

The sale was held May 25, 1949, and started off with Thoroughbred horses in the morning, followed by Arabians in the afternoon. *Witez II bore hip number 131 and was the first Arabian to be sold.

Hurlbutt had run into an old friend at the sale, Fred Arth, and they agreed to partner on the bay, 15-hand stallion. As Hurlbutt later recalled, "The bidding

Potter ®

Burrtez, a gelded son of Witezar and grandson of *Witez II, was an AHSA Horse of the Year who excelled in a variety of events, including polo. He was owned by Burr Betts, but his rider here is Walter Chapman.

Photo by Alan Potter, courtesy of Mona Betts Benson

started at about $2,000. This Yank over there bid $2,500 and I bid $2,600. That went on and up.

"And here Mr. Arth was standing back there tapping me on the shoulder saying, 'Stop! Stop! Stop!' Then they bid $8,000 and I bid $8,100—and walked off. Finally, someone came running after me and said, 'Well, you bought a horse!'"

Frances Hurlbutt, who was home minding the ranch, was not at all surprised when Earle brought *Witez II home. "Earle always gets what he wants," she said with a laugh during the same Trust video interview.

The Hurlbutts relieved Arth of his share the next year, and started using *Witez II in their breeding program. They had never planned to show the horse, but friends convinced them otherwise. Subsequently, trainer Rocky Wright led *Witez to the stallion grand championship at the 1951 Southern California

All-Arabian Show—one of the largest shows at that time.

His second and last show appearance came in 1953, again with Rocky Wright, at the same event.

Said Hurlbutt, "He was very dignified, as horses go. During the judging he would stand there and just look way away, not moving around at all. The judge put his hand in front of his eyes to see whether he could see or not. He just blinked an eye and didn't move at all."

The Polish refugee was named both show grand champion and Pacific Coast Champion Stallion. (The great Fersara was the Pacific Coast Champion Mare— see Bint Sahara's chapter.) *Witez II was

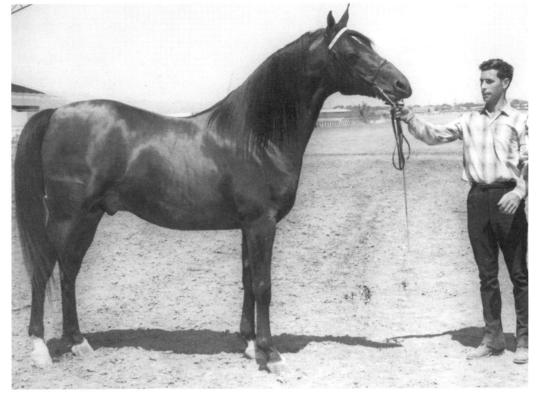

*Nafatez was another
good son of *Witez
II, and was out of
Nafa. In this 1958
photo he was the
reserve champion
stallion at the Las
Vegas Arabian show.
The back of the photo
lists Lou Gardella of
Van Nuys, Calif., as
the horse's owner.*

Photo by Williamson

**A look at modern-
day show records
indicate a good
number of top
horses trace to
*Witez II.**

15 years old at the time.

Three of the stallion's sons also were at that show. Zitez was Pacific Coast Reserve Champion; Nitez (x Nafa), a yearling, was the reserve champion of the regular show; and Natez (x Nafalla) won the 2-year-old colt class. Natez was later named Pacific Slope Champion Stallion in 1955 and 1957.

The next year, 1954, six sons competed in the 3-year-old colt class at the Pomona All-Arabian Show. Natez won it.

Offspring

In all, *Witez II sired 223 registered purebred Arabian horses. Of these, 16 were national winners (but many good ones showed before there were U.S. National Champion classes) and 48 were regular show champions—during an era in which Arabian shows were far and few between.

Of his outstanding offspring, several were particularly superior:

Witezar (x Gezana), a 1955 bay stallion,

was the 1965 AHSA Horse of the Year over all breeds, a Canadian Reserve National Champion Stallion, a U.S. Top Ten Stallion, and western pleasure winner. He was the sire of Witezarif, four-time (1970 through 1973) winner of that ultimate endurance race test, the Tevis Cup in California; and Burrtez, who won the AHSA Horse of the Year title.

Bolero (x Nafalla), another 1955 bay stallion, was the 1961 U.S. Reserve National Champion Stallion (with a total of six national halter titles) and won other championships, including a U.S. Top Ten Native Costume award at age 15. He sired the wonderful cutting horse Xenophonn, who won three U.S. national championship titles in open and novice cutting, and three U.S. reserves in open and ladies cutting from 1979 through 1982. (Refer to Xenophonn's chapter.) Bolero also sired Zarabo, the 1968 U.S. National Champion Stallion.

Natez, Bolero's older full brother who was mentioned earlier, was foaled in 1951. He was a U.S. Top Ten Stallion and sired Indian Genii, the 1967 U.S. National Champion Mare and a producer of national winners.

The American-born Ofir (x Tiara), a chestnut stallion born in 1953, set early records for 2½-mile races.

Ronteza (x Ronna), a 1954 bay mare,

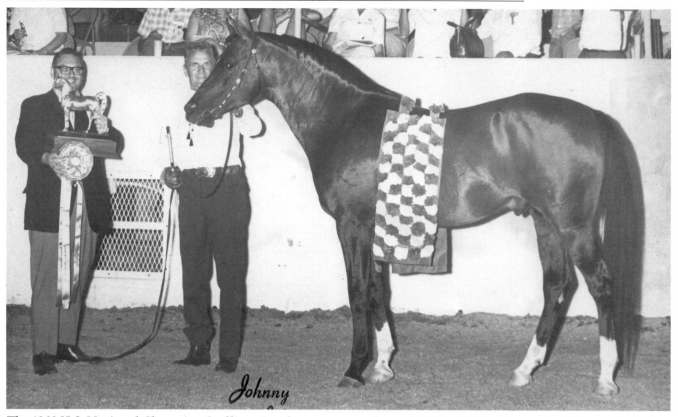

The 1968 U.S. National Champion Stallion, Zarabo, was a grandson of *Witez II. Zarabo was by Bolero, who's pictured in the Zenophonn chapter.   Photo by Johnny Johnston

The American-born Ofir (*Witez II x Tiara) set early records for 2 l/2-mile races. He's shown here in the winner's circle at Laurel Race Course in 1959 in Washington D.C. The jockey is Charles McKee and the trainer, Jack Mobberley. This Ofir is not to be confused with the Polish Ofir, who sired *Witez II.

Amatez was a good-looking son of *Witez II who was the grand champion gelding at Scottsdale in 1963.

Photo by Pat Close

Nitez, by Witez II and out of Nafa, was a halter champion and full brother to Nafatez.   **Photo courtesy Arabian Horse Trust**

and Sheila Varian made history as the first Arabian and first woman to win (in November 1961) the Cow Palace's tough reined cow horse championship against all breeds. (See chapters on Bay-Abi and Bay El Bey for more information.)

In fact, a look at modern-day show records indicate a good number of top horses—especially in performance—trace to *Witez II in their pedigrees. They include, but are not limited to: Bint Miss Fire, Hearrts on Fire, Aza Destiny, Cyrk, Aladdinn Echo, Laddinn's Fire, and Padron's Mahogany.

An Arabian horse breeders' group, the *Witez II Alliance, was formed in the mid-1990s to encourage the breeding of horses who carry the stallion's bloodlines.

During his lifetime, *Witez II became quite a celebrity. The Polish government put his likeness on a commemorative stamp. Famous author Marguerite Henry used his photo in her book *All About Horses*, and he was a model for many book covers and calendars.

A fictionalized book of his life, *And Miles To Go*, was written by Linell Smith, published in 1967, and became wildly popular. (Movie rights to the book have been sold.)

Fan clubs were established and letters and visitors came in from around the world. Children especially adored *Witez II, and Frances Hurlbutt said she answered every one of their thousands of letters.

The Trust video shares the experience of one little girl who, after being allowed to sit on the stallion on her birthday,

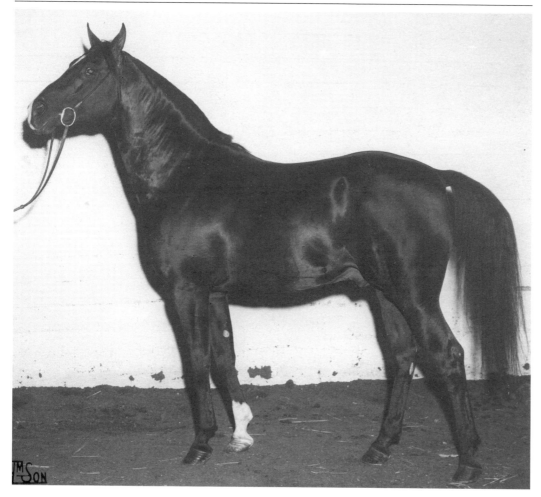

Natez, another *Witez II son, is shown here at the Cow Palace (in San Francisco) where he was named 1957 Pacific Coast Champion Arabian Stallion. He was also a U.S. Top Ten Stallion and sired Indian Genii, the 1967 U.S. National Champion Mare.

Photo by Williamson

Black Magic, by *Witez II and a full brother to Natez, was named grand champion stallion at the Estes Park (Colo.) Arabian show in the mid-1960s.

Photo by Alexander

*Perhaps the most famous *Witez II daughter was Ronteza, owned, trained, and shown by Sheila Varian of Arroyo Grande, California. In 1961 Sheila and Ronteza won the tough reined cow horse championship against all breeds at the Cow Palace.*

During the 1961 Cow Palace cow horse competition, Ronteza slipped and fell while working the cow in the light-weight eliminations. Says Sheila, "I can remember what seemed like hours deciding if I should stay on or jump off. I stayed on, Ronteza jumped up, caught up with the cow within 10 feet, and finished circling her. She was just that kind of horse!"

wrote to the Hurlbutts: "When I got home, I found three of his hairs on my coat. I put them in a jewel box. They are my most precious possession."

That *Witez II's profile was incorporated into the Hurlbutts' farm name and Calarabia logo is of no surprise. And when the flag with the Polish eagle on it flew from the Calarabia barn roof, passersby knew they were welcome to visit the bright bay horse.

Colorado

Although the bay stallion spent most of his life in America with the Hurlbutts, he was leased to Burr Betts in Parker, Colo., from 1960 to 1964. Betts, an insurance executive in Denver and later a president of IAHA, was establishing an Arabian breeding program at his Circle 2 Ranch in nearby Parker. He had become familiar with *Witez II, liked him and his offspring very much, and convinced the Hurlbutts to lease the horse to him.

It was Betts who owned and campaigned both Witezar and Witezar's son, Burrtez, to their AHSA Horse of the Year titles. Witezar ultimately proved to be one of the greatest sons of *Witez II. And Burrtez was not just a show horse; he also served as Betts' personal riding gelding for trail rides and ranch work.

Betts either acquired or bred many daughters of *Witez II, as well as several sons, who contributed to the success of his breeding program. This program also made horses of *Witez II breeding available to many Arabian enthusiasts in the Rocky Mountain and Midwest regions.

On January 3, 1965, the Hurlbutts hosted a birthday party for *Witez II with trainer Rocky Wright as honored guest. Just a few months later, on June 9, *Witez II died at Calarabia. He was 27.

"My favorite memory of him is the very last day of his life," Frances Hurlbutt said in the Trust interview. "I used to go out and give him some apple peelings and some carrots and things at night. And he looked so beautiful. He had gained weight. He was nice and sleek, and had copper tints in his

*This classy granddaughter of *Witez II is Royal Zara. By Witezar, she produced many fine foals for Betts Circle 2 Arabians. Riding her through this trail course is Mona Betts Benson.*

Photo by Scott Trees

coat. There were a couple of mares across the way that he was flirting with. And his brand stood out. I could put my head on his shoulder and pat him. He was in such good shape and such good spirits, and he was so pretty. . . ."

Foaled to face a horrible war, *Witez II died that night in tranquil peace.

43

3 XENOPHONN

No horse has had as much direct influence on the purebred Arabian working western divisions.

PROFESSIONAL horse photographer Jerry Sparagowski peered into his camera as the cowboy on the bay stallion adjusted the flower garland around his horse's neck. The pair had just won the 1982 U.S. National Arabian Open Cutting Championship, and were being awarded two trophies, a gold belt buckle, the tricolor

Xenophonn won the 1982 U.S. National Open Cutting Championship with Tom Miller aboard. Don Burt (left) and John Wheeler hold some of Tom's awards.

Photo by Jerry Sparagowski

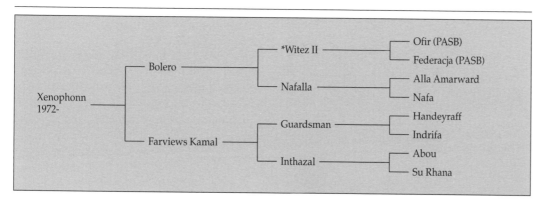

Xenophonn
1972-
├─ Bolero
│ ├─ *Witez II
│ │ ├─ Ofir (PASB)
│ │ └─ Federacja (PASB)
│ └─ Nafalla
│   ├─ Alla Amarward
│   └─ Nafa
└─ Farviews Kamal
   ├─ Guardsman
   │ ├─ Handeyraff
   │ └─ Indrifa
   └─ Inthazal
      ├─ Abou
      └─ Su Rhana

ribbon, and a new saddle. It took four people on the ground just to hold all the loot for the photograph.

The crowd in Freedom Hall on that typically cool Louisville, Ky., October day whooped and hollered and warmed up the place. Few had ever seen an Arabian horse work cattle like the bay. He was a supreme athlete, a superior performer.

Everyone smiled, the flash went off, and the cowboy began walking his horse toward the out-gate.

"Excuse me," a young man called out, trotting to catch the pair as they made their way back to the stall area. "That's the best I've ever seen a horse move in my life," he said earnestly. "I'm a farrier and I was just wondering, if you wouldn't mind, could I look at his feet and see how he's shod? I think maybe I could learn something."

The lean, gray-haired cowboy pulled up, paused, then smiled apologetically and said, "Well, sir, I guess I'm not very good advertisement for horseshoeing. He's barefoot." With that, the pair turned and quietly walked back to the stables . . . and into the history books.

No horse has had as much direct influence on the purebred Arabian working western divisions—especially cutting—than has the bay stallion Xenophonn (pronounced Zen-o-phon), better known as "Zee." And when you talk about Zee and the Zee horses, you had better mention Tom Miller and his family, as well. Like

Halter and Performance Record: 3 U.S. National Championships in open and novice cutting; 3 U.S. Reserve National Championships in ladies and open cutting.

Progeny Record:

Purebred Foal Crops: 17
Purebred Foals Registered: 149 (as of 1998)
U.S./Canadian National Winners: 27
Class A Champions: 35
IAHA Legion of Honor Award Winners: 1

the ancient Bedouins, the Millers consider their Zee Arabians to be part of the family and have virtually dedicated their lives to producing and showing cutting horses who descend from Xenophonn.

"Around here we call him The Old Horse," offered Tom. "Or just Zee. Xenophonn is too hard to say, too much of a mouthful."

Miller, who lives near Red Bluff, Calif., explained that the family shows all of its horses, most of whom descend from Zee, without shoes. "I figure if a horse is built

45

Speed Princess with Arlene Miller in the saddle. This mare was co-champion at the New Mexico Turquoise Circuit in 1980 with Xenophonn. Tom Miller holds the trophy.   Photo by Jim McCaulley

right, there's no one who can put better grab on a horse than 'the man upstairs.' Now, you get a shelly-footed one, you would have to shoe him. But our horses all have good feet.

"We raise our youngsters kind of rough and tough; they are all turned out and run in the hills until we bring them in for training. They're strong and agile, good horses." Added Miller, "You know, genetics is a wonderful thing. You can take care of a lot of problems in the breeding barn."

Through October 1998 Zee had sired 149 registered offspring, and, of those, 27 have won national titles (39 and counting) in the working western divisions, more than any other stallion.

Zee himself has a total of three U.S. national championships in open and novice cutting and three U.S. reserve national championships in ladies cutting and open cutting, won from 1979 through 1982.

An Arabian horse with a strong, natural cow sense is somewhat unusual in the breed. In addition, some who possess it are incapable of putting it to good use because of the distinctive "rear end alignment" many Arabians possess that limits their ability to crouch down low with their back legs tucked under their bellies. This classic cutting and stock-horse position allows the horse to better follow a steer's quick movements. Instead, the typical Arabian's hips and hocks are better conformed for an airy, easy, energy-efficient canter across miles of desert sand.

At first glance there is little in Xenophonn's pedigree that predicts his finely honed cow sense and his apparent ability to pass this gift on to his offspring. His pedigree does, however, contain bloodlines known for athleticism and good dispositions with beautiful Arabian heads to boot.

Through his sire, the *Witez II son Bolero, Zee inherited the strength, balance, and courage for which Polish Arabian horses are known and respected around the world. Bolero also has a line to England's Crabbet horses, who typically can use their hind legs quite well. They also have a more rounded croup and, therefore, different hip structure than some Arabian bloodline groups with flat croups.

Zee's maternal lines carry strong Crabbet ties, as well, through the two *Raffles sons Handeyraff and Indraff, both of whom sired some good western horses. A dose of old Egyptian blood from his tail

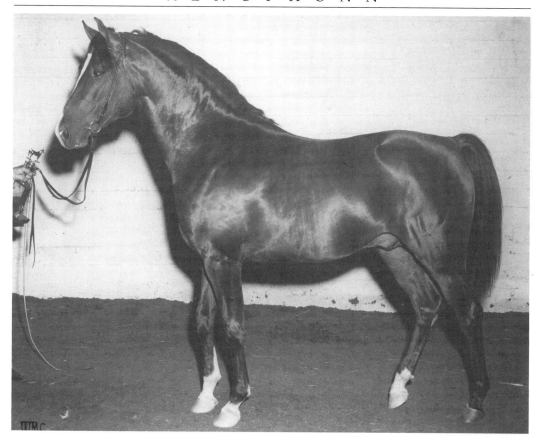

The back of this mid-1950s photo states that Bolero, Xenophonn's sire, was the champion stallion at the Cow Palace. Bob McDonald is listed as owner.

Photo by John H. Williamson

female line—through *Fadl and *Sulejman—gave Zee a touch of the exotic and increased stamina and endurance. Still, there aren't any cutting horses, per se, among his direct antecedents.

Zee, foaled on May 27, 1972, was bred by southern Californian Dr. Harvey A. Cohen, and soon was sold to Red and Charlene Fletcher. They placed Zee with well-known cutting horse trainer Bill Mowery (now deceased), who started the stallion and began showing him.

Tom Miller happened upon Zee about that time. "We were going to cuttings and we'd see him around here and there. You could see the talent in him. He was pretty good," offered Miller, who grew up riding ranch horses and lived near De Beque in western Colorado at the time.

"The Fletchers had been after us for a while to take Zee and ride him, so finally we did. I pretty much knew how he would go from watching him with Bill, and that's how I found him to be. He was an extremely talented athlete; he had wonderful style and lots of natural cow. He was pretty well-trained, but he had a few small problems that we managed to work out. Soon we were winning everything with him," said Miller.

Early in 1981, the Millers moved to Cali-

Owner Eleanor Hamilton, Rogers, Minn., in 1997 on Hesa Zee (Xenophonn x Something Special). Ridden by Oregon trainer Russ Brown, the stallion has been the Scottsdale reining champion, Canadian reserve national reining champion, and a U.S. Top Ten in reining.

Photo by Sue Wooldridge

Judd Miller riding Zee Trixie (Xenophonn x Impressive Lady), U.S. Arabian Reserve National Champion Open Cutting Horse.
Photo by Jim Bortvedt

fornia. "I knew I was never going to change the weather in Colorado, so we decided to go somewhere more pleasant," explained Miller. Around that same time, Red Fletcher was seriously injured when a tractor turned over on him. Sadly, he decided to sell Zee.

"We'd been winning so much with him that we just decided to buy him," said Miller. "You might say Mr. Fletcher's bad luck led to our good luck, but we were sorry it happened to that good man, no matter what."

Zee was off to California and to his first season in the breeding shed. "He'd only had one foal, born in 1980," Miller said.

"He had his first (breeding) season with us when he was 9 years old. He was showing at the same time. We've kept him busy ever since." That first crop of six foals, born in 1982, included three who later won national titles: Zee Prince, Zee Trixie, and Zee Ruler.

Miller described the specific attributes Xenophonn possesses and also consistently passes to his sons and daughters. These traits enable them to be the superior working western horses they are.

"He's a natural," Miller began. "When he stops and turns, you can see that he is mentally and physically equipped to do the job asked of him. So many can't do it. They may want to, but they aren't physically able to do it. Or they might be able

Zee Princess (Xenophonn x Speed Princess) with Judd Miller aboard, won the 1987 U.S. Arabian National Cutting Futurity Championship.

Photo by Jim Bortvedt

physically, but don't have the mind to work in this way.

"Zee's hocks are set low; he can really get in the ground, but then he can get up again too. There is a lot about him—the way he looks and how he works—that reminds me of the great Quarter Horse cutting horse sire Doc Bar.

"You know, there can be more differences within a breed than between breeds," Miller added. "There aren't many differences between a good working cow horse who is a Quarter Horse and one who is an Arabian, compared to all the conformational differences between a Quarter Horse race horse and a Quarter Horse cutting horse, for example."

Miller continued, "Zee is extremely dominant in color—mostly all bays. He never sires a chestnut, and only has grays with homozygous gray mares. Zee has a good, straight neck, not set on too high, a strip on his face, and four stockings. He's a good-looking horse.

"And he is really good-minded and he passes it on. We use all of our horses here; there are no prima donnas. We've used him to pony babies and to pony other stallions. There is never a problem. Our stallions each have a runway out from their sheds, which are right next to each other (mainly Zee and a couple of his sons), and

Two U.S. National Arabian Show Champions in 1990: Zee Queen with Jimmie Reno won the open cutting, and Princess Zee with Judd Miller won the futurity. Both are by Xenophonn and out of Speed Princess.

Photo by Dennis Photography

As serious breeders, the Millers remain focused on their ideal Arabian horse, despite roller-coaster markets and flash-in-the-pan fads. This has contributed greatly to Zenophonn's extraordinary success.

there is never any trouble between them, no fighting. They all have good minds.

"He teases all his own mares; we hand-breed him as we do all our stallions. We do ship semen on Zee, but only Zee."

Added Miller, "You know, he's never taken a lame step in his life, or been sick. In 1997, he settled a bunch of mares again at age 25."

In 1997 Zee finally moved into a box stall. According to Rod Matthieson, a Minnesota trainer who manages the national-winning reining horse Hesa Zee (by Xenophonn) for owner Eleanor Hamilton, it took unusual weather to do it.

"The Millers had been having a lot of rain, much more than usual, and, as you know, their horses—all their horses—are turned out all of the time," explained Matthieson. "Well, Arlene (Tom's wife) really got after ol' Tom and made him put

The Old Horse in a nice, dry box stall. I believe that was the first time he's been in a stall on the ranch, ever, and the only other time was years ago at horse shows. That shows you how tough and healthy the Millers' horses are because they all look and perform beautifully."

Notable Offspring

The Millers are as proud of their broodmare band as they are of Xeno-phonn and rightfully so. Many are working western champions themselves and are champion producers.

The best cross with Zee, by far, has been the mare Speed Princess (Ferana, by Ferseyn, x Teyma Miller), bred by the Millers. Foaled the same year (1972) as Zee, she, too, was still producing foals as of 1997. She has always been bred exclusively to Xenophonn.

Speed Princess herself has two U.S. National Cutting Championships (a futurity and a ladies title) and three U.S. National Top Ten open cutting awards. Her six U.S. Arabian Nationals-winning offspring include Zee Princess, 1987 U.S. National Cutting Futurity Champion; Zee

The Millers horseback, as they are most often seen. That's Tom (on Smooth Zee), Arlene (on Lakota Khedive), son Judd (Zee Brownie), and granddaughter Amanda (on AA Monte Carlo), who had just participated in her first cutting competition, winning the $1,500 novice class.
Photo by Amy Joy

Prince, 1987 U.S. Reserve National Cutting Futurity Champion; Zee Queen, 1989 U.S. National Cutting Futurity Champion and Top Ten Open Cutting and 1990 U.S. National Open Cutting Champion; Princess Zee, 1990 U.S. National Cutting Futurity Champion; Z Princes Miracle, with two 1995 U.S. Reserve National Championships in futurity cutting and non-pro futurity cutting; and Zee King, named the 1997 U.S. National Futurity Cutting Champion.

A close second to Speed Princess's record is that of the mare Impressive Lady (Gay Apollo x Sheykha), who also was bred by the Millers and had five Zee offspring win four national reserve titles and one national championship in various cutting classes. Those five include Zee Trixie (reserve open), Zee Witez (reserve futurity), Ima Trixie Too (reserve futurity), Zee

Impressive (reserve non-pro futurity), and Zee Jada (champion novice cutting).

As it is with most influential stallions, the right human partnership often makes the difference between laurels and obscurity. As serious breeders, the Millers remain focused on their ideal Arabian horse, despite roller-coaster markets and flash-in-the-pan fads. This has contributed immeasurably to Xenophonn's extraordinary success.

Offered Tom: "I always say that we breed for three things. One, eye appeal. They have to be pretty. Two, athletic ability. If they can't move well, you might as

Speed Princess in action. In 1977 she was the U.S. National Arabian Cutting Futurity Champion and Ladies Cutting Champion. Also a Top Ten winner three times in open cutting, she has been the most successful cross with Xenophonn.

Photo by Potter

well just get a piece of clay and mold yourself a pretty horse.

"And three, a trainable mind. This is the most important. They must be able to take a lot of work, respond well, retain what they learn, and understand what you are trying to get across. If they can't think very well, then you are up against it; pretty and even athletic aren't going to help much.

"Zee does put on pretty. People come up to us all the time when we ride Zee horses and say, 'Boy, that's a pretty horse.' And that's whether they are the most

knowledgeable or it's their first time at a horse show. Zee horses attract people."

Xenophonn made his mark in the cutting arena mainly because it is the Miller family's first love. (Their son Judd has won more national Arabian cutting futurities than anyone else, ever, and Tom's grandchildren now show at the Nationals.) But Zee horses have all the attributes to dominate other working western divisions as well. The best example is the stallion Hesa Zee (Xenophonn x Something Special).

Oregon trainer Russ Brown wanted a reining horse who would take him to the top at the Big Three: Scottsdale, the Canadian National Show, and U.S. Nationals. In February 1992, the Millers offered him Hesa Zee and the pair soon

52

began sliding into the winner's circle. In fact, their first win was the 1992 Arabian National Reining Futurity, which they took by an incredible 7 points.

Brown purchased Hesa Zee and together they won Scottsdale in 1993. In 1995 they won the Canadian Reserve National Reining Championship and a U.S. Top Ten in reining. In 1993, Rod Matthieson saw Brown ride Hesa Zee and began a friendly campaign to purchase the horse for his boss, Eleanor Hamilton. "We finally talked Russ into selling him at the 1995 Canadian Nationals. Russ kept showing him the rest of the year, and then we took him home to Minnesota. Eleanor shows him in amateur reining and I ride his offspring," Rod said.

Russ consoles himself with Hesa Zee's full brother, Zee Mega Bucks, foaled in 1994. At the 1998 U.S. Nationals, Russ won the National Championship Reining Futurity on Zee Mega Bucks.

"The mental attitude of Zee horses is wonderful," offered Brown. "They don't flee. You can do anything with them. When it's time to go to work, they go to work. With Hesa Zee, we've bred a mare with him and the next day won a reining. And they are built to do their job. Sometimes I wish all my horses were Zees."

Matthieson concurs. "He's the best Arabian I have ever thrown a leg over. He is my idea of a good working western horse. We are crossing him on our Crown Musc (by *Muscat) daughters and others with great results. And he's attractive too. He's used in the print ads for Pfizer's Strongid C product.

"Xenophonn's body has one of the most perfect trapezoids I've ever seen on a horse, any horse," added Matthieson. "Don Burt came up with using an imaginary trapezoid to measure horses to determine how they will function. (Editor's note: A trapezoid is a four-sided geometric figure with only two sides parallel, in this case superimposed on a horse's body. To have a good trapezoid, a horse should have matching shoulder and hip angles, a short back, and a long underline.) Zee and his offspring all function beautifully."

The Millers and their Zee horses have changed the horse world's view of Arabian cutting horses. They are good and they are competitive. "Back when Zee

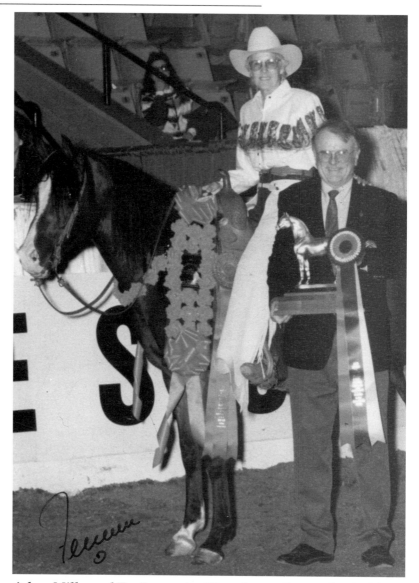

Arlene Miller and Zee Impressive (Xenophonn x Impressive Lady) won the 1994 U.S. Arabian National Reserve Non-Pro Futurity Championship.
Photo by Ferrara

Princess won the Oregon Cutting Horse Association open cutting trials in 1987, the show office people kept saying they couldn't find her registration number. It took some talking to convince them to check with the Arabian registry. They simply didn't believe me. They know the Zee horses now, though."

Added Tom: "The Old Horse, he's made quite a difference. For the Millers and for Arabian cutting horses."

4   *ALADDINN

He was the first U.S. National Champion Stallion to sire four sons who won the same title.

*A 1990 photo of the striking bay stallion, *Aladdinn, who was the 1979 U.S. National Champion Stallion.*

Photo by
Jerry Sparagowski

AS IF HE possessed the lamp of his namesake, *Aladdinn has brought magic to breeding programs and show rings across the country and, in some instances, around the world.

Flashy, he is not, although many of his offspring are. Rather, a better title might be "The Quiet Hero," especially when compared to some other top stallions of his generation.

*Aladdinn, albeit handsome, confor-mationally correct, and quite elegant, cannot, for example, claim the star-spangled brilliance and grassroots popularity of other well-known stallions.

"Frankly, *Aladdinn has had to grow on us," said his current owner, Rick Taylor of Provo, Utah. "The first time I really got chills was when we released him at liberty for the Saturday night finals crowd at the 1998 Scottsdale Show. It was then I first began to understand his power, his

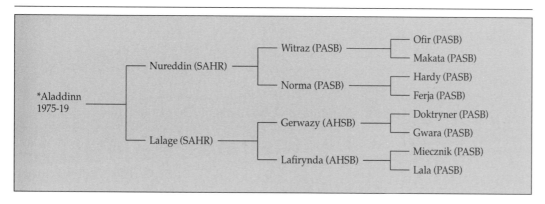

```
                                            ┌─── Ofir (PASB)
                        ┌─── Witraz (PASB) ─┤
                        │                   └─── Makata (PASB)
     ┌─ Nureddin (SAHR)─┤
     │                  │                   ┌─── Hardy (PASB)
     │                  └─── Norma (PASB) ──┤
*Aladdinn ─┤                                └─── Ferja (PASB)
1975-19    │
     │                  ┌─── Gerwazy (AHSB)─┬─── Doktryner (PASB)
     │                  │                   └─── Gwara (PASB)
     └─ Lalage (SAHR)───┤
                        │                   ┌─── Miecznik (PASB)
                        └─ Lafirynda (AHSB)─┤
                                            └─── Lala (PASB)
```

own particular brand of magic."

In fact, only two other sires have shaped the breed as much in modern times as has *Aladdinn. Furthermore, he claims records even the immortal *Bask and ever-popular Khemosabi cannot touch.

*Aladdinn is the only stallion to win a European championship—1978 Swedish National Champion Stallion—and then go on to be named a U.S. National Champion Stallion, which he did (unanimously) in 1979. He also was the 1979 Scottsdale Champion Stallion. Those two wins, both with a young Gene LaCroix on the other end of the lead shank, represent the only times he was shown in the United States.

Furthermore, *Aladdinn possesses the genetic material that enabled him alone to sire four sons who also took the very same U.S. National Champion Stallion title: AAF Kaset in 1984, Strike in 1985, Almaden in 1987, and Exceladdinn in 1989. To date, no other stallion has ever accomplished such a feat.

*Aladdinn was foaled on February 13, 1975, on the farm of his breeder, Eric Erlandsson, in Sweden. After winning the national title there in 1978 at the tender age of 3, he was exported to this country on August 31, 1978. The Arabian Horse Registry of America lists his importer as the same Eric Erlandsson who bred him, and also lists a Scottsdale, Ariz., address. However, common knowledge has it that Dr. Eugene LaCroix of Lasma Arabians, Scottsdale, actually brought the stallion to America.

The importation made great sense and was an astute move for Lasma. The LaCroixes' famous *Bask was aging, and they wanted a new, young stallion to carry their prestigious breeding program into the 1980s and beyond.

At that time, American breeders were enamored with bloodline groups. It was

Halter and Performance Record: 1979 U.S. National Champion Stallion.

Progeny Record:

Purebred Foal Crops: 20
Purebred Foals Registered: 1,172
U.S./Canadian National Winners: 63
Class A Champions: 267
IAHA Legion of Honor Award Winners: 19
IAHA Legion of Supreme Honor Award Winners: 6
IAHA Legion of Merit Award Winners: 1
IAHA Legion of Supreme Honor/Merit Award Winners: 1
Race Starters: 31
Race Money Earned: $184,198

*This is not a very good picture, but it's the only we could find of Nureddin, the sire of *Aladdinn. Nureddin sired just six foals, all in Sweden.*

Courtesy Arabian Horse Times Archives

*AAF Kaset was the first of *Aladdinn's sons to win the U.S. National Champion Stallion title (in 1984). He is out of the Polish mare *Kaseta, by Negatiw.*

Photo by Rie Jones

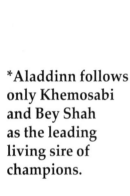

*Aladdinn follows only Khemosabi and Bey Shah as the leading living sire of champions.

popular to breed only straight Egyptian, or straight Spanish, or true Russian, or pure Polish horses and "never the twain shall meet." In fact, Arabian horses with salad bowl or "domestic-bred" pedigrees tended to bring lower prices no matter what their actual quality and/or talents.

The LaCroixes had made a name for themselves and for their program partially because of their Polish-bred horses, who tended to be bay and extremely athletic, thanks, in part, to Poland's heavy emphasis on Arabian horse racing. Rest assured, however, that the LaCroixes never hesitated to use horses of other bloodline groups in their efforts to pro-

duce the very best Arabian horses in the world. The Lasma program often met with tremendous success in this endeavor.

Upon examination of *Aladdinn's Polish bloodlines, it is easy to see why the LaCroixes had high hopes for the young stallion.

*Aladdinn's sire, the bay Nureddin, shared the same sire as the immortal *Bask: Witraz, by Ofir. Witraz also sired Bandola, dam of three national halter winners; *Caliope, dam of seven champions; Arfa, dam of U.S. and Canadian National Champion Mare *Arwistawa; Celebes, sire of six Polish national champions; and more. Unfortunately, Nureddin sired only six foals, all born in Sweden.

*Aladdinn's dam, the gray Lalage, had three American champions: *Aladdinn, *EA Amurath, and *Ali Mirr. Lalage was a mare of Polish breeding, but was bred in England by Patricia Lindsay, who had imported the mare's parents from Poland.

Her sire, Gerwazy, was by the well-known Polish stallion Doktryner, sire of U.S. National English Pleasure Champion *Muzulmanin, and out of the Wielki Szlem daughter Gwara. Gwara was the dam of *Gwadiana, who produced nine champions and four national winners.

Gerwazy also sired *Karadjordje and *Blue Danube, both of whom won U.S. National Top Tens in halter and park and then sired national winners.

Lalage's dam was Lafirynda, a Miecznik daughter, who was a full sister to Ela, dam of national winners *Eskadra, *Essaul, and *Espartero. In addition, Lafirynda's dam, Lala, was a full sister to Amneris, dam of U.S. and Canadian National Champion Stallion *Aramus, and of Aquinor, sire of five national champions, including U.S. National Champion Stallion *Elkin and U.S. National Champion Mare *Elkana.

It is no wonder that *Aladdinn's heritage of champion producers would cause him to do the same, and for his offspring and their offspring to continue this amazing tradition.

So great was *Aladdinn's promise that he was syndicated for seven figures to forty-two shareholders even before he won his national championship. To say the least, *Aladdinn soon proved himself worthy of his investors' faith.

The enchanted smoke from *Aladdinn's lamp seems to envelop all who descend from the dapper little bay. Both get and grandget tend to inherit many of the same fine characteristics that make *Aladdinn himself such an outstanding individual: large eyes set in clean heads, excellent necks and shoulders, sound straight legs supporting good, tight backs, especially strong hindquarters that promote balance and athleticism, and an overall smoothness that draws all the parts together. Many are bay.

Perhaps best of all, they often possess his willing, sensible, quiet demeanor, a personality particularly well-suited to the stresses of the horse show world.

Through 1997 *Aladdinn had sired

*Almaden is a dark bay son of *Aladdinn out of the *Bask daughter La Ambir. Named 1987 U.S. National Champion Stallion, he now stands at stud in Brazil and has sired the Brazilian National Champion Stallion, Cajun Prince HCF. Photo by Judith

1,172 registered purebred Arabian foals. At this writing, *Bask, Khemosabi, and *Aladdinn alone share the honor of having more than 1,000 registered purebred foals. Of his offspring, 63 are national winners and 267 are show champions. *Aladdinn follows only Khemosabi and Bey Shah as the leading

*Aladdinn's most
famous daughter is
SS Follow Me, out of
Contessa-B, and
owned by Dunromin'
Arabians in Pine
Plains, New York.
She was the 1986 U.S.
National Champion
Futurity Filly and the
1990 U.S. National
Champion Mare.
From her first five
foals, she has pro-
duced two national
Top Ten winners.

Photo by
Jerry Sparagowski

Aladdinn Echo, by *Aladdinn and out of the heavily *Raseyn-*Raffles-
bred mare Gaamara, was six times a U.S. National Top Ten winner in
halter. Two of his best sons are Echo Magniffico, the unanimous 1992
U.S. National Champion Stallion, and Ray-Dorr-Echo, a U.S.
National Champion Futurity Colt. Aladdinn Echo stands in Brazil.

Photo by J.R. Little

living sire of champions.

In addition, several have found success
on the racetrack, as well as in other all-
breed disciplines and competitions.

*Aladdinn seems to sire better sons than
he does daughters, with some notable
exceptions, of course. Furthermore, many
carry the success they find in the show
ring right on into the breeding shed.

To follow are just some of *Aladdinn's
most notable sons. First to come to mind
are his previously mentioned four U.S.
National Champion Halter Stallion sons:
AAF Kaset, out of *Kaseta; Strike, out
of Gwyndalyn; Almaden, out of La
Ambir; and Exceladdinn, out of Jortaala.
All have gone on to sire champions of
their own. AAF Kaset, with 14 national
winners and Strike, with 19 national winners, top the list. Strike has sired the
most Class A or better show winners,
with more than 100 to his credit.

Also of note is the red chestnut Alada
Baskin, out of Launa Baske Tu, who was
twice a U.S. Reserve National Champion
Stallion and who has sired 15 national
winners himself. In one particularly superior effort, four of his sons were among the
winners of the U.S. National Futurity
Colts class in 1993: Alada Baskin I, HC
Wacek, Legacy of Gold, and Allionce.

Legacy of Gold later became the 1995 U.S. National Champion Stallion, and Allionce has won multiple national championships in pleasure driving and English pleasure junior horse divisions.

Houston, out of Mustabright, is an *Aladdinn son with an incredible record in performance. He is the only horse ever to win the U.S. National Formal Driving Championship four times (1988 through 1991). Houston also was the 1987 U.S. National Reserve Park Champion, 1989 Canadian National Formal Driving Champion, and Canadian National Reserve Park Champion. Houston also is a sire of national winners.

Another stellar performer is Allience, an *Aladdinn son who is out of the mare A Love Song, the product of the mating of two national halter champions, *Bask and *Elkana. Allience has won the park championships at both the U.S. and Canadian national shows, as well as many other park and English pleasure awards .

Another son, Sensation Al Z, out of *Wenta, was the first stallion ever to be a national performance champion and have an offspring win a national performance championship title at the same show. He was the 1993 Canadian National Western Pleasure Champion while his daughter, HR Alexis, out of JR Dorinda, was the Canadian National Champion Western Pleasure Junior Horse.

Other sons of note include, but are not limited to: Aladdinn Echo, Armagnac, Laddinns Fire, and *Celaddinn. In all, 41 *Aladdinn sons have sired national winners, with many more who have sired at least one show winner.

Perhaps *Aladdinn's most famous daughter is SS Follow Me, out of Contessa-B. She was the 1986 U.S. National Champion Futurity Filly and the 1990 U.S. National Champion Mare. Even more impressively, from only five foals she already has two national winners in halter: 1995 U.S. Top Ten Futurity Gelding Yankee Moon and 1998 U.S. Top Ten Mare (Amateur Owner To Handle) Follow The Sun.

Other illustrious daughters include Ombra Rose, out of *Pliska, the 1986 Canadian National Champion Futurity Filly; and Gwyndyna, out of Gwyndalyn, the 1990 Canadian National Reserve Champion Futurity Filly, to name but two. *Aladdinn daughters have won national

Exceladdinn was a striking red chestnut son of *Aladdinn out of Jortaala. Jortaala was by *Exelsjor and out of Vaalentine, by Amerigo (the sire of Khemosabi). Exceladdinn is being used for breeding in Brazil.
Photo by Jerry Sparagowski

The gray stallion Strike, out of the *Bask daughter Gwyndalyn, was the U.S. National Champion Stallion in 1985. He is *Aladdinn's best-siring son with more than 20 national winners and over 100 AHSA Class A show winners among his offspring.

Photo by Stuart Vesty, courtesy Gallun's Training Center

The *Aladdinn son Alada Baskin, out of Launa Baske Tu, was twice a U.S. Reserve National Champion Stallion. He has sired numerous national winners, including four sons who went Top Ten in the 1993 U.S. National Champion Futurity Colt class. One of those, Legacy of Gold, later became the 1995 U.S. National Champion Stallion, and another, Allionce, won national championships in pleasure driving and English pleasure junior horse.

Photo by Judith

Sensational Al Z, by *Aladdinn and out of *Wenta, in 1993 won the "triple crown" of Arabian showing by winning the western pleasure championships at Scottsdale and the Canadian and U.S. nationals. He was ridden by Bob Hart Jr., shown here.

Photo by Stuart Vesty

championships in junior owner divisions in western pleasure and halter.

Although it has been noted that *Aladdinn sires more good sons than daughters, 31 daughters have produced national winners. Best among them is Ladie Love, out of Gift of Love, who has three national Top Ten winners among her offspring, all by Medalion.

Another top *Aladdinn daughter is Scoundrel, out of DS Aluzja, who, similar to the feat of the *Aladdinn son Sensational Al Z, was the first mare to win a national performance championship as the 1990 Canadian National Hunter Pleasure Champion, and have an offspring do the same at the same national show. Fizjon, by Wizjon, was the 1990 Canadian National Country Pleasure Champion.

The amazing statistics on *Aladdinn and his descendants could easily continue for many more pages, but what about the horse himself?

As a syndicated stallion, *Aladdinn spent most of his breeding career living quietly at the Lasma East breeding facility near LaGrange, Ky., owned for some years after the LaCroixes by Japanese businessman Ryohei Ishikawa and managed by his son, Kazu. There, *Aladdinn and several other top stallions were carefully tended by a battery of

Houston is a top performance son of *Aladdinn. Out of Mustabright, Houston won the U.S. Formal Driving Championship four times, was the 1987 U.S. Reserve National Champion Park Horse, and in 1989 was the Canadian National Formal Driving Champion and reserve Park Champion. At the whip is James Bowman. Owners at the time were Jeannie Bauer and Deb Parent.

Photo by Rob Hess

With the Rick and Paula Taylor family in Provo, Utah, *Aladdinn seems to have at last come home. "He seems happy, content, and enormously self-confident," notes Christy Egan, well-known writer and a friend of the Taylors. "He loved having his picture taken that day in the mountains with the little girls on his back. I think he has found a sense of self, and of peace."

Photo by Rick Van Lent

Here's another picture of *Aladdinn (left) and the Taylor family, with *Nariadni on the right.

Photo by Rick Van Lent

capable managers, veterinarians, and other professionals. However, unlike most of the other horses featured in this book, *Aladdinn for many years was never strongly linked to any one particular human being. And then along came Rick Taylor.

Taylor had made a name for himself in the Arabian horse business by buying the famous Russian stallions *Muscat and *Nariadni. He hadn't planned to purchase *Aladdinn, but when the opportunity arose, he grabbed it.

"When *Aladdinn came to us, we had heard he had some breeding problems," offered Taylor. "He arrived here (in Utah) on a snowy, wintry day, which instantly began to brighten as he stepped off the trailer.

"We had two mares in heat, and he appeared in very good health, so we decided to breed the mares. He enthusiastically bred each one within 30 minutes of his arrival. Both became pregnant, and we've had very few problems since. I should have young colts who do as well as *Aladdinn! So far, between 60 and 70 percent of the mares he breeds get in foal from the first cover."

At the Taylor Ranch, *Aladdinn soon settled into the hands-on riding and management program in which the Taylor family strongly believes. For perhaps the first time in his life he is the star of the stable, loved and pampered, massaged and petted, and, yes, worked.

"*Aladdinn loves the racetrack, loves to gallop there. It's like riding a powerful train engine," said Taylor who often rides the horse himself on the ranch's ⅞-mile training track. "I believe horses are happiest when they are treated like horses, not hot-house flowers. It has been thrilling riding a legend like *Aladdinn, for me and for my whole family. Just being with him is special."

*Aladdinn lives in the late *Muscat's stall, and seems to be very comfortable there, according to Taylor. "*Aladdinn loves Slurpees® and really loves carrots. He has been a gentleman from the beginning.

"*Aladdinn is very prepotent, an extraordinarily consistent sire," Taylor continued. "We've noticed that his offspring are laid-back, confident, easy-going—wonderful to work with.

"It is an honor to have *Aladdinn. Having him here has catapulted our business in a way that would take three lifetimes to achieve with any other horse, and especially with breeders from other countries."

The Taylors receive scores of visitors and lots of letters and phone calls, all asking about *Aladdinn.

"I believe in fate," stated Rick Taylor. "There is some reason why paths cross. Maybe in the case of these three stallions—*Muscat, *Nariadni, and *Aladdinn (the first two are deceased)—we were able to help bring back, even for a short time, the glory and fame they once enjoyed years ago. I hope so. Our stallions have done far more for us than we ever did for them.

"And as our relationship with *Aladdinn grows, so will the stories we have to tell. We love him more and more as time goes on."

*This picture of *Aladdinn was taken in 1984, just as his offspring were beginning to win top halter titles in the national show rings.*

Photo by Jerry Sparagowski

5 SAMTYR

He is one of the all-time leading sires of Arabian racehorses.

ANY WORDS written here must be as much a tribute to the man beloved by many and known simply as "Dr. Sam," as to his mighty red horse, Samtyr. Together, they epitomized the challenges faced and rewards reaped in modern Arabian horse racing in America.

At least through 1996, Samtyr (pronounced Sam-TEER) reigned as the all-time leading sire of Arabian racehorses. Ten times he was Arabian Racehorse Sire of the Year—from 1980 through 1988 and again in 1993. (As much as possible, all race records and earnings reported here are based on information from the Arabian Jockey Club's official data.)

His offspring have won well over $2

Samtyr was a good-looking, well-built chestnut with a lot of speed. The identity of this exercise rider is unknown.

All photos in this chapter are courtesy of Mrs. Bettye Harrison

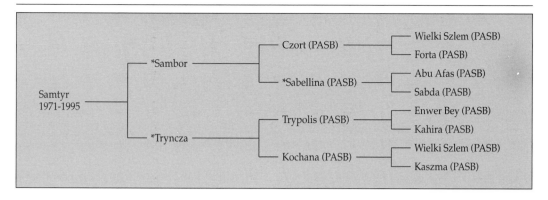

Samtyr
1971-1995

- *Sambor
  - Czort (PASB)
    - Wielki Szlem (PASB)
    - Forta (PASB)
  - *Sabellina (PASB)
    - Abu Afas (PASB)
    - Sabda (PASB)
- *Tryncza
  - Trypolis (PASB)
    - Enwer Bey (PASB)
    - Kahira (PASB)
  - Kochana (PASB)
    - Wielki Szlem (PASB)
    - Kaszma (PASB)

million—an enormous amount in Arabian racing circles. Of his 262 foals, 113 have been race starters who galloped to 353 wins through 1997. His 11 stakes winners share 28 stakes triumphs through the same time period. The average money earned per starter is an incredible $19,010.

When one considers that several Samtyr offspring are still racing, and more than 50 are just now old enough to begin training, it becomes apparent that the statistics will only increase, even though Samtyr is deceased.

On the other hand, simple statistics don't begin to describe the late Sam Harrison, M.D., of Sa-Arabet Arabians in Loudon, Tennessee.

Like a fearless, determined Don Quixote, Dr. Sam charged where few men of good sense dared even to tiptoe. Tireless in his quest to make Arabian horse racing a respected, successful, and profitable sport, he slowly but surely knocked over the windmills of doubt and prejudice as he attained one seemingly impossible goal after another.

In so doing, Dr. Sam often was called crazy, but he really didn't care. "Heck, it's all just a whole lotta fun," he once said with his familiar big grin. "There's just no greater thrill than having your horse win a race. That's the bottom line."

Sam Harrison was born of a long line of physicians and horsemen from Loudon County, Tennessee. Both his grandfather and father were family practitioners who often made their rounds horseback, and the young Sam Harrison grew up with a much-beloved pony. In the early 1940s, he left home to attend medical school. Later he served in World War II and the Korean conflict. Dr. Sam then returned to Loudon to set up his medical office.

As Dr. Sam's practice and family grew, he bought some horses to show locally,

Halter and Performance Record: Race record, 10 (8-2-0); Winner 1975 IAHA Championship Race.

Progeny Record:

Purebred Foal Crops: 21
Purebred Foals Registered: 262
IAHA Legion of Honor Award Winners: 1
Race Starters: 113
Race Money Earned: $2,148,118

and in 1963 he acquired his first Arabian, the gray gelding Hajahn, by Haj-Amin out of Ababa, bred by the famous Cedardell Farms, Plano, Illinois. He was soon actively involved with the breed.

Dr. Sam had always enjoyed horse racing, so it wasn't long before he purchased his first Arabian racehorse, *Dimrak (El Azrak x *Dimatra, by Wielki Szlem), in 1972, about the same time he bought the weanling Samtyr. *Dimrak not only earned some money on the track for the Harrisons, but *Dimrak daughters in time would prove to be excellent crosses with Samtyr.

In addition to being a noted Arabian racehorse owner and breeder, Dr. Sam was a founder in 1983 of the Arabian Jockey Club Inc., the forerunner of the current AJC, and the Arabian Racing Cup series. The latter offers financial incentives and futurity races for participants. By 1995 Dr. Sam had successfully pushed for the first Arabian Cup Championships, patterned after the Thoroughbred industry's Breeders' Cup race day. He also created the annual Darley Awards program, first held in 1987, which is roughly equivalent to the Eclipse Awards given each year to outstanding Thoroughbred racehorses. The

Samtyr had excellent conformation, including straight legs, short cannons, and strong bone. This picture was taken in the winner's circle in May 1975 at Santa Fe Downs in New Mexico. Pat Torres is up, with trainer Nancy Kirkpatrick holding the horse.

best Arabian racehorses and their owners and breeders are honored each year during the Darley Awards banquet and ceremony.

Dr. Sam published the *Arabian Racing News,* the first edition of which appeared in 1977, and began publishing the Annual Racing Record Book in 1981. The Arabian Jockey Club, based in Denver, now compiles and publishes all records.

In essence, Dr. Sam was the hardest worker and greatest cheerleader Arabian horse racing—and the entire American racing industry in general—had ever seen. He personally encouraged, and some might say pushed, more owners and breeders into the game than ever before.

"I just didn't let them not be involved," Dr. Sam told Sharon Moreau of *Arabian Finish Line* magazine a few months before he died from cancer at age 72 on November 21, 1997. "There is a certain group of

people who are interested in horse racing and also in the historical Arabian breed. Although Arabians are not the fastest breed, they are the origin of all the 'hot' breeds and therefore of all the speed breeds. People love to tell bigger and better stories to their neighbor about the history of their horse, and with Arabians it can go so far back no one can tell whether it's true or not, so that makes them king of the hill. Arabian racing is also easier to get involved in, and even a small investment can put you at a higher level than with a Thoroughbred. It's all a lot of fun!"

Through all the fun, Dr. Sam's wife, "Miss Bettye," also a horse lover, was his faithful companion. Although she was not as actively involved as Dr. Sam, Arabian horse people grew to love them both.

"Sam thought that Samtyr was simply the best Arabian stallion in the whole world—not just in Tennessee, not just in racing—but the best in the whole world—period," said Miss Bettye. "When he believed in something, whether it was the stallion or racing or whatever, he believed in it completely. He was very determined."

66

Background

Samtyr, foaled on April 16, 1971, was bred by Leon Rubin of Sir William Farm, Hillsdale, New York. Rubin was an early player in Arabian racing ventures. Samtyr was considered to be pure Polish as both his sire and dam were imported from that Eastern European country. For many years, some considered Poland the producer of the world's best Arabian racehorses.

*Sambor, the sire of Samtyr, was by the Wielki Szlem son Czort and out of *Sabellina, who was by Abu Afas and out of Sabda. *Sambor was a successful race horse, with a record in Poland of eight races (3-2-1). The 3-2-1 means three wins, two seconds, and one third-place finish. In the United States, *Sambor's record reveals six races (3-2-0) in exhibition and pari-mutuel racing.

Like his son, *Sambor also sired some good runners. He has several times led the leading sires list, and through 1997 was in third place (just behind *Wiking) on the list of leading Arabian racehorse sires of all time with $1.4 million won by his 95 starters (for an average of $15,717 per starter) through 1997.

Although he carried Poland's best racing lines, *Sambor also found success as a halter and park horse. He was the 1971 Region VII Champion Stallion and Champion Park Horse, and the 1974 East Coast Champion Stallion. *Sambor was awarded his Legion of Merit title in 1971.

In addition to Samtyr, *Sambor sired such winners as:

• Sam Tiki, out of Kyla Tiki, winner of the Florida Derby and a Darley Award winner.

• Sir William Nissam, 1984 Race Colt of the Year and IAHA Derby winner.

• Sir William Bogdan, 1985 California Derby winner.

• Sir William Tryczam, 1976 IAHA Derby winner and 1981 U.S. National Top Ten in western pleasure.

*Sambor also sired SW Saruchna, the dam of 1986 U.S. National Champion Stallion MS Santana, by *Bask.

Samtyr's dam, *Tryncza, foaled in Poland in 1958, was an extraordinarily good producer. She was by Trypolis, who was unraced, but became one of Poland's leading sires of winning race and show horse lines—especially through his daughters.

Dr. Sam Harrison enjoyed riding his Arabians as well as racing them.

*Tryncza's dam, *Kochana (by Wielki Szlem and out of Kaszmir), raced 13 times with a record of 6-0-3, including 3 stakes wins, one of which was the Polish Oaks.

*Tryncza also produced the following horses:

• Sir William Tryczam, Samtyr's full brother and who was mentioned earlier.

• *Tryptyk, by Aquinor, a Swedish National Champion Stallion and European Senior Champion Stallion.

• *Tryneg, by the famous Negatiw, a U.S. and Canadian National Top Ten Park Horse.

• *Tinian, also by Negatiw, a multiple stakes winner in Poland and a Canadian national performance champion.

• Sir William Tyncza, by *Etiw, dam of Vladin (by MC Bask,), an IAHA Derby winner and the 1987 top money-earner.

Samtyr took the Governor's Cup Handicap by 5 lengths over Las Nutron in September 1975 at the New Mexico State Fair track in Albuquerque. Pat Torres is up, with trainers Vic Oppegard and Nancy Kirkpatrick next to the horse. Holding the award blanket (from right to left) are Dr. Sam and Bettye Harrison and their two sons, Mark and Scott. The others are unknown.

Both *Tryncza and *Sambor were imported from Poland by Samtyr's breeder, Sir William Farm's Leon Rubin.

Career

In the autumn of 1971, Rubin placed the 6-month-old Samtyr in his farm's production sale. Dr. Sam had never seen the youngster, but he was determined to buy him.

"Sam picked out Samtyr strictly from his pedigree," said Miss Bettye. "He liked his sire very much. Of course, his dam was very good, too. Sam had researched Samtyr's whole background and knew this was the colt he wanted. Sam had his money together—actually himself and nine partners to start with—and he took us to New York and we did it. There was never any doubt he would buy the horse.

"I was completely against us ever having a stallion here, you know," Miss Bettye added. "Then Sam just slipped this cute little baby in on me!"

Dr. Sam paid $3,500 for Samtyr, which worked out to $440 for each partner, once insurance and shipping were added, and the young red colt came home to Tennessee.

Samtyr's first race trainer was Ingun Littorin in California. As a 3-year-old,

Samtyr had a record in seven non-pari-mutuel races of 4-1-2. As autumn came, a change seemed in order, and trainer Vic Oppegard took the colt to Santa Fe Downs in New Mexico, one of the few U.S. tracks writing races for Arabians in the 1970s.

Samtyr was a smashing success. He started in six races and won them all, setting four track records in the process between Santa Fe and the track in Albuquerque. Carrying top weight of 127 pounds, he capped his career by winning the 1½- mile IAHA National Championship Race in Albuquerque. Still considered today to be a very fast Arabian horse, Samtyr's best time was 6 furlongs in 1:17.4 on June 1, 1975.

Never out of the money, Samtyr finished his career with a pari-mutuel record in 10 races of 8-2-0. It was time to go home and see if Dr. Sam's belief in Samtyr as a breeding horse would hold true.

Sire Record

Samtyr as an individual had excellent conformation. He was powerful behind as well as through his shoulders, had a deep heart girth and large windpipe, short cannons and strong bone, straight legs and round feet, a beautiful large eye, and an intelligent personality.

"I remember seeing Samtyr for the first

Samtyr's first son, Saam, won the IAHA Super Derby at Chicago's famous Arlington Park in 1980. James Milner was the jockey, and Buzz Smith the trainer. Equus finished second in the race, and Glymarr, third. Saam went on to be a successful endurance horse in later years.

time at Paramont Farm in Kentucky (where Jim Brown stood the horse in the mid-1980s)," wrote Sandy Wollpert in the September 1997 *Arabian Finish Line* magazine. "A beautiful, perfectly balanced, strong-legged chestnut stallion was galloping fast out on the track by the barn. Being partial to chestnuts, and especially to good-legged ones, I asked who he was."

It wasn't long before the track would prove, with great regularity, that Samtyr successfully passed on his best traits to his offspring. "Tough-minded, good-legged, balanced, and fast—that's what a typical Samtyr baby seems most often to be," added Wollpert.

As luck would have it, the very first colt out of the gate was Saam, foaled in 1977 to the mare Count's Jewel, by Count Me, whom Dr. Sam had purchased years before from Gina Manion in Indiana. Saam was named IAHA Race Colt of the Year in 1980, and 1981 Racehorse of the Year. He won the IAHA Derby and five major stakes races, setting several records along the way. In 3 years, he ran 38 races, finishing with a record of 20-10-3, and earning $24,791 in the days when Arabian races paid very little.

Saam retired sound and then became a top endurance horse, counting the grueling Tevis Cup 100-Mile 1-Day Race among his successful finishes.

Other Samtyr offspring quickly followed Saam's lead. Samorc, out of Majorca de Washoe, by *Mohacz, at ages 3 and 4 won seven stakes and was 1981 IAHA Race Colt of the Year and 1982 Racehorse of the Year.

Samorc's full brother, Bobbie's Sam, was 1982 IAHA Race Colt of the Year and won the 1982 IAHA Super Derby, the first pari-mutuel Arabian race run at Chicago's Arlington Park.

Tyrix , out of Dimfixa, by *Dimrak, exploded on the scene in 1983, winning the IAHA Derby and that year's IAHA Race Colt of the Year award (three in a row for Samtyr sons).

The next year, 1984, Tyrix won Arabian racing's crown jewel, the first $52,500 Armand Hammer Classic. Tyrix beat out the full brothers Samstar and Sam's Count (both by Samtyr and out of Count's Jewel, like Saam), who finished second and third, respectively.

Recalled Bob Van Hoose, with great amusement, "I can still hear Dr. Sam singing the song, 'Oh Lord, It's Hard to be Humble,' all the way to the winner's circle after his Tyrix came from last place to beat my Samstar by a neck in that first Armand Hammer Classic!" Tyrix, Samstar, and Sam's Count dominated racing that year. Tyrix had lifetime earnings of $67,466.

The Arabian community, and even the Thoroughbred racing industry, was finally beginning to take note of Arabian racing emerging as a viable sport—almost entirely and directly through the efforts of Dr. Sam and his hot Samtyr runners.

Other big names, such as Alec and Louise Courtelis of Town and Country Farms, began playing a major role. In addition, the number of races and horses started continued to grow, as

One of Samtyr's greatest sons was Tyrix, shown here after winning the inaugural running of the prestigious Armand Hammer Classic in 1984 at Pompano Park in Florida. From left: Bettye Harrison, Dr. Sam Harrison, Sandy and Buzz Smith (trainers), Tyrix with jockey Manuel Criollo aboard, Dr. Armand Hammer and Merv Griffin with trophy, Alec Courtelis, and Kentucky Gov. Martha Layne Collins.

did the number of bloodlines represented by Arabian race horses. More stallions assumed top siring spots as purses increased.

Samtyr's offspring remained among the hottest, however, and continued to dominate racing headlines. The aforementioned Sam's Count (foaled in 1979) was the first Arabian whose lifetime earnings exceeded $100,000. His official record in 74 races over a 5-year period was 23-17-10, with 12 major stakes wins—a testament to soundness, if nothing else. His $113,796 in official lifetime earnings made him one of Samtyr's highest money-earners through 1997.

His full brother Samstar won several stakes and had a record in 76 races of 17-16-10 with $43,481 in lifetime earnings.

Sam's Fix, a full brother to Tyrix, got a late start in racing but still won four stakes. He made history when he became the first Arabian ever claimed in a claiming race.

The Samtyr son Saaray, out of HCC Malosca, by *Wosk, won the 1986 ARC Classic, defeating the Polish stallion *Wiking, and then ran second to *Wiking in the 1987 Armand Hammer Classic. Saaray's full sister, Bettye Sam, also was a winner.

Other Samtyr get who dominated the 1980s include the mare Samtyra, out of Dimfixa, by *Dimrak, who won Darley Awards in 1987 and 1988, and the mare Jessorca, out of Dimorca, by *Dimrak, who was a Darley Award winner and won the prestigious Paramont Arabian Cup Oaks. Jessorca's full sister, Kimorca, also was a stakes winner. Other winning Samtyr-bred runners include Forest Hill Rage, Abac, Edenstreak, Raja Sam, Saaka, Tyrixa, Samraja, Miss Reed, Cain, Tyx, Unisys, Electyra, Alive Alive O, and many more.

In summary, it is important to note that the Arabian Horse Trust Racing Hall of Fame inductee Dimfixa, by *Dimrak, produced these aforementioned top racehorses: Tyrix, Tyx, Samtyra, Tyrixa, and Sams Fix. All were sired by Samtyr and bred by Dr. Sam. It should also be noted that Counts Jewel, by Count Me, produced Samstar (sire of U.S. National Champion Racehorse Charlie Valentine), Sams Count, Saam, Cool Sam, and Counts Star. Again, all were sired by Samtyr and bred by Dr. Sam. That's an impressive record in anybody's book.

Samtyr's top money-earner overall through 1997 was the powerful gray stallion TC Tomtyr, out of Kellowna by Kello-Gwalor. Foaled in 1988, TC Tomtyr won, over a 5-year period, more than $218,000 with an official record of 22-10-1 in 36 races. He finished out of the money only three times.

By 1984, the top three Arabian lifetime money earners were all by Samtyr. Left to right: Samstar, Sam's Count, and Tyrix.

Illustration by Karen Kasper

Samtyr's second leading money-earner through 1997 was Sam's Count, as previously stated.

Interestingly, the third leading money-earner is a full brother to TC Tomtyr, the gray stallion Tomanchie. Foaled in 1990, his record through 1997 was 6-1-0 in seven races,with $104,245 in lifetime earnings. Both TC Tomtyr and Tomanchie were bred by Tom and Eunice Luckett of Louisville, Kentucky.

Fourth among Samtyr's top money-earning offspring is Sam Taire, out of Joras Debonair, by Jora Honey Ku. In 29 races over 4 years and a record 11-7-4, that horse had earnings of $102,925.

Samtyr's fifth-ranked money-earner through 1997: Sams Louisa, a bay mare out of Scimitar Georgia, by Fadi. She won $94,424 in 37 races (16-8-2) over a 6-year period.

The Twilight Years

Dr. Sam syndicated Samtyr in 1984 for $500,000. After his stint in Kentucky, the red stallion, for the most part, reigned supreme with Dr. Sam at home on the farm in Tennessee.

"Samtyr's temperament was extremely good," recalled Miss Bettye. "He was very nice to be around. Sam always attributed it to the fact that Samtyr was left in the field with the mares; he was never confined. It made a big difference.

"We sold him to Jim Wagner of Godolphin Racing Inc. in the early '90s, and extended the payments over 3 years, with Jim to make each payment as long as the horse continued to produce for him. This worked out well, and we were paid in full by the time the 3 years were up. So, I think Jim was happy and he had a few more good foals by the horse."

A banner year for the Harrison program was 1995, when the first Arabian Cup Championships were held, when Samtyr and Dimfixa were inducted into the Arabian Horse Trust Racing Hall of Fame, and when Dr. Sam was inducted into the AHT Tent of Honor.

Samtyr died in 1995 at the age of 24.

George Bernard Shaw once wrote, "You see things and say 'Why?' But I dream things that never were; and I say 'Why not.'" That could have been the motto of Dr. Sam Harrison's life, but he had his own motto which those in racing heard time and time again, and which perhaps best sums up his famous red horse and his love of Arabian horse racing. Quite simply: "The best you bet!"

6

*NABORR

Imported from Poland, he became a very successful sire in the United States.

ON OCTOBER 14, 1969, one man and one horse, in one moment at one horse sale, dramatically changed the face of the Arabian horse industry. That event proved to be the catalyst for an explosion in popularity, value, and prices for purebred Arabians that would rise to spectacular heights through the mid-1980s and continued to support high prices for the best individuals into at least the late 1990s.

"I looked up and I could see this white-haired man way up in the middle of the back bleachers, keeping sort of a low profile," the late Jimmy Dean once told this author and her husband. Dean's Tip Top Sale and Auction Service of Sanders, Ky., was managing Anne McCormick's estate sale, a 60-horse lineup that included her

Naborr at age 20 in 1970 in the Arizona desert, soon after he was purchased by Tom Chauncey for the then-record auction price of $150,000.

Photo by Polly Knoll

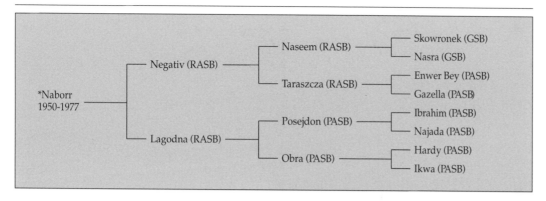

```
                                    ┌─ Skowronek (GSB)
                    ┌─ Naseem (RASB) ─┤
                    │                 └─ Nasra (GSB)
   ┌─ Negativ (RASB) ┤
   │                 │                 ┌─ Enwer Bey (PASB)
   │                 └─ Taraszcza (RASB) ┤
*Naborr              │                 └─ Gazella (PASB)
1950-1977 ┤
   │                                   ┌─ Ibrahim (PASB)
   │                 ┌─ Posejdon (PASB) ┤
   │                 │                 └─ Najada (PASB)
   └─ Lagodna (RASB) ┤
                     │                 ┌─ Hardy (PASB)
                     └─ Obra (PASB) ───┤
                                       └─ Ikwa (PASB)
```

famous Russian-born stallion, *Naborr.

"Well," said Dean, "the man sitting there was Tom Chauncey, but nobody knew who Tom Chauncey was then. The auctioneer looked up there and said, 'Sir, are you bidding? Or are you just waving at somebody?' And he said, 'I'm bidding.'

"We knew that the horse would bring a lot of money," Dean continued. "He was kind of a myth, and everybody was speculating on what he would bring. People were makin' up syndicates and gettin' their money together, and it was the darndest thing you ever saw."

The auctioneer that day, Dean Parker, recalled that until the McCormick sale, the highest-priced Arabian horse at auction had gone for $25,000, and the highest-priced mare for $14,500. "*Naborr was one of those rare horses. He never stopped but he stopped perfectly balanced. He never walked but he walked calmly. He just had a carriage, a presence, a presentation about himself that was fantastic," Parker said in an *Arabian Horse Breed Journal* interview.

Continuing, he added, "You know, the privilege of having sold him is not that he brought a record-breaking price. I have sold quite a few horses since then for more money. It is the idea that I sold such a great horse. It's one of the highlights of my life."

Tom Chauncey (now deceased) recounted his version of the purchase in the same magazine. "I was going to buy the horse whatever he cost," Chauncey said. "I didn't tell my wife (Deedie). The only person I did talk to was (entertainer) Wayne Newton. He wanted to go to $40,000.

"Wayne was doing a show for General Motors that day. If Wayne had stayed, we'd have wound up bidding against each other." Instead, a month later they became partners on the stallion.

During the early bidding, not even Deedie, who sat right next to Tom, real-

Halter and Performance Record: 1954 Reserve National Champion Stallion—Moscow, USSR.

Progeny Record:

Purebred Foal Crops: 23
Purebred Foals Registered: 413
U.S./Canadian National Winners: 46
Class A Champions: 151
IAHA Legion of Honor Award Winners: 6
IAHA Legion of Supreme Honor Award Winners: 1
IAHA Legion of Merit Award Winners: 19
IAHA Legion of Supreme Merit Award Winners: 2

Naborr, foaled in Russia, had beautiful eyes and a white coat he inherited from his sire, Negatiw.* **Photo by Polly Knoll

*Even at age 27,
*Naborr remained
healthy and vigorous.*

Photo by
Jerry Sparagowski

***Naborr descended
from a line known
for its tremendous
stamina and
endurance.**

ized he was bidding. "When she found
out," offered Chauncey, "she said, 'Well,
it's your nickel!'"

The bidding progressed rapidly by
$5,000 increments until it stalled at
$100,000. Chauncey entered the game
at $102,000. The action continued
between the snowy-haired Phoenix businessman and a California syndicate
made up of Robert Brunson, Mary Ann
Hannah, and C.V. Wood Jr., of the
McCulloch Corporation.

When all was said and done, nearly
an hour after *Naborr entered the sales
ring, Tom Chauncey had purchased a
19-year-old Arabian stallion for $150,000.
So incredible was that price in 1969,
that it made the pages of the *Los Angeles
Times* and several national television
news programs.

"That's when all the monkey business
(of high prices) started," said Jimmy
Dean, "at one of my sales." When
Chauncey went outside with his new
horse, the crowd did too. Of course, there
were many more horses to sell, and after
two or three colts brought only about
$1,800 each, the auctioneer realized he
needed that crowd back. At that point,
Chauncey sent word, and Dean Parker
announced, that Chauncey would take a
few outside mares to be bred to *Naborr
for an amazing $10,000 stud fee each. The
crowd returned to their seats.

"The next colt that came in," recalled
Dean, "was a ratty, moth-eaten yearling
colt, and he brought $7,000, and from then
on the prices went up. That was the beginning of those high prices. The whole thing
went just like a grass fire."

Just who was this *Naborr, this mythic
horse who ignited the blaze? His story
begins in Poland, travels through the
former Soviet Union, back to Poland, and
finally to the United States.

*Naborr (pronounced Na-BORE and
spelled Nabor in Europe) descended from
a line known for its tremendous stamina
and endurance, even under the harshest

conditions. His forebears and he himself proved this on several occasions.

In 1936, the Soviet Union purchased from Lady Judith Wentworth, of England's Crabbet Park Stud, a group of horses that included the 14-year-old Skowronek son Naseem, out of Nasra. The Russians hoped to dramatically improve their Arabian breeding program at the state-owned Tersk Stud, located in the Caucasus Mountains near the Turkish border.

Three years later, in 1939, Hitler invaded Poland. Within 2 weeks, the Russians, claiming they needed to protect their borders from the Germans, attacked Poland from the east. They soon "liberated" the one remaining Arabian stud, Janow Podlaski, and confiscated the 50 best horses, who were shipped to Tersk. Among them were Lagodna, *Naborr's dam, and Taraszcza, *Naborr's paternal grandam.

In 1941, Hitler directly invaded Russia, and the Tersk horses were evacuated. The stallions went by truck, but the broodmares, yearlings, and a few foals walked the 1,000-plus miles to safety in the Trans-Caspian area (a story in itself). The herd was returned to Tersk in 1943.

In 1944, the Soviets bred Taraszcza of Poland to Naseem of England to produce, in 1945, the stallion Negatiw (also spelled Negativ). When the 4-year-old Negatiw was bred to the Polish-born Lagodna (Posejdon x Obra), the resulting foal, born on April 13, 1950, was *Naborr.

By 1954, *Naborr had matured nicely and was named reserve champion stallion at the Moscow show. His sire, Negatiw, was champion. *Naborr was purchased at age 5 by the Michalow State Stud of Poland to be used as part of its rebuilding process following the devastation of two world wars.

Ignacy Jaworowski, later the director at Michalow, wrote of his first sight of *Naborr in 1955: "(His) remarkable Arabian type, mild Saklawi beauty, dry, fine head with black, expressive eyes, swan neck, and milk-white hair unusual for his age were really very impressive. He resembled the Arabian horses painted by Juliusz Kossak, the best painter of oriental horses."

Jaworowski cared for *Naborr for 7 years, riding him occasionally and observing him often. "His good, docile character, full of dignity and inborn intelligence, was

*Kaborr, by *Naborr and out of Bint Kholameh, was often referred to as the "spittin' image" of his sire.*   Photo by Jerry Sparagowski

A head shot of Kaborr, who won a Canadian National Championship in both stallion halter and western pleasure.

Photo courtesy of Tom Chauncey Arabians

The *Naborr son *Aramus (Ah-RAH-moos) became famous for two reasons. First, in 1970 he won both the U.S. and Canadian national champion stallion titles, and second, he was owned by the famous entertainer and long-time Arabian horse breeder Wayne Newton. *Aramus was also a Canadian National Park Champion and U.S. National Formal Driving Champion.

Photo by Polly Knoll

captivating for anybody who had been in close touch with him," Jaworowski continued. "He was a very sound horse, he had never been ill.

"*Naborr is a proven producer of pure-bred Arabian horses. His great prepotency resulted extremely well in the breeding of the Polish Arabian horses. From among all the colts, *Naborr's children were always easy to recognize. They were always gray. They inherited very fine heads, light, full of harmony, conformation, and a very subtle Saklawi beauty. Mating with the Amurath Sahib bloodline and the line of Miecznik had given especially phenomenal results."

Dr. Eugene LaCroix, who imported the legendary *Bask and established one of the finest Arabian horse breeding programs in the world, recalled seeing *Naborr in Poland in 1962.

"It wasn't until I saw *Bask and *Naborr that I saw what the painters had been painting for centuries. They were like something that was merged out of the past. The Poles had been breeding the Arabian horse for 500 years, and they hadn't lost sight of his elegance," he said in an interview for *The Arabian Horse Breed Journal*.

LaCroix noted the consistent high quality of the Polish Arabians and noted that the best were by two stallions: *Naborr and Witraz. "We considered buying *Naborr, but they gave me the idea that he couldn't be bought," said LaCroix. So, he purchased four horses: *Bask (see his chapter in this book), *Bajram, *Gwadiana (dam of *Gwalior, by *Naborr), and *Gwazdawa (a *Naborr daughter), with options on 23 more.

After Dr. LaCroix returned home to Scottsdale, he decided to again ask for a price on *Naborr. "I was surprised when they offered him to me." The Poles had recently acquired *Naborr's sire, Negatiw, from the Soviets, and may have been more willing, then, to part with *Naborr.

So, why didn't the white stallion claim a spot alongside *Bask as a major sire at LaCroix's Lasma Arabians? In a name: Anne McCormick.

Mrs. McCormick was a somewhat eccentric woman given to wearing pounds of silver and turquoise jewelry, Indian-type clothing, and fur coats. As the wife of the chairman of the board of the International Harvester Company, she had the means and the contacts required to accumulate some of the finest horses available—and keep them in grand style. Her McCormick Ranch, located near Scottsdale, had pink barns, and its gravel roadways were dyed a bright green and kept perfectly raked at all times.

"Mrs. McCormick heard about the deal, so I went down there to show her the pictures of *Naborr," Dr. LaCroix related. "I told her I had already made arrangements to buy the horse. But she said, 'Why don't you let me buy the horse?' She was really quite firm about it." So, Anne McCormick bought *Naborr.

As told in the *Bask chapter, on January 23, 1963, a ship set sail bound for New York City, carrying what would prove to be a very precious cargo indeed. Included among the 15 Arabian horses aboard were both *Bask and *Naborr. En route, the ship hit a terrible storm. Huge waves tossed it about for days on end. The horses were miserable and hay supplies ran low.

By the time the ship made port on March 9, 1963, the 15 horses were a sorry lot. *Naborr, however, looked quite good, considering. He had lost only about 50 pounds and seemed to be quite healthy. Jaworowski, who traveled with the horses, attributed it to *Naborr's calm, mature demeanor, his inbred ability to endure harsh conditions, and "very good food conversion" tendencies, which he often passed on to his offspring. "Nothing seemed to bother him," he said.

Offspring

From 1963 until Chauncey acquired him in 1969, *Naborr was used mainly on McCormick's mares and was only available to outside breeders on a limited basis. During those 6 years, he sired 82 registered purebred foals. Under Chauncey's ownership, a period of 8 years, *Naborr sired nearly 260 foals. Not bad for an old fellow!

While all those youngsters were growing up, several offspring foaled earlier in Poland were imported to the United States and met with tremendous show ring success during the 1960s and 1970s. The more prominent among them were:

• *Gwalior (out of Gwadiana, by Amurath Sahib), three times a U.S. Reserve National Champion Stallion, 1971 Canadian National Champion Stallion, and a U.S. National Reserve Champion Park Horse.

• *Druzba (out of *Druchna, by Rozmaryn), a U.S. and Canadian Top Ten Stallion.

• *Faraon (out of Forta, by Kuhailan Abu Urkub), Canadian Top Ten Stallion.

• *Gwiazdor (out of *Gwadiana, by Amurath Sahib), Canadian Top Ten Stallion.

• *Mirzaz (out of Mira, by Wielki Szlem), a U.S. Top Ten Park Horse.

• *Werbor (imported en utero and out of *Antwerpia), a U.S. and Canadian Top Ten Stallion.

• *Eskadra (out of Ela, by Miecznik), Canadian Reserve National Champion Mare, U.S. Top Ten Mare, and U.S. Top Ten Park Horse.

• *Wirginia (out of Werbena, by Wojski), U.S. National English Pleasure Champion.

• *Lawina (out of Lawenda, by Doktryner), a Canadian Top Ten Mare.

Easily the most memorable and beloved of *Naborr's Polish offspring who later came to America were his son *Aramus (out of Amneris, by Amurath Sahib) and his daughter *Dornaba (out of Darda by Amurath Sahib).

*Aramus in 1970 won both the U.S. and Canadian national champion stallion awards, and he was a U.S. National Formal Driving Champion and Canadian National Park Champion. He and his descendants have had phenomenal success in the show ring, and have proven to be very popular with Arabian horse lovers around the world.

His soulmate was the well-known singer, entertainer, and long-time Arabian

Mrs. McCormick was a somewhat eccentric woman given to wearing pounds of silver and turquoise jewelry, Indian-type clothing, and fur coats.

*Riffle, by *Naborr and out of *Rifilla, was a Canadian National Park Champion and U.S. National Formal Driving Champion. Owned by Vantage Point Arabians, he's shown here with Ron Palelek in the saddle.*

Photo by
Johnny Johnston

horse breeder Wayne Newton. Newton has often claimed that it was "love at first sight" when he saw *Aramus in 1970.

"There is no doubt that *Aramus is the reason I am in the Arabian horse business today," said Newton.

*Dornaba was the 1966 National Champion Mare in both the United States and Canada, and a U.S. Reserve National Champion English Pleasure Horse. Asked to name the top three most beautiful mares ever to grace an arena, most Arabian enthusiasts will include this incomparable female. Selected in Poland by Dr. Howard F. Kale, along with another *Naborr daughter, *Eskadra (mentioned earlier), *Dornaba was an amazing individual. She became pure white, having turned snowy at an unusually young age, and was both elegant and extraordinarily athletic.

After her retirement from competition, she was a good broodmare, producing such horses as Canadian National Champion Mare Jewel Drift, by *Silver Drift. Unfortunately, she died at a relatively young age.

All told, 46 *Naborr sons and daughters won 122 national top tens or better. Further, more than 150 of his offspring have won over 500 Class A or better championships over the years.

The Elite

Best known among *Naborr's national-winning offspring foaled in North America are:

• Gai-Adventure (out of Gavrelle, by Ferzon), the 1974 U.S. National Champion Stallion bred by Dan Gainey and owned at the time of his win by Verl Shel and the Beehive Syndicate.

• Silver Caprice (out of Miss Century, by Ga'Zi) and Sterling Silver (out of Wahida, by Ferseyn), both Canadian Top Ten mares.

• Riffle (out of *Rifilla), Canadian National Park Champion, U.S. National Formal Driving Champion, and U.S. National Formal Combination Champion, trained and shown by Ron Palelek.

• Ibn Naborr (out of Arizona Rose), a Canadian National Stock Horse Champion.

*Considered by some to be the most beautiful Arabian mare ever, *Dornaba was the 1966 U.S. National Champion Mare in both the United States and Canada, and was a U.S. Reserve National English Pleasure Champion. She was by *Naborr and out of the mare Darda. *Dornaba was imported from Poland by Dr. Howard F. Kale.*

• Naborro (out of *Mimika), a U.S. Top Ten Park winner.

• Kaborr (out of Bint Kholameh, a Wrigley-bred mare), Canadian National Champion in both stallion halter and western pleasure. He was also the first *Naborr foal born at Tom Chauncey Arabians, and was one of *Naborr's most look-alike sons.

Not only did *Naborr's record-breaking purchase change the face of the Arabian industry, it led to the capture of a man's heart as well. As Chauncey explained in a 1975 interview, he had no intention of going into the Arabian horse breeding business, let alone allowing it to change his life. He had owned Thoroughbred race horses and Quarter Horse ranch horses, and enjoyed riding, but this was different.

"When you own a horse like *Naborr, you go where he takes you," said Chauncey.

The white stallion soon took the white-haired man down the road to some raw desert property north of Scottsdale. Before long, barns and paddocks were built, and some wonderful mares added

to the Chauncey family. Wayne Newton sold his half of *Naborr back to Chauncey (Newton had since acquired *Aramus), and the rest is history.

*Naborr's last foal was born on October 1, 1978, nearly 9 years after his sale to Tom Chauncey. In fact, his last foal crop, in 1978, numbered 36, all sired when the stallion was 27 years old.

Chauncey and *Naborr remained good friends until the end. Before *Naborr's death, Chauncey said, "He is white-headed, just like me. And he is stubborn as hell. He knows what he wants. Once he makes up his mind, nobody is going to change it. But the stubbornness is sprinkled with drops of one other trait that makes it all worthwhile. With kindness, you can get him to do what you want.

"I never go out to the barn at any time of day or night that he doesn't talk to me, and it is always in a very low chortle. We understand each other."

7

*MUSCAT

He was one of the most regal and majestic stallions in the history of the breed.

AN EARLY WINTER darkness shrouded the city of Brest on Poland's eastern boundary with the Soviet Union. Near its heavily guarded border crossing, an American and his Dutch friend sat in a truck and peered nervously through the gloom.

Surely after all this time, after the thousands of dollars spent, after the pleas and complicated negotiations . . . surely after so much heartache and sweat . . . surely the van would be there.

Behind their seat, in the back of their own van, the men could hear their living cargo. Two valuable breeding stallions, American Standardbred trotters, stamped in the cold, snorted and fussed. They were ready too.

It was January 8, 1978, and the Cold War was at its height. Two Westerners deep in communist territory were, at best, in a somewhat uneasy situation. At worst, they were at the mercy of every bureaucrat and policeman for miles around. For the American, especially, that day could have engendered his worst nightmare or the realization of his fondest dream.

With relief, the men saw that the others had indeed arrived. The time had come.

*A 1986 photograph of the striking red chestnut stallion, *Muscat, when he was 15 years old. The photograph was taken on the lawn of Karho Arabians in Scottsdale.*

Photo by
Jerry Sparagowski

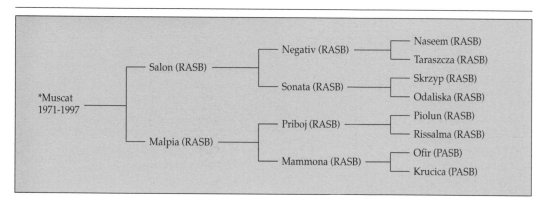

			Naseem (RASB)
		Negativ (RASB)	Taraszcza (RASB)
	Salon (RASB)		Skrzyp (RASB)
		Sonata (RASB)	Odaliska (RASB)
*Muscat 1971-1997			Piolun (RASB)
		Priboj (RASB)	Rissalma (RASB)
	Malpia (RASB)		Ofir (PASB)
		Mammona (RASB)	Krucica (PASB)

Carefully unloading the two stallions, they walked forward and handed them over to the men standing there. A moment later, the American, Howard F. "Howie" Kale Jr., took the lead shank on a brilliant chestnut Arabian stallion. He ran his hand down the horse's neck and looked into his eyes. *Muscat—probably the best Arabian stallion in the world at that time—looked back. Said Kale of the now-famous border exchange: "It was one of those rare moments of fulfillment in life."

The tension quickly gave way to camaraderie as the vodka flowed and toasts were made all around. The Soviets had what they wanted far more than cash: two of America's promising Standardbred breeding stallions. One was the young Centennial Way, who was out of the wonderful mare Kerry Way, the 1966 Hambletonian winner (one of very few mares to win this most prestigious race), and by a son of Speedy Scot, one of the best trotting sires of the 1970s.

And Kale, at last, had *Muscat.

As soon as politeness allowed, Kale and his Dutch friend, Robbie den Hartog Jr., began the long trip back to Holland. They dared not stop for long and spent 34 straight hours in the van, including an agonizing 6-hour hold-up on the East German border. Finally, the two men and their precious stallion arrived jubilant, albeit exhausted, at the den Hartog family's Kossack Stud stables at 6 a.m. on January 10.

Kale's incredible journey to Brest actually began in England 3½ years earlier when he arrived there to look for a stallion to take his family's 30-year Arabian horse breeding program (located in Washington state) to the next level. Kale and his parents, Dr. Howard and Marybeth Kale, had had success with the stallions *Silver Drift (a full brother to *Serafix, who has a chapter in this book) and Tornado, a *Bask son,

Halter and Performance Record: Triple Crown Winner, 1980: Scottsdale Champion Stallion, Canadian National Champion Stallion, U.S. National Champion Stallion.

Progeny Record:

Purebred Foal Crops: 23
Purebred Foals Registered: 1,028
U.S./Canadian National Winners: 47
Class A Champions: 171
IAHA Legion of Honor Award Winners: 8
IAHA Legion of Supreme Honor Award Winners: 1
IAHA Legion of Excellence Award Winners: 1
IAHA Legion of Merit Award Winners: 1
Race Starters: 14
Race Money Earned: $31,287

*This well-known photograph of *Muscat clearly shows his unusual facial markings. Regarding the pronunciation of *Muscat, Howie Kale says Muss-COTT, while the Russians say MOOSE-cott. However, he was affectionately known as Scotty.*

Photo by Polly Knoll

Muscat's famous trot is captured in this 1986 photograph. Note his glorious tail.

Photo by
Jerry Sparagowski

*Howard "Howie" Kale Jr. and his beloved *Muscat in February 1987 at Scottsdale.*

Photo by Polly Knoll

among others, and were ready to go on.

While on the 1974 trip to England, Kale saw the beautiful stallion Nashmeshnik (Arax x Neposeda, by Priboj), who, he found out upon inquiry, had been imported from the Tersk Stud in Russia. However, the horse was not for sale. Then Kale recalled that while in Poland a few months earlier he had seen the lovely *Namiet (*Salon x Naturshitsa, by Arax), who also was Tersk-bred. Were there any more like them back at the farm? Kale was determined to find out.

In London's J.A. Allen Horseman's Book Store, Kale asked Mr. Allen if he knew anything about Russian Arab horses. The owner nodded and climbed to the shop's third floor, where he pulled out Volume II of *The Russian Arabian Stud Book.* Never mind that it was printed in the Cyrillic alphabet; Kale knew that, quite possibly,

*SR Nadom, a chestnut stallion by *Muscat and out of Nazra, by Sport, was foaled at Tersk and imported by Saddle Rock Ranch in California. He was three times a U.S. National Top Ten Stallion and also won a Canadian Top Ten Stallion Award.

Photo by
Jerry Sparagowski

he held an extremely valuable piece of the world's Arabian horse breeding puzzle.

A brilliant and determined man, Kale holed up in a London hotel and began to translate the entire book, letter by letter. Hundreds of hours later, he emerged with his head filled with such names as Ofir, Naseem, *Naborr, and Aswan, names Kale recognized from his own extensive knowledge of international bloodlines. He also realized the Russians had been quietly breeding Arabian horses in a way that was difficult or impossible to do anywhere else, given that they had access to some rare bloodlines and, more importantly, were crossing them in remarkable ways.

Kale knew he had to go to the Soviet Union and in June 1975, he arrived at Tersk for the first of many visits. His life would never be the same.

The Tersk breeding program was based, for the most part, on specific importations made over many years. As Kale explained to this author, "The Russians imported the French stallion Kann and six mares in 1930, followed in 1936 by a group from

Lady Wentworth at the Crabbet Stud in England. The Russians were smart; they agreed to buy the three stallions and nine mares she wanted to sell, then they chose ten more they really wanted to buy and presented her with an all or nothing scenario. They got the horses they wanted."

More outstanding Arabian horses were acquired as "spoils of war" from the Polish breeding farms during World War II. Mix in the Nazeer son Aswan, a gift to the Soviet Union from Egypt in 1963, and you have the basis of the Tersk Stud's superb Arabian horse breeding program in the 1970s. However, only a very few North American breeders even knew that it existed.

Kale was thrilled by the horses he saw there, and realized that the Russian breeding and record-keeping practices were far superior to many others. He also knew he had to own some of these horses.

There was, however, one problem: Neither the Arabian Horse Registry of America ("The Registry") or the World

This is the bay stallion MHR Muscateal, the 1995 U.S. National Reining Champion, ridden by John Slack. By *Muscat and out of the *Bask daughter MHR Princess Bask, he is owned by Heidi and Audrey Zinke, West Covina, California. Photo by Cappy Jackson

Arabian Horse Organization (WAHO) would accept the Russian studbooks.

Ed Tweed, of the Brusally Ranch in Scottsdale (see the chapter on Skorage), in the 1960s had imported a few Tersk Arabians, including Park and *Sportsmenka. Tweed's horses were turned down for registration at that time.

Nevertheless, Kale convinced his father and several other breeders that it would be wise to try to acquire some of these horses and work on registering them later.

"It was no surprise to me that the first group out of Tersk was the best," explained Kale. "I was determined to get 20 of the best they had. It took five trips to get the first package together. I told them (the Russians) that only the best would be good enough to make it in the United States. I said, 'If you value your reputation in the United States, these are the ones I'll take. If you don't, goodbye.' If they were second-class, there was nothing for me—I wasn't interested.

"Taming Dan Gainey and Jay Stream (the presidents of The Registry and WAHO, respectively) was not easy. My first trip to Tersk was in 1975. Our first imports were in 1976, and none of the horses were registered until 1979." (All of Tweed's Tersk horses, except Park, were also registered then.)

The first group of horses included the stallion *Nariadni (Nabeg, by Arax, and out of Nariadnaia, by Aswan). "*Nariadni was our first choice for our personal program as the best complement for our *Silver Drift daughters," said Kale. "He would build best on earlier generations of excellence."

Indeed, *Nariadni would eventually become a championship-winning show horse and a very good sire in the United States. He was a lovely chocolate chestnut stallion of exquisite type, with a particularly beautiful and symmetrical head and a delightful personality.

But there was another stallion at Tersk on that June day in 1975 who out-and-out stole Howie Kale's heart. He was a stallion some later called *Nariadni's "big brother," so closely were their lives aligned, though not their blood. He was a stallion who was the other member of the pair Kale still refers to as "my right hand and my left hand." He was the big red horse *Muscat. He was 4 years old, and he was not for sale, at any price.

Mussiah, described as a strong, elegant horse, stands at the Taylor Ranch in Utah. He is by *Muscat and out of the Tersk-bred mare *Nissa. *Nissa is by the Egyptian stallion Aswan and out of Napersnitsa, who traces to the wonderful English Crabbett stallion Naseem.

Photo by J.R. Little

*Muscat was that one in 100,000 foals who is the super-happy combination of what he came from.

*Muscat's sire, *Salon, was one of Tersk's top breeding stallions. "*Salon was a very good horse who had some problems," said Kale. "Malpia (*Muscat's dam) was a wonderful mare who was a little plain. *Muscat was that one in 100,000 foals who is the super-happy combination of what he came from. Of the millions and millions of genetic possibilities from two parents, a few end up at the top end. Only one or two of those will hit the super jackpot, taking all the best that two parents are capable of producing and taking that to a new level of greatness. *Salon and Malpia had every right to produce *Muscat, but no obligation. . . .

"*Muscat ended up with a unique combination that left behind almost everything but the good stuff, enabling him to pass it on," said Kale. "The Russians knew it. They basically sold *Salon when they got *Muscat. They were not about to let him go."

*Muscat, who was foaled on April 15, 1971, was best noted for his excellent conformation and a dynamic, cadenced trot, in which he moved with strength and animation off all four corners. In addition, his overall beauty contributed to his striking presence, highlighted always by a unique question-mark blaze that made him instantly recognizable everywhere he went.

Tersk's director, Alexander "Sasha" Ponomarev, so believed in *Muscat's value that he started to breed the horse when he was only a 3-year-old, the first time in 40 years that a Tersk stallion was used before age 4. Again and again Ponomarev told the big American, "No," and again and again, Kale asked to buy the horse.

Finally, Kale simply went over Ponomarev's head. In Moscow, he contacted Alexander Martinenkov, director of horse

The famous "Amber sisters," both by *Muscat, were almost full siblings and often appeared together in the same show rings and sales arenas. Amber Silk (left) was twice a U.S. National Top Ten Mare and once a Canadian Top Ten Mare. Amber Satin was the 1987 U.S. National Champion Mare. The mares' dams were the full sisters Silk N Silver and Satin Silver (respectively), who were by Tornado, a *Bask son, and out of Silver Sprite, a *Silver Drift daughter.

Photo by Jerry Sparagowski

breeding in the Ministry of Agriculture, and asked him, "What does the Soviet Agricultural Department want more than it wants *Muscat?" The answer? Two of America's very best Standardbred stallions.

In addition to obtaining and shipping the horses, Kale had to guarantee them against all defects for 120 days, but could ask for no guarantees on *Muscat. He had to accept the stallion "as is." So, after 2½ years of precious time, hundreds of thousands of dollars spent, and 13 trips to the Soviet Union, Howie Kale stood holding *Muscat's lead shank at the Polish-Soviet border.

"My motivation wasn't money or entertainment," explained Kale. "He was my ninth stallion, not my first. I *knew* it was worth the effort to work that hard because I *knew* what he would sire; I *knew* what his pedigree predicted. He inspired me. 'No' was simply not an acceptable answer. I was not unaware of the economic impact of what he would sire, but I would have made much more money using that same energy doing something else.

"He simply inspired me to give of my time and energy to an unreasonable degree. He gave me a great gift; he made me work harder and go through more hell than I ever realized I was capable of doing. With him, I knew what I could contribute. There was no mystery in that promise. His promise was *that* strong."

Show and Sire Record

*Muscat fulfilled his promise in at least two ways. First, he simply blew the socks off his competition in the show ring. On what will long be remembered as "Russian Sunday" at the huge February 1980 Scottsdale All-Arabian Horse Show, *Muscat—with Howie Kale himself showing him—was named grand champion

HK Breeze is a good example of the *Muscat-*Nariadni cross. He is by *Muscat and out of Crown Narada (*Nariadni x Jewel Drift, by *Silver Drift). He stands at the Taylor Ranch in Utah.

Photo by Javan

*Muscat fulfilled his promise in at least two ways.

stallion. (In addition, several other Tersk-bred horses won awards in various classes at this, the first Scottsdale show at which they were eligible to compete.)

*Muscat then went on to win both the Canadian and U.S. national champion stallion titles in that same year, an accomplishment considered the Triple Crown of the Arabian horse show world. He was the first horse ever to win all three titles in the same year.

Second, he sired just over 1,000 foals, 171 of whom won championships in both halter and performance, including 47 who grabbed more than 90 national titles. Among his best were the following

national winners:
• Ford Prima Donna, out of *Pristan, by Aswan.
• Mmusket, out of ROK Ofirka, by Bask Tez.
• Vaguely Noble, out of SX La Quinta, by *Serafix.
• *SR Nadom, foaled at Tersk, out of Nazra, by Sport.
• Mustasia, out of *Anntasia, by Antey.
• Muscap, out of Caprisan, by Tornado.
• Lady Muscata, out of First Lady, by Tornado.

The exotically beautiful stallion *Nariadni (Nabeg x Nariadnaia), pictured here, and *Muscat were stablemates and comrades most of their lives. Both were imported from Russia by Howie Kale, and their bloodlines were often crossed in the Kale breeding program, as well as in others. Both horses were later purchased by the Taylor Ranch in Utah.

Photo by Rik Van Lent Jr.

• Barodd, out of *Nahodka, by Arax.
• MHR Muscateal, out of MHR Princess Bask, by *Bask.
• Moudriey, out of Brieah, by The Egyptian Prince.
• Musknitsa, out of *Prokaznitza, by Arax.
• Amber Satin, out of Satin Silver, by Tornado; the 1987 U.S. National Champion Mare.
• Amber Silk, out of Silk N Silver, by Tornado; a U.S. Top Ten Mare.

Both Amber Silk and Amber Satin several times shared the same sale and show arenas.

*Muscat offspring continue to have great influence in show rings and breeding programs around the world. Through 1997, 21 sons had sired North American national winners and 18 daughters had produced national winners.

To house his illustrious group of Russian horses in Scottsdale, Kale built the magnificent Karho Farms, an ivory-pillared horse palace located on Bell Road, famous in that era for its outstanding Arabian farms. There, *Muscat and *Nariadni reigned as the king and crown prince of Tersk Arabians throughout the glittering, high-dollar glory days of the 1980s horse industry.

During that time, *Muscat was presented to standing-ovation crowds at Karho auctions, during which his daughters often brought six-figure prices. In 1985, this author watched as the aforementioned Amber Silk topped all Scottsdale sales that year when she sold for $1.7 million. Although horse prices among all breeds plummeted in the late 1980s when U.S. tax laws changed, *Muscat and *Nariadni offspring continued to demand top dollar.

New Homes

Kale had syndicated *Muscat early on. In 1989, when 72 percent of the shares were purchased by Ryohei Ishikawa, the stallion was moved to Lasma East International Centre, LaGrange, Kentucky. In

*Barrodd, pictured here in 1989, was the 1983 U.S. Reserve National Champion Futurity Filly. She is by *Muscat and out of *Nahodka, by Arax.*

Photo by
Jerry Sparagowski

1990, *Muscat went to stand at Midwest Station II, Rogers, Minnesota.

Then, in late 1994, a Utah horseman named Rick Taylor learned that the *Muscat syndicate's controlling interest was up for sale. Taylor and his wife, Paula, had fallen in love with and subsequently leased *Nariadni in 1991. So. . . .

"We knew that bringing them back together to live at the same farm was the right thing, the honorable thing to do," offered Taylor. "They were in Russia together. They built Karho together. They went to Kentucky together. And they ended up together here in Utah with us, right up until their deaths."

Taylor believes it is impossible to talk about *Muscat without *Nariadni. He was dedicated to continuing Kale's plan to breed them each to the daughters of the other— the left hand and the right hand working together for the betterment of the whole.

"The interaction between the two was incredible," Taylor said. "It was apparent from the day *Muscat came off

the trailer here until the day he died. They *knew* each other.

"*Muscat was so regal, so majestic. He didn't even look at *Nariadni, but *Nariadni zoomed in on him like only *Nariadni could do. *Muscat paid him absolutely no attention until he was within 10 feet or so of him, then he paused and looked his way as if to say, 'Oh, so you're here, too?'

"They had strikingly different personalities," Taylor continued. "*Nariadni was an alpha stallion. He would stop at every stall as he went down the alleyway, squeal or snort and strike his foot one time, receive the standard 6-inch head drop from the other stallion, and move on. He

A photo of Amber Satin when she was named the 1987 Buckeye Sweepstakes Champion Mare. She was shown by David Boggs.

Photo by Rob Hess

knew he was No. 1, and he was going to *show* you who was boss.

"*Muscat, on the other hand, would regally survey his kingdom in such a way that said he knew he was the king and he expected that you—and everyone else— knew it too. There was no need to *show* it.

"The two had a game they played, every day, over and over, for hours on end. They were stabled at opposite ends of the barn, each able to go outside into their respective paddocks at any time, and able to see each other clearly. *Nariadni would

walk out of his stall and look for *Muscat. If *Muscat wasn't out, *Nariadni would go back inside. But if *Muscat was there and saw *Nariadni, *Muscat would calmly walk out to the fence, at which point *Nariadni would fiercely rush the fence, snorting and blowing. *Muscat would just look at him. Then, with a calm regal air, he would turn and walk quietly back into his stall, infuriating *Nariadni. This would go on *all* day, over and over."

Both horses were groomed daily, massaged, and fed a special diet. Both had scores of visitors and bred as many mares as age would allow. "They bloomed," offered Taylor.

And, for the first time in many years, they were ridden, often. "My wife, Paula, especially loved riding *Nariadni," said Taylor. "And our children did too. (They have nine.) He was like riding the wind; it was as if you were following the clouds across the sky. He was much lighter of foot

*Here's a photograph of Dr. Howard F. Kale Sr., a physician, who won the 1972 U.S. National Native Costume Championship on Ross'zi, no kin to *Muscat.*

Photo by
Johnny Johnston

than either *Muscat or *Aladdinn (whom they also have; see his chapter).

"*Muscat was like riding an engine; you could feel the train engine power in every fiber, feel it under you, feel it in the reins. He loved to be out in the fields, moving swiftly and elegantly across the wide open spaces."

On *Muscat's last day, appearing happy and healthy, he bred a mare, walked back into his stall, and dropped dead of a heart attack. It was July 25, 1996. He was 25 years old.

"When *Muscat died, *Nariadni was not the same horse. I noticed it the very next day," said Taylor. "He was still gorgeous, but the spark was gone. And it was that way until he died almost exactly a year after *Muscat's death. It was August 2, 1997. He was 24.

"These horses did far more for us, for my family, than we ever could do for them. We owe them so much. We are honored to have had them here."

*The *Muscat son BPL Kirov is shown here winning the 1987 Scottsdale Junior Colt Championship with Michael Byatt. BPL Kirov was out of the U.S. Top Ten Mare *Karny. Patricia Dempsey holds the plaque and ribbon.*

Photo by Rob Hess

8   *PADRON

He won all there is to win at halter in North Amercia.

WHEN A LITTLE chestnut colt, bred by Dr. and Mrs. J.M.M. Blaauwhof, was foaled in a Dutch stable near Kerkdriel on May 13, 1977, there was every reason in the world to believe he would become a champion.

First of all, his pedigree was a delectable blend of the best British, Egyptian, and Russian bloodlines available. His sire, Patron (Aswan x Podruga), was three times National Champion Stallion of Holland. His dam, *Odessa, had parents who won national titles. *Odessa's sire, Bright Wings, was the 1966 British Reserve Junior Champion Stallion, and her dam, Serinda, was the 1969 British

*This conformation shot of *Padron (pronounced Pa-DRONE) was taken at John O'Brien's Sandspur Arabians in Scottsdale in the late 1980s.*

Photo by Jerry Sparagowski

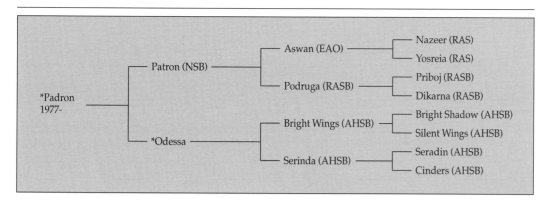

```
                           ┌─ Aswan (EAO) ────────┬─ Nazeer (RAS)
              ┌─ Patron (NSB) ─┤                   └─ Yosreia (RAS)
              │              └─ Podruga (RASB) ────┬─ Priboj (RASB)
*Padron ──────┤                                    └─ Dikarna (RASB)
1977-         │              ┌─ Bright Wings (AHSB) ┬─ Bright Shadow (AHSB)
              └─ *Odessa ─────┤                      └─ Silent Wings (AHSB)
                             └─ Serinda (AHSB) ─────┬─ Seradin (AHSB)
                                                    └─ Cinders (AHSB)
```

National Champion Foal.

The youngster was cute, too. Born with a distinctive crooked blaze down his dished face, the colt's two opposing white socks (off fore, near hind) and a sassy straw-colored mane accented his powerful body and strong legs.

But he had something more. The colt they called *Padron had that magic "something," that charisma that reaches out and embraces an audience. When *Padron appeared, you could not look away.

Neither could judges. At the tender age of three months, he was named Dutch Junior National Champion, and then won three more junior championships in that country.

Such a horse is seldom a secret. Soon, *Padron was on his way to the United States, imported on February 11, 1978, by Robert and Donna Stratmore of Make-Believe Farm, Alamo, California. He spent a couple of years growing up, and then destiny beckoned.

Few reach Olympus alone, and neither did *Padron. By his side was David Boggs, charismatic in his own right, and one of the most successful, innovative Arabian halter horse showmen of the latter decades of the 20th century. One of the handful of trainers who ever even came close to matching him was his own brother, Bob Boggs.

First paired in September 1980, David Boggs and *Padron embodied youthful energy, with a style and zest for life that knew no bounds. During the next 24 months, and with the management guidance of veteran horseman Billy Harris, Boggs would show *Padron to virtually all of his major wins: champion stallion at the Cow Palace, Region III Champion Stallion, Minnesota All-Arabian Supreme Champion, Scottsdale All-Arabian Supreme Champion (1982), Canadian National Champion Stallion

Halter and Performance Record: 1982 United States National Champion Stallion; 1982 Scottsdale Champion Stallion/Supreme Champion; 1981 Canadian National Champion Stallion; 1977 Dutch Junior National Champion.

Progeny Record:

Purebred Foal Crops: 19
Purebred Foals Registered: 770
U.S./Canadian National Winners: 50
Class A Champions: 179
IAHA Legion of Honor Award Winners: 3
Race Starters: 3
Race Money Earned: $6,347

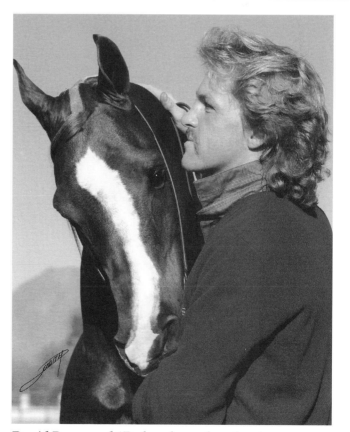

*David Boggs and *Padron have shared a strong relationship for 20 years.*   Photo by Judith

David Boggs is all smiles as he and *Padron leave the ring after winning the 1982 U.S. National Stallion Championship. The man on the right is Robert Stratmore of Make-Believe Farm, Alamo, Calif., the owner of *Padron at that time.

Photo courtesy Jo West Lauter

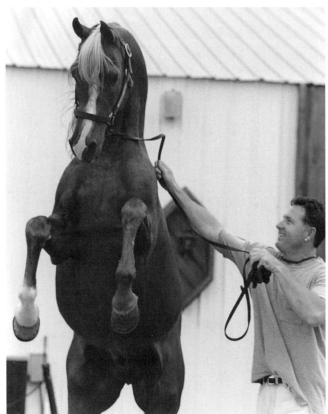

*Padron was taught to rear, and it became one of his favorite tricks. He's shown here with Greg Hazlewood, one of Midwest's successful associate trainers.

(1981), and the 1982 U.S. National Champion Stallion title.

While Boggs had seen some success before meeting *Padron (he showed the *Naborr son Kaborr to his 1979 Canadian National Champion Stallion title), this stallion was his first *really* big show horse. Some might even say the horse made the man. But they would be wrong; the horse and the man made each other.

By the end of their run, Boggs and *Padron had formed an incredible bond. So strong was their relationship that, over the stallion's entire life, it defied the weakening forces of time, distance, and even species differentiation. To the Arabian community, the words "David and *Padron" began to sound as familiar as "cream and sugar" or "silk and satin."

As Boggs summed it up, "Maybe there's a little of him in me, and a little of me in him. I don't know. I do know that what I feel for this horse goes beyond words."

In early 1983, *Padron was purchased by Lasma Arabians (the LaCroix family) when the Make-Believe Farm horses were dispersed. That same year in October, *Padron Associates acquired the stallion. The group was headed by Boggs and John O'Brien, a Californian who owned Sandspur Farm, and included Arnold

94

Although *Padron was trained to ride, he was never shown under saddle. He's pictured here with Bill Porcher, Midwest Training Centre's longtime western trainer.

Photo by Judith

Fisher, Carroll Buzzell, Andrew Weil, James Talbot, and Gordon Schuster. Shortly thereafter, *Padron was syndicated for $11 million.

For investors to put up so much money, however, both proof and promise must be firmly in place. *Padron's personal attributes had just been proven, in that he had won all there is to win at halter in North America.

So what about his potential as a sire? Many show ring stars have failed to shine as brightly when back home in the breeding shed.

Luckily, *Padron's ability as a sire was predicted by his strong pedigree. His sire, Patron, in addition to the afore-

mentioned wins, had sired the top stallions *Puschkin, *Patronne, *Patent, and *El Kasaka before an untimely death cut short his career.

Patron's sire, Aswan, was one of the most valuable stallions at Russia's Tersk Stud. A gift to the Soviet Union from a grateful Egypt after the Russians helped build the Aswan Dam, the straight Egyptian Aswan was a son of the immortal

*The *Padron daughter PR Padrons Jewel (out of CHF Serenata) was the 1988 U.S. National Champion Futurity Filly. She was bred by Syl Crooker of Park Ridge Arabians, Mankato, Minn., who sold her to Paolo Gucci just before her national win.* **Photo by Judith**

Nazeer (see the chapters on *Morafic and *Ansata Ibn Halima).

Along with some excellent mares, Aswan sired several outstanding sons. Among the best were U.S. National Top Ten Park Horse *Magnat, 1981 U.S. National Champion Stallion *Marsianin, German champion Kilimandscharo, Dutch National Champion Mag, and the good Polish sire, Palas.

Patron's dam, Podruga, was a daughter of the wonderful sire Priboj, who was known

for siring athletic ability and great heart.

*Padron's dam, *Odessa, carried lines through her sire (Bright Wings) and/or her dam (Serinda) that brought the breed such good horses as *Pietuszok, Topol, Naseem, *Silver Drift, Blue Domino, *Oran Van Crabbet, Indraff, and *Serafix.

In addition, *Padron's pedigree traces at least 12 times to the incomparable stallion Mesaoud, to whom *Padron compares closely in both color and bearing.

Also in place was proof of Boggs's total devotion to the Arabian horse breed and to *Padron himself. As long as there was a Midwest (Training Centre and Station II), there would be management, promotion, and marketing support available.

And, based on its history, the chances of Midwest's longevity were very good, indeed. David was young, but the Boggs family had been around a long time.

During the 1960s and 1970s, Don and Shorty Boggs, David's parents, were a hard-working, fun-loving couple from Minnesota who raised lovely Arabians and eight handsome children. The two youngest boys, Bob and David, showed a special interest in the horses.

"I remember sitting in school, when I was supposed to be studying, and designing tack trunks," said David, with a grin. "That's all I ever wanted to do, work with horses, show horses, breed them. There wasn't anything else that interested me."

Bob, the youngest, added, "I just don't remember a life without horses."

While still in high school in 1977, the two boys started Midwest Training Centre, Inc., a business which has grown to encompass two farms, scores of employees, millions of dollars in horse flesh, truckloads of trophies, and countless clients—both modest and wealthy— literally from around the world.

The Boggs brothers' show ring entrances—at a full run with shiny golden-blond hair streaming, much like their horses' tails—were for years a part of their flamboyant style, a style both emulated and maligned by their competitors.

No matter. Both men, and several key assistants, have become known for taking Arabian horses to the very top in halter competition, with a bunch of perfor-

**Padron has an
exotic head and cap-
tivating personality.*

Photo by Judith

mance awards thrown in for good measure. Midwest showmen can count nearly
100 national championships, about as
many reserves, and almost 400 national
Top Tens to their credit.

Regional championships number
between 300 and 400, and Class A Show
wins easily surpass 1,000. (No one has
kept an accurate record of the actual
number of wins at the regional and
Class A levels.)

What's more, the Boggs brothers and
their assistants have had similar success in
countries ranging from Brazil to France.

Back home, the syndicate agreement
stipulates that David Boggs and John
O'Brien share the care of *Padron, with
each party taking turns every two years
standing the stallion. When *Padron is
with Boggs, he lives in a special stall
with a huge window that looks into
David's office.

When the stallion is presented to his
admirers—whether they be casual visitors or at the gala parties for which Mid-

west is known—he always gives a grand
performance. David has trained him to
rear and dance on command (which he
did a bit more of when he was younger),
and their rapport is ever apparent.

At Midwest's annual New Year's Eve
parties (to which guests fly in from around
the world), *Padron is still the star of the
evening, despite his advancing years and
aging, low back. After scores of young
show horses and other breeding stallions
are presented to the guests, his entrance is
always the *grande finale* for which the
crowd excitedly awaits.

One of the more exciting experiences

The flashy Padrons Esperanza was the 1991 Canadian Reserve National Champion Western Pleasure Junior Horse. A *Padron daughter out of Ms April, she's pictured here with Midwest trainer Randy Anderson aboard.

Photo by Judith

for this author was seeing *Padron ridden under English tack by consummate horseman Bob Battaglia during a training session at Sandspur, in Scottsdale, in the late 1980s.

The pair were positively electric. *Padron's coat gleamed in the desert sun as his legs flashed in perfect cadence at the trot, his hocks bending as much as his knees, his neck arched, tail up, ears alert—in near-perfect silhouette. It was a shame that he was never shown under saddle.

Through all the traveling, all the years, and all the horses, Boggs has maintained a remarkable loyalty to *Padron—and the stallion hasn't let him down.

Offspring

All told, *Padron has sired 50 North American national winners, 12 international champions, and more than 180 show ring champions from 770 registered purebred foals. Some have multiple titles in both halter and performance (particularly in the western divisions), and many bear his flaming red-gold color.

With far too many to list here, just some of *Padron's national titleists include:

• PR Padrons Jewel (out of CHF Serenata), 1988 U.S. National Champion Futurity Filly.

• Padron Perfection (out of Ferzons Dream), 1988 Canadian National Western Pleasure Junior Horse Reserve Champion.

Arguably *Padron's best son, Padrons Psyche (out of Kilika, by *Tamerlan) is pictured here in 1991 when he was named the U.S. Reserve National Champion Stallion at the tender age of 3. He was shown by David Boggs.

Photo by Judith

• Padruska (out of MHR Port Geisha), 1988 U.S. National Western Pleasure Reserve Champion.

• Sassy Padron (out of Miss Sassy Coy), 1988 U.S. and Canadian National Reserve Champion Futurity Filly.

• Padrons Chantille (out of SX Bint Cobah), 1990 U.S. National Western Pleasure Reserve Champion.

• Padrons Love (out of Maria Blanca), 1989 Canadian National Western Pleasure Junior Horse Champion and U.S. Reserve Champion.

• Padrons Esperanza (out of Ms April), 1991 Canadian National Western Pleasure Junior Horse Reserve Champion.

• Padrenta (out of The Yenta), 1990 U.S. National Reserve Champion Futurity Filly.

• GLF Kassanova (out of Karamalika), 1991 Canadian National Reserve Champion Futurity Colt.

• Padrons Psyche (out of Kilika), 1991 U.S. Reserve National Champion Stallion.

Through 1997, 15 sons and 16 daughters have sired or produced 54 national winners, some with several titles. A few had even found success on the race track.

*Padron's best-siring—and most look-alike—son is Padrons Psyche, out of Kilika, a daughter of the Tersk-bred *Tamerlan (Arax x Trapecia). Psyche is somewhat line-bred, with three lines to Aswan, two to Arax, and four to Priboj—but he carries a most unusual and extremely rare tail female dam, Dafina, a desert-bred mare imported to England from Saudi Arabia by Lady Wentworth in 1927.

Psyche was bred by the McPherson Family Trust of California, but raised by Ernie and Marlys Weber of Er Mar Arabians in Minnesota. When he was just a baby, Psyche was "discovered" at a small Midwestern horse show by highly-regarded trainer Gene Reichardt. The colt's amazing presence and excellent conformation impressed even Reichardt (who has seen it all!), and he rushed to a telephone to call Walter Mishek, owner of many national-winning Arabians and publisher of the *Arabian Horse Times* magazine.

Reichardt convinced Mishek to buy the youngster sight unseen, right on the spot.

*Here's a 1996 *Padron grandson, *JJ Ibn Padron, by Padron's Image and out of the mare Ledhjeene.*

Photo by Judith

Although somewhat reluctant, Mishek did so. It was like winning the lottery.

Psyche immediately started campaigning with Reichardt at shows all around the Midwest. In 1991, he was the first 3-year-old colt in 27 years to be named a U.S. Reserve National Champion Stallion. His ownership by this time had passed to Larry Lengacher of Four Star Arabians in Indiana.

Since that win, Psyche has sired 16 national winners, including NW Siena Psyche and Estoriah, both U.S. National Champion Sweepstakes Fillies; Magnum Psyche, a U.S. National Champion Sweepstakes Colt; GA Hal Psyche, the 1995 U.S. and Canadian National Champion Futurity Colt; FS Ritz, twice the Canadian National Reserve Champion Stallion; RA Mahalo, a Canadian National Champion Futurity Colt; All Psyched Up, a Canadian National Champion Futurity Gelding; and JBK Mystic Fawn, the 1996 U.S. and Canadian National Champion Mare.

The year 1997 was a stellar year as Psyche was the leading halter sire for both the U.S. and Canadian national shows. He is now proudly owned by Joe and Cathy Zehr of La Cabreah Arabians, Fort Wayne, Indiana.

Although *Padron's sons, daughters, and grandget easily and mightily attest to his gifts as a sire, the coppery Dutch-born stallion stands for something far more than his legacy of show ring champions.

In his own way, *Padron represents the "Golden Era" of Arabian horses—that period of years which began in the mid-1970s and slowed in the late 1980s, and when the sky itself was truly the only limit. When some mares sold for a million dollars, and stallions for even more. When horse sales became Hollywood productions, and horse shows featured the best and the brightest in glittering array.

But beyond all that, *Padron represents the courage, creativity, stamina, and hard work required to survive after "the fall." When prices plummeted and countless farms disappeared in 1987 and 1988, there had to be something substantial, something real, in place in order to survive.

With *Padron, and through it all, rode Midwest and the Boggs brothers. They soared to the heights, teetered on the brink of destruction—and then managed to not only survive, but prosper. While learning from the past, they moved willingly into a future they saw—and see—as promising and bright.

As David has said on more than one occasion: "One day, when I'm too old to run, I want to be the caretaker of the world's greatest Arabian stallions." He can still run, and so can *Padron, but Boggs works toward that very goal.

The year 1998 found *Padron taking his turn in the care of John O'Brien, with Michael Byatt—one of North America's most prominent horse trainers—carefully managing the stallion's breeding schedule at Byatt's farm, Arabco, near Cumming, Georgia.

Said Byatt in a recent *Arabian Horse Times* article: "It is my stated wish to be able to breed a horse which will be remembered 100 years from now. To live with *Padron, a stallion which will be remembered a thousand years from now, is truly a blessing."

As for his longtime comrade, Boggs said, "Not a day goes by that I do not think of this great horse. *Padron has given me so much more than I can ever describe. He has been my friend, my confidant, and, most importantly, my inspiration. He has contributed immeasurably to the improvement of our breed, and he has done it with a style all his own."

*Padron might say the same about David Boggs.

*Say You Say Me, by *Padron and out of Oakridge Sarsur, won the prestigious Nations Cup in 1990 in Aachen, Germany, in the division for mares ages 4-6. She was shown by Bob Boggs and owned by A.C.E. Arabians, Ermelo, Holland.* Photo by Judith

*Padron Perfection, by *Padron and out of Ferzons Dream, was a 1987 U.S. National Top Ten Futurity Filly and 1988 Canadian Reserve National Champion in junior horse western pleasure.* Photo by Judith

*ANSATA IBN HALIMA

"There was something indefinable about his ability to touch the lives of others."

*ANSATA IBN HALIMA is often credited with helping to inspire in America a renewed interest in Arabian horses bred in Egypt. When he and two fillies were imported into the United States in 1959 by Donald and Judith Forbis of Ansata Arabian Stud, breeders from across the continent traveled to Oklahoma to view the trio.

"Ibn Halima, Bint Mabrouka, and Bint Zaafarana were our first children . . . our first love. There's nothing quite like your first love . . . ," said Judi Forbis.

*Ansata Ibn Halima's success as a sire in succeeding years only increased a grow-ing fascination with the "Horses of the Pyramids," while founding a dynasty of Ansata descendants. Today, they portray a special consistency in type, a certain look recognized around the world.

In truth, that look is the result of careful line-breeding and judicious outcrossing, over many years, on the bloodlines of the immortal stallion Nazeer, sire of *Ansata Ibn Halima, the two fillies mentioned, and other important horses. (See the chapter on *Morafic.)

It's only because Nazeer was never imported into or registered in the United States that he does not rate a

*Ansata Ibn Halima in 1969, the year he was named the grand champion stallion at Houston. That's Tom McNair at the halter and Judith Forbis with the trophy.

Photo by Jim Keeland

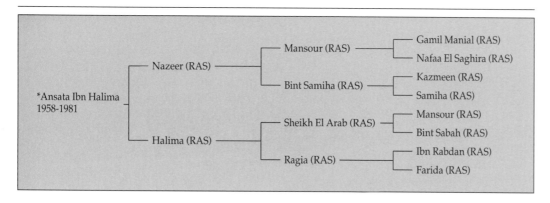

```
                                                    ┌─ Gamil Manial (RAS)
                                    ┌─ Mansour (RAS) ─┤
                                    │                └─ Nafaa El Saghira (RAS)
                  ┌─ Nazeer (RAS) ──┤
                  │                 │                 ┌─ Kazmeen (RAS)
                  │                 └─ Bint Samiha (RAS) ─┤
*Ansata Ibn Halima│                                   └─ Samiha (RAS)
1958-1981         │
                  │                                   ┌─ Mansour (RAS)
                  │                 ┌─ Sheikh El Arab (RAS) ─┤
                  │                 │                 └─ Bint Sabah (RAS)
                  └─ Halima (RAS) ──┤
                                    │                 ┌─ Ibn Rabdan (RAS)
                                    └─ Ragia (RAS) ───┤
                                                      └─ Farida (RAS)
```

chapter in this book. To say that Nazeer has had a tremendous influence on the Forbises' Ansata breeding program, and upon that of the entire Egyptian Arabian community, is a gross understatement. Perhaps no other single Egyptian stallion has so greatly affected the modern Arabian horse.

Judi wrote in her book, *The Classic Arabian Horse,* of the first time she saw Nazeer, at age 25 in 1959, at the Egyptian Agricultural Organization's (EAO) El Zahraa Stables near Cairo:

"He pranced out of his shaded box stall into the bright October sun and stood majestically scanning the palm-fringed blue horizon before trumpeting a love call to his mares. As he posed beneath the arched trellis of bright pink bougainvillea, a vision in white elegance, he was the classic Arabian personified, a model Vernet, Delacroix, or Schreyer would have been overjoyed with. Indeed, he reminded one that 'beauty is its own excuse for being'."

The look with which Nazeer stamped his offspring has been described as that of eagles or "the wide-eyed look of the desert." He is aptly named, as nazeer in Arabic means "observer or director of all he oversees." Although he stood just 14.3 hands, Nazeer appeared much taller through his carriage and attitude. His sons and daughters inherited the same demeanor.

In addition, Nazeer is credited with siring horses of excellent overall conformation, with good substance and size. It is no surprise, then, that an incredible 70 percent of Nazeer's get with American

Halter and Performance Record: Legion of Merit winner; 3 times—1966, '67, '69—U.S. National Top Ten Stallion; Region VI Park Champion.

Progeny Record:

Purebred Foal Crops: 19
Purebred Foals Registered: 261
U.S./Canadian National Winners: 13
Class A Champions: 59
IAHA Legion of Honor Award Winners: 1
IAHA Legion of Merit Award Winners: 3

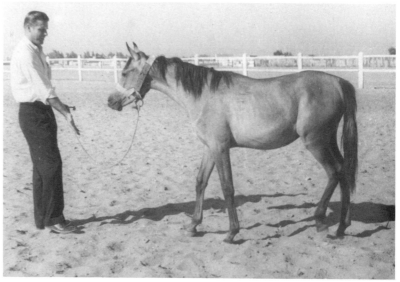

Don Forbis and Ibn Halima (as a weanling) meet for the first time in a sand paddock in Egypt.   Photo by Judith Forbis

*Three yearlings, who later became famous, at the El Zahraa Stud Farm near Cairo, Egypt. From left: *Ansata Ibn Halima, *Ansata Bint Mabrouka, and *Ansata Bint Zaafarana. They were the first three Egyptian Arabians imported by Don and Judith Forbis.*

Photo by Judith Forbis

*A 1978 photograph of Dr. Mohamed El Marsafi, director of the El Zahraa Stud in Cairo, and *Ansata Ibn Halima. The occasion was Ansata's 20th anniversary in Lufkin, Texas.* Photo by Jerry Sparagowski

foals have produced national winners. His descendants can be found in more than 20 countries around the world, with the highest numbers living in North America.

*Ansata Ibn Halima's dam, Halima, was a solid bay mare by the exquisite stallion Sheikh El Arab and out of Ragia, who traced to the ancient desert strain called Dahman Shahwan, noted for pretty heads, arched necks, excellent tail carriage, and athletic ability. The cross was a wise decision.

"It was October 28, 1957," recalled (the late) Dr. Mohamed El Marsafi, director of the EAO's farm (from an audiotape recorded at *Ansata Ibn Halima's 20th birthday celebration), "when the mare Halima, one of the outstanding mares by Sheikh El Arab, was bred to Nazeer, the most significant stallion in the EAO and one of the great breeding stallions in Egypt at that time. This combination was based on a long, careful study by General Tibor (von Pettko Szandtner, a Hungarian who was head of the EAO at that time) to have, for the first time, double Mansour in one individual.

"All our optimistic expectations were proved on September 16, 1958, when Ibn Halima was born under my own

The bay Halima, dam of *Ansata Ibn Halima, in Egypt, circa 1959.

Photo by Judith Forbis

care and was weaned and joined his comrades in the kindergarten paddocks on February 20, 1959. On October 5, 1959, it was my pleasure to receive at the EAO in Egypt a young, charming couple presenting themselves as Mr. and Mrs. Donald Forbis. They were looking for pure Egyptian Arabians. Their choice was Ibn Halima, 1 year at the time, and Bint Zaafarana and Bint Mabrouka, 10-month-old fillies."

Judi Forbis recalled that she and Don had been searching the Middle East for several years, trying to find just the right classic Arabian horses from which to build the breeding program of their dreams. They were disappointed at every turn, finding nothing they liked anywhere.

General von Szandtner, the brilliant head of Egypt's breeding program for 10 years, had only been gone 2 weeks when the Forbises arrived in Cairo. Only after much discussion—and apparently impressed by the Forbises' fervor—did the new director, Dr. Marsafi, agree to show the couple those young horses who were being "saved" for Egypt's breeding program. Most Arabian horse breeders in America had long considered Egypt played out in terms of high-quality horseflesh. Don and Judi discovered otherwise.

Judi Forbis: "In the paddock of young

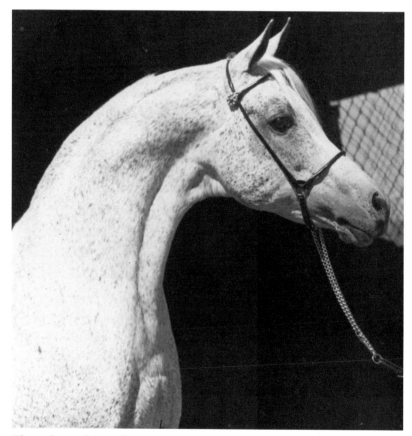

The soft-eyed "gentle one," *Ansata Ibn Halima—pronounced On-sah-ta Ib-n Ha-LEE-ma.
Photo by Jerry Sparagowski

Ansata Ibn Sudan, one of *Ansata Ibn Halima's best sons, was named 1971 U.S. National Champion Stallion. He was shown by Maurice Wingo for the Ansata Arabian Stud.

Photo by
Johnny Johnston

The legendary Egyptian Arabian stallion Nazeer with his groom at El Zahraa Stud in Cairo. He sired *Ansata Ibn Halima, *Morafic, and scores of other famous horses. **Photo by Judith Forbis**

horses, Ibn Halima (later registered as *Ansata Ibn Halima) really stood out among all of them. He had that classic essence, the beautiful head, the beautiful eye—one of the kindest eyes I've ever seen—a nobility. His name reflected what he was—the Son of the Gentle One."

As the Forbises strolled the paddock, Judi and the Nazeer daughter Bint Mabrouka formed an uncanny bond. The filly refused to leave her side, even when the other youngsters raced away for their noon meal. Judi had to have her. The other filly, Bint Zaafarana, was simply one of the loveliest fillies either Forbis had ever seen. Don especially saw the potential in Ibn Halima as a stallion prospect. He told Judi, "If you're going to take two fillies home, you absolutely have to have a colt."

The newly married young couple desperately wanted to purchase the three yearlings. Dr. Marsafi set the price for the trio at $15,000—an incredible sum in 1959. After much discussion, however, the price for the mares was set at $10,000—with Ibn Halima thrown in as a bonus.

The purchase took every cent the couple had. "We examined our bank account and said a prayer," Judi recalled. "We were newly married, had no home, no ranch, and no nest egg. Yet, we knew that our search had ended there in Egypt. This visit was to change our lives."

As Don and Judi would continue to live and work in the Middle East for several more years, the horses were shipped to Oklahoma to be cared for by Don's father, Nolan Forbis, at a rented barn. News of their arrival quickly spread.

"Well, the first pictures of these three to hit the newspapers and magazines immediately sparked a great interest," said Judi. "People wondered, 'How did these beautiful animals appear, when Egypt had supposedly run out of good horses?'

"And I remember one of the first visitors was Jimmy Dean, who was a *Raffles breeder. But people who loved classic horses, who saw the picture of these classic horses, saw the answer to what was needed to carry on. Later, when we had the opportunity to show Ibn Halima, it just revolutionized people's thinking about the Egyptian Arabian horse."

Judi also noted that when General von Szandtner, who had returned to Hungary, saw the news reports, he wrote a friend that, had he still been the EAO director, he would never have let the three horses go. "Had we arrived in Egypt just a few weeks earlier, we would never have gotten Ibn Halima," stated Judi. "Our lives would have turned out completely differently."

The Forbises had a very good reason for choosing to use the prefix "Ansata" when they registered Ibn Halima and the two fillies (plus hundreds more as time went by). "To the ancient Egyptians, the Ansata Crux, or Key of Life, symbolized life and reproduction. Ansata is a sacred emblem of the continuity of life, even of immortality."

Because all three horses were by Nazeer, the Forbises were in a linebreeding program. Ibn Halima's first foal was out of Bint Zaafarana, hence a "double-Nazeer" colt, who, by winning several championships and a Canadian Top Ten Stallion title, first proved the power of that inbred cross. Named Ansata Ali Pasha, he was owned by Willis Flick, Miami, Florida.

In 1965, Douglas and Margaret Marshall

Judith Forbis and Ansata Ibn Sudan stroll through one of Ansata's pastures shortly before his death. Photo by Jerry Sparagowski

of Gleannloch Farms near Houston, Tex., leased *Ansata Ibn Halima to breed to their Egyptian mares. Their trainer, Tom McNair, showed the stallion in halter and park classes, as the Forbises still lived abroad.

Ibn Halima arrived at Gleannloch, 7 years old and virtually untrained. "He was a bit set in his ways," recalls McNair, "and we had to redo some things as far as his thinking was concerned, but the horse

Judi Forbis and Ansata Halim Shah, a 1983 U.S. Top Ten Futurity Colt and another important son of *Ansata Ibn Halima. Now deceased, he was one of the more influential sires of Egyptian Arabian horses.
Photo by Jerry Sparagowski

let down a hair. I could have dropped the lead line and walked away."

*Ansata Ibn Halima was three times a U.S. National Top Ten Stallion, in 1966, 1967, and 1969, won numerous park championships, including the Region VI title, and was a Legion of Merit winner. His sons and daughters did even better.

"Ibn Halima really became a household name in the Arabian horse breeding community," offered Judi. "As a mature horse, Ib had an ethereal quality about him that was more than just physical beauty. There was something indefinable about his ability to touch the lives of others. He was the kind of horse who attracted so many people because I think the gentility and quality of this horse came through even in his pictures. . . . He had a certain quality that he was able to give to his foals—a prepotency, I guess you would have to say— that stamped the 'Halima look.'"

*Ansata Ibn Halima sired 263 registered foals, the last born in 1982. Four were National Top Ten Futurity Colts, and nine were National Top Ten (or better) open halter horses, including the 1980 U.S. National Champion Mare Fa Halima, out of Sabrah, and the 1971 U.S. National Champion Stallion Ansata Ibn Sudan, out of Judi's special mare (*Ansata) Bint Mabrouka. In addition, Rahalima (out of Bint Rahma) was twice a U.S. Top Ten winner in Park.

In recalling Ansata Ibn Sudan's national championship, Judi explained, "Ibn Halima was the king, truly regal, and Don grew especially fond of him. They had a wonderful relationship. But in my heart, no horse will ever replace his son, Ansata Ibn Sudan.

"Nobody who ever saw this horse show will ever forget him, because he loved the show ring," Judi continued. "He loved to walk in. He loved to exhibit himself. He loved to show off. And he walked into the show ring that year (in which he won the national championship), and, I will never forget it. Maurice Wingo showed him, and

had a tremendous amount of talent. For that day and time he had more action than most of the horses we were dealing with, and he did exceptionally well as a park horse. At halter, he was one of the easiest horses I've ever shown. You'd get his feet situated like you wanted them, put his head and neck where you wanted them, and he would just stand there and look off as if he were seeing something a hundred miles away. And he stayed that way, never

*El Hilal, probably
*Ansata Ibn Halima's
best son in terms of a
breeding stallion.
Photo courtesy of
Vantage Point Farm.*

Photo by
Johnny Johnston

**During the last
years of his life,
El Hilal annually
was among the top
10 living sires of
show winners in
the world.**

he had never laid a hand on that horse until he walked him in the ring. And the horse just took over."

Judi called Ansata Ibn Sudan "Buzz"—for Buzzard—and he was like her child. Always. Although Don delighted in presenting the younger stallion to his adoring public, Ansata Ibn Sudan and Judi Forbis simply loved each other. If Judi failed to greet him when she arrived in the barn each morning, he beat the walls until she went to him. Other times, Ibn Sudan played dead in his stall just to get her attention. He was leased out to other farms in the early years when the Forbises lived abroad, but he always came home. Ibn Sudan sired 259 registered get,

including National Top Ten winners in both halter and performance.

Probably *Ansata Ibn Halima's best son, in terms of a breeding stallion, was El Hilal. Bred by the Marshalls, El Hilal was foaled in 1966 to the Nazeer daughter *Bint Nefisaa (x Nefisa), and, hence, "double-Nazeer." Purchased as a weanling by noted horsewoman Sheila Varian, El Hilal eventually was syndicated by Ron Palelek, of Vantage Point Farm,

*Rahalima, owned by Bevans Arabians, winning a park horse class with Dick Koehler riding. By *Ansata Ibn Halima and out of Bint Rahma, Rahalima was twice a U.S. Top Ten Park winner.*

Photo by
Johnny Johnston

Vantage, Washington. He spent most of his life with Palelek.

El Hilal won two Canadian National Top Ten titles, a U.S. Top Ten Stallion award, and other wins. During the last years of his life, El Hilal annually was among the top 10 living sires of show winners in the world. In addition, he had more champions and national winners than any other living Egyptian stallion—

over 150 known champions and 44 national winners, from more than 618 registered foals.

According to the Forbises, stud fees paid on *Ansata Ibn Halima built their first ranch near Lufkin, Texas. "He knew he was the king of that ranch," said Judi. "He observed everything we did everyday, from turning out mares to who was on the hot walker. . . . He'd let us know if we didn't perform to his expectations."

As the king, Ib had the right to certain idiosyncrasies. For instance, he hated to go through water. If you were riding and he saw a puddle before you did, the brakes went on—and you kept going,

110

often into the water. Top trainer Tom McNair managed to get him into water only by backing him in.

Judi also recalled his very "cold" back. "You always had to warm him up before mounting. I remember sitting on a fence one time and suddenly slipping onto his back, thinking I'd go for a bareback ride around the paddock. I ended up on the ground looking up, while he calmly looked down upon me, as if he was saying, 'You should have been more thoughtful. Warm me up first. Don't do that again.' I didn't, and from that experience I can truthfully say I've been dumped by the best."

At age 22, Ib, who had always been healthy, colicked severely. He was rushed to Texas A & M, and recovered, only to colic once more 2 weeks later. Back to Texas A & M, where, again, he rallied. Upon his return home, he received a host of local Arabian owners who came to say goodbye to him before the Forbises moved to their new farm in Arkansas.

"I knew by now that Ib's days were drawing to a close," said Judi. "The two mares who came with him from Egypt were already gone. We had only three Nazeer offspring left: Ib, *Ansata Bint Bukra, and *Ansata Bint Nazeer. I told Ib and the old mares, 'You just can't die in Texas. You're going to have to come with us to Arkansas.' Somehow I felt that he knew he had to make the trip.

"The second week of September 1981, we began moving horses," Judi continued. "I rode in the van with Ib during the 6-hour trip. Our vet traveled with us and we stopped several times. When we arrived, several of our friends met us, and Ib gloried in all the attention and excitement. His eyes sparkled like a young stud who had been away for a long time and just returned home."

*Ansata Ibn Halima seemed delighted by his new home with its view of the mare pasture. Soon, however, he colicked again. "Before dawn on the morning of

The *Ansata Ibn Halima daughter Fa Halima was the 1980 U.S. National Champion Mare. Photo courtesy of The Pyramid Society.
Photo by Johnny Johnston

his 23rd birthday, we knew his time had come," said Judi softly. "Nothing more could be done.

"The sun had just heralded the new morning as I walked him out of his stall. Slowly we crossed the field to pasture number one where his mares had gathered to pay him tribute. *They knew!* He trumpeted his last call to them, which they acknowledged. Then they turned and ran to a distant corner, tails flagging a final farewell. They stood—as if suspended for a moment in time—watching from afar as he was laid to rest beneath the shadow of a giant oak tree."

10 *MORAFIC

Most people agreed there had never been an Arabian horse quite like him before—and there would never be one quite like him again.

*MORAFIC was a horse of the imagination; a horse of dreams. So unusual was he, so exotic in form and feature, that a few dared to call him grotesque. Most, however, pronounced him to be astonishingly beautiful.

His face was long, with tapered nose and deeply dished, almost "broken" in profile. The large, dark eyes, which enhanced his appearance, were set in such a way that he seemed royally aloof, yet somehow sad, as if he had seen too much of the world. His chest was a bit narrow, but his tail carriage and movements were both elegant and extreme, vents for a fiery nature within. Most people who saw *Morafic agreed there had never been an

*The elegant *Morafic, photographed at Gleannloch Farms in Texas.*

Photo by
Johnny Johnston

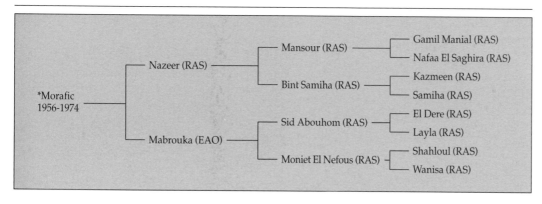

			Gamil Manial (RAS)
		Mansour (RAS)	
	Nazeer (RAS)		Nafaa El Saghira (RAS)
			Kazmeen (RAS)
*Morafic		Bint Samiha (RAS)	
1956-1974			Samiha (RAS)
			El Dere (RAS)
		Sid Abouhom (RAS)	
	Mabrouka (EAO)		Layla (RAS)
			Shahloul (RAS)
		Moniet El Nefous (RAS)	
			Wanisa (RAS)

Arabian horse quite like him before—and that there would never be one quite like him again.

*Morafic (pronounced Mo-RAF-ick) was the firstborn son of the chestnut mare Mabrouka, from whose lineage he most probably inherited his long nose. Mabrouka, foaled in 1951, was the daughter of one of the most famous Egyptian Arabian mares of all time—Moniet El Nefous.

This *grande dame* of Egypt also produced *Bint Moniet El Nefous and *Fakher El Din (both by Nazeer), *Soufian (by Alaa El Din), *Tuhotmos (by El Sareei), and *Ibn Moniet El Nefous (by *Morafic, her own grandson). All became well-known show ring champions and/or valuable sires or producers in the United States.

Moniet El Nefous also produced two full sisters to Mabrouka (by Sid Abouhom). The first was Lubna, known for her two famous grandsons *Sakr and *Asaad (through her son, *Sultann). *Sakr was a multiple U.S. National Champion (see his chapter) and *Asadd was a double U.S. National Champion. The other full sister to Mabrouka was Mona, a prolific producer whose best-known daughter was *Bint Mona, the only imported Egyptian mare to produce four national winners.

Of *Morafic's dam, Mabrouka, well-known Arabian horse breeder, pedigree expert, and author Judith Forbis once wrote: "Mabrouka began her career as a broodmare with a colt, which, had she done no more than produce him, would have assured her equine immortality." That colt, of course, was *Morafic.

Mabrouka also produced several other good horses, including *Ansata Bint Mabrouka, a full sister to *Morafic, who was a halter champion and who produced 1971 U.S. National Champion Stallion Ansata Ibn Sudan, the first "straight"

Halter and Performance Record: Class A park champion; aged stallions, 2nd place—1966 Scottsdale Show; champion stallion, Houston Livestock Show.

Progeny Record:

Purebred Foal Crops: 17
Purebred Foals Registered: 207
U.S./Canadian National Winners: 30
Class A Champions: 58
IAHA Legion of Honor Award Winners: 4
IAHA Legion of Merit Award Winners: 11
IAHA Legion of Supreme Merit Award Winners: 3

Egyptian Arabian to win that title.

*Morafic's sire was the legendary Nazeer. (For more on Nazeer, refer to the chapter on *Ansata Ibn Halima.) The mating of Nazeer to Mabrouka was planned by the famous Hungarian horseman General Tibor von Pettko Szandtner, who, during the 1950s, played an important role in the revitalization of the Egyptian Royal Agricultural Society's breeding program.

Foaled on February 19, 1956, at the RAS's El Zahraa Stud Farm near Cairo, *Morafic quickly became known for his unique appearance and was often paraded for visitors. American breeders, such as Don and Judith Forbis, Sara Loken, Richard Pritzlaff, and Douglas and Margaret Marshall, were just beginning to discover the treasures of El Zahraa, and were especially intrigued by the young grey-white stallion.

Judi Forbis, the eventual owner of

Perhaps no other photograph better shows the unusual shape of *Morafic's head than this one taken in 1959 just after he was returned from the racetrack to El Zahraa.

Photo by Judith Forbis

This classic photo is probably the most famous head study of *Morafic. Said photographer Polly Knoll, "When I suggested we photograph *Morafic without a halter, his trainer, Tom McNair, was a little skeptical, particularly about using the barn doorway. But the black background exemplified his beauty without obstruction."

Photo by
Polly Knoll

*Morafic's full sister, *Ansata Bint Mabrouka, described him thus: "He looked you square in the eye, demanding equal status with man as a child of the universe, and he exulted in his right to be here. His children inherited his free spirit, courage, intelligence, and dignity. A vision in pure white, *Morafic's elegance, spirit, and regal bearing proclaimed his aristocratic birthright. I believe his noble purpose for being here was to excite the imagination and create human interest in preserving the classic beauty of his Egyptian heritage. In ancient times, Pharaoh himself would have claimed him to draw his battle chariot!"

As were most young Egyptian Arabian horses, *Morafic was sent to the racetrack. He was strong and talented, but proved difficult to control, frightening his jockeys and trainer. After going through a fence and receiving a neck blemish he carried for the rest of his life, *Morafic was returned to El Zahraa to begin his career as a sire.

Of all the foreign visitors who saw *Morafic, the ones most taken with him were the Marshalls. Douglas and Margaret owned Gleannloch Farms, near Houston, and had spent countless hours and thousands of dollars during the 1950s combing the Middle East in search of the perfect Arabian horse. As Douglas once recounted, "While in Syria, we were told by Mutib El Sh'alan, Amir of the Ruala tribe, that exceptionally beautiful horses came only one in a thousand. Since he estimated they still had 1,500 horses, he thought there might be one or two. He promised us he would search the desert tribes and gather up those horses.

"We came back the next year, but he told us he was sorry, he couldn't find horses as beautiful as those in the famous old paintings. So, we went to Egypt. . . ."

Added (the late) Margaret Marshall, "And that is where we found them. The most beautiful were in Egypt."

Their first visit was in 1959. In 1961 the Marshalls arranged to import three Nazeer daughters and two other mares. One, the El Sareei daughter *Salomy, was in foal to *Morafic when she arrived in 1962 in the United States. That foal was *Saba El Zahraa, later to be a U.S. National Top Ten Stallion, and the first *Morafic offspring to be imported. Also in 1961, the Marshalls approached Dr. Mohamed El Marsafi, director of the Egyptian Agricultural Organization (formerly the RAS), and asked to buy *Morafic. All agreed that as soon as he had sired "enough" horses in Egypt, the Marshalls could buy him.

Three years passed without a word said about a purchase. In 1964 the Marshalls tentatively asked again. Marsafi and his colleagues agreed, provided the EAO was immediately paid in full, and *Morafic stayed one more year to breed as many Egyptian mares as possible. Finally, in 1965, the white stallion left his desert homeland to live in the lush pastures of southeastern Texas.

*A 1966 photograph of *Morafic with Douglas B. Marshall, the stallion's greatest admirer.*   **Photo courtesy of the Arabian Horse Trust**

It is interesting to note that while *Morafic was still in Egypt, the Marshalls' trainer, Tom McNair, asked that he be ridden. "The grooms turned pea-green with fear," McNair recalled. One carefully jogged him around, and then McNair stepped aboard. He quickly discovered that *Morafic was one big bluffer. Smart and overloaded with energy from constant stall confinement, the stallion tested those who tried to handle him. "But he didn't really have a mean bone in his body," said McNair.

*Mabrouka, the dam of *Morafic, pictured in 1959 in Egypt. A photo of *Morafic's sire, Nazeer, is shown in the *Ansata Ibn Halima chapter.*

Photo by Judith Forbis

*Morafic in his prime at age 16 in 1972 at Gleannloch Farms.

Photo by Polly Knoll

*Tom McNair showed the *Morafic daughter *Nahlah to the reserve national champion mare title at the 1967 U.S. Nationals.*

Photo by Ed Smyth

The trainer also recalled the actual process of loading *Morafic onto the plane at the Cairo airport. The stallion and 12 other horses being exported to the United States were walked the 20 miles from the stud farm to the airport. In order to get the horses into the belly of the KLM transport plane, a scissors lift without railings on two sides was used to raise them 18 feet into the air. None of the horses had ever been transported anywhere, not even in a truck.

When it was *Morafic's turn, he was amazingly calm—even with planes landing and taking off all around him. McNair was holding him when, just as he was about to step aboard the plane, a KLM official suddenly grabbed for *Morafic's halter and pulled. The horse pulled back, banging his face on the plane door just below his eyes. It scared McNair so badly that he froze, but the stallion was no fool. "One of his hind feet went off the back of the platform, but he realized there was nothing but air for 18 feet down, so he moved it back up," said McNair. "He just had a little bloody face, is all, when he finally was loaded up."

Upon his arrival in the United States, the 9-year-old *Morafic had some challenging adjustments to make, in terms of both culture and environment. At that time in

*Ibn Morafic (out of *Kahramana, by Antar) was his sire's namesake and the 1976 U.S. National Champion Futurity Colt. In 1978 he won a U.S. Top Ten in English pleasure and a Canadian Top Ten in halter. A winner of the Legion of Supreme Merit title, he's shown here with owners Douglas and Margaret Marshall.*

Photo by Polly Knoll

*Ruminaja Ali, a son of Shaikh Al Badi and *Bint Maisa Saghira, and grandson of *Morafic, was the 1979 U.S. National Champion Futurity Colt and the 1983 U.S. Reserve National Champion Stallion. As a sire he continued the prolificacy of both his sire and paternal grandsire in siring national champions.* Photo by Polly Knoll

*It was through his son Shaikh Al Badi (pictured) that *Morafic launched a dynasty of stallions who won national halter titles generation after generation. Shaikh Al Badi (out of *Bint Maisa El Saghira, by Nazeer) was himself the 1972 U.S. Reserve National Champion Futurity Colt.* Photo by Polly Knoll

Egypt, stallions were kept in stalls almost continuously. Horses who were turned out—mainly mares and youngsters—spent their time in small sand lots. *Morafic had never grazed. He had never run free.

Now, instead of a simple diet of berseem hay and, occasionally, dates, *Morafic could graze on rich Bermuda grass and consume regular meals of grain. The Marshalls carefully restricted his time in the pasture, and closely monitored both diet and exercise during those first months, but *Morafic always kept his lean desert look and never attained American "show shape."

*Morafic made his show ring debut in February 1966 at the prestigious Scottsdale (Arizona) Arabian Show. The judges didn't know quite what to do with this unusually beautiful but lean, high-headed desert horse. With McNair showing him, *Morafic placed second of 27 in the aged stallion class—and first in the conversations of those at ringside.

At the Oklahoma Spring Arabian Show in June, McNair showed the stallion to a park championship and a third place in halter. (Also at that show, the *Morafic daughter *Nahlah won the mare championship and the English Pleasure Stakes, with Rhita McNair aboard.) Then it was on to a show in Fort Worth where *Morafic was named senior champion and grand champion stallion. His final show was in April 1967 when he won the stallion championship and the most classic award at the famous Houston Livestock Show.

Although his show career was brief, *Morafic made quite an impact in the ring. Many who saw him recalled that his ears and tail were always up and his movements were powerful and regal, yet graceful. He was the same at home, at Gleannloch, where he began a full-time career as that renowned farm's most important stallion.

From the time he was imported in 1965, and during 1966 and 1967, *Morafic was bred to only a handful of outside mares. His published stud fee was $5,000—a whopping price in those days. At the end of 1967, the Marshalls decided to permanently close his book to outside mares—with only a few exceptions. For the rest of his life, other breeders only had access to him—except in rare instances—through sales of his offspring and Gleannloch mares sold with breeding rights to Gleannloch stallions.

*Morafic sired, in all, 207 purebred Arabian foals: 56 in Egypt (11 of which were imported to the United States) and 151 in North America (of which only 15 were bred by someone other than members of the Marshall or McNair families). Of those, 58—36 percent—became show ring champions at Class A levels or above. And of the 58, an incredible 30 (52 percent) won national awards.

In 1971, both U.S. national halter futurity champions were by *Morafic. Dalul was champion colt, and Il Muna was champion filly. Another *Morafic daughter, Muzahrafa, was reserve to Il Muna. Another year, 1975, three of his daughters were U.S. national halter futurity winners: Shafeekah was national champion; Doriah was reserve; and Shahira was a top five.

Bint Bint Rafica (out of *Shamah, by Sameh) was but one of many famous *Morafic daughters. A U.S. National Top Five Futurity Filly in 1974, she was described by Bob Dressler, D.V.M., as "a wonderful riding horse with a light, airy movement and happy disposition. She was also an outstanding producer for us." Dressler was a Gleannloch Farms manager. Photo by Bob Dressler, D.V.M.

Records indicate that *Morafic is the leading imported Egyptian Arabian sire of national winners, and the leading Egyptian sire of producers of national winners. In other words, he had "it," and his offspring could pass "it" on, as well. In fact, the line of national winners that descends

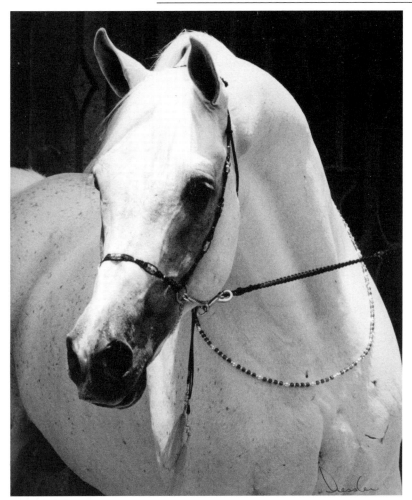

Al Metrabbi, out of the mare *Sammara, was the only colt ever produced by crossing *Morafic on one of his own daughters. Al Metrabbi was the 1970 U.S. National Champion Futurity Colt, won a U.S. Top Ten in trail, and was a Legion of Supreme Merit winner. For many years he was an important stallion—and friend—for the Tom Atkinson family of Anchor Hill Farm, Rogersville, Missouri.

Photo by Bob Dressler, D.V.M.

through the sire line from *Morafic is nothing short of amazing.

Consider this bunch of boys. The *Morafic son, Shaikh Al Badi, was the 1972 U.S. Reserve National Futurity Champion. Shaikh Al Badi sired Ruminaja Ali, the 1979 U.S. National Champion Futurity Colt and the 1983 U.S. Reserve National Champion Stallion. Ruminaja Ali sired Ali Jamaal, the 1985 U.S. National Champion Futurity Colt and the 1990 U.S. National Champion Stallion. Then, Ali Jamaal sired BST Dajamaal, the 1993 U.S. National Champion Futurity Colt. And this lineup is only a tiny taste of the vast smorgasbord of champions who descend from *Morafic.

The stallion's greatest admirer by far was Douglas Marshall. Rarely did a day pass that he failed to visit *Morafic's stall—once in the morning on his way to the office, and again in the evening upon his return home. Said Marshall of his exotic friend, "He was special; really incredible. It's difficult to put into words . . . I think he was the most important stallion that was ever brought over. I'm being prejudiced, but if you look at the percentages of champions from the number of foals he sired, it's fantastic. Plus, the percentage of great sons he sired from that number is higher than with any stallion I know."

Among *Morafic's best sons were national winners (and often top sires) such as Al Fahir, Al Fattah, Al Metrabbi, Dalul, El Risaan, *Ibn Moniet El Nefous, Ibn Morafic, Mosry, Rayek, *Refky, *Saba El Zahraa, Shah Nishan, and Shaikh Al Badi, and exceptional sires such as Ansata Shah Zaman, Ben Morafic, *Khofo, Moraftakhar, Shaker El Masri, The Egyptian Prince, and Wazir Ibn Morafic—among others.

While *Morafic's male offspring tended to dominate, many of his daughters also became show ring stars and/or top-producing broodmares. In fact, during the 1980s *Morafic daughters were so valuable that their price tags sometimes topped a quarter of a million dollars—if you could find an owner willing to part with one.

Of *Morafic's fine daughters, several deserve mention as national winners and, in some cases, also top producers: Bint Bint Hanaa, Bint Bint Mona, Bint Bint Rafica, Bint Romanaa, Dalia, Doriah, Hebet Allah, Ilaha, Il Muna, Muzahrafa,

*Nahlah, Shafeekah, and Tarafic—to name only some.

As halter champions tend to dominate the lists of both winning sons and daughters, it is apparent that *Morafic's greatest contribution to the breed is exquisite beauty and Arabian type, especially that seen in young halter futurity contenders. This legacy lives on into the third, fourth and fifth generations of today.

*Morafic's influence was felt not only in North America, but around the world, as well. The EAO in Cairo exported seven *Morafic daughters to three countries: the United States, the (former) Soviet Union, and Germany. Also from Egypt, 13 sons went to the United States, Morocco, Hungary, and Germany. The Marshalls sent *Morafic sons to Australia, Mexico, England, South America, and South Africa. From these exportations—and others— have come many generations of offspring who continue to have an enormous impact in show rings and breeding programs around the globe.

*Morafic's last public appearance was at the October 1973 Stallion Spectacular at the Gulf Coast Arabian Horse Club Show in Houston. Nominated as a "Living Legend" of the breed, he was reunited with two of his EAO stablemates, paternal siblings *Ansata Ibn Halima and *Talal. There, *Morafic preened and posed for an adoring crowd who rarely got to see the famous horse in person. Those who were there said it was as if he knew it would be his last public appearance, that in 5 short months he would be gone from this earth.

*Morafic died in March 1974 following colic surgery, which revealed a series of blood clots to the mesenteric artery that feeds the large intestine. A fighter until the end, he died on his feet as he stood in the recovery room. He was 18. His last two foals, the colts Choukran and Sayeed, were foaled in 1975.

*Morafic's death was devastating for everyone at Gleannloch Farms, but particularly to Douglas Marshall. Twenty years later, he said, "You know, I can close my eyes and I still see him as if he were right in front of me. His tail plumed, his head held so high. A king. I will never forget him."

*The Egyptian Prince (*Morafic x *Bint Mona, by Nazeer), foaled in 1967, became renowned as a broodmare sire, consistently placing high on such lists in the late 1970s and '80s.* **Photo by Jerry Sparagowski**

*This is the *Morafic daughter Il Muna, a full sister to The Egyptian Prince. Foaled in 1968, Il Muna was the 1971 U.S. National Champion Futurity Filly. *Morafic offspring had a lock on the futurities that year, with another *Morafic daughter, Muzahrafa, winning the reserve title and a son, Dalul, winning the colt title.*

Photo by Johnny Johnston

11   *SAKR

"*Sakr was an electrifying kind of horse."

TO THE CHORUS of scores of people screaming "Sic 'em, *Sakr!", one of the most famous and popular Arabian show horses of his generation would blast into the ring, snowy legs flashing, silver tail streaming, black eyes dancing. His rider, Tom McNair, would grin from ear to ear and just hold on tight. *Sakr was back in town—and it was show time.

Although McNair was tall and lean, and *Sakr of average Arabian size, the stallion became a giant under saddle—dwarfing the master trainer into insignificance. *Sakr loved his fans and his show ring as much as he loved life, for there he epitomized his Arabic namesake, "The Falcon," and there he soared in his own heaven on earth.

"*Sakr (pronounced like soccer) was an electrifying kind of horse," offered McNair. "Sometimes, especially at the big shows, even the great horses can get lost and not be seen in their classes. *Sakr was not that way. When he came into an arena, you knew it, the audience knew it,

*A 1974 photograph of *Sakr, one of the most popular Arabian show horses of all time.*

Photo by
Jerry Sparagowski

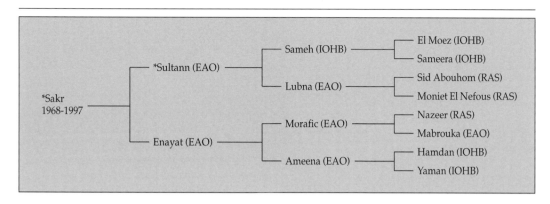

```
                              ┌─ Sameh (IOHB) ──────┬─ El Moez (IOHB)
              ┌─ *Sultann (EAO) ─┤                     └─ Sameera (IOHB)
              │                  └─ Lubna (EAO) ───────┬─ Sid Abouhom (RAS)
*Sakr ────────┤                                        └─ Moniet El Nefous (RAS)
1968-1997     │                  ┌─ Morafic (EAO) ─────┬─ Nazeer (RAS)
              └─ Enayat (EAO) ───┤                     └─ Mabrouka (EAO)
                                 └─ Ameena (EAO) ──────┬─ Hamdan (IOHB)
                                                        └─ Yaman (IOHB)
```

every single time. What an entrance!

"Riding him in the show ring was one of the biggest thrills of my life—just to be up there in the saddle. And most people seemed to love him. Not everyone liked the way he traveled, but they sure remembered him. One year we had buttons made up for the Nationals that read 'Sic 'em, *Sakr!' because that's what people would yell and scream when we'd ride in. When he died, I had several people send those buttons back to me. It was really neat. That meant a lot.

"*Sakr had a great, huge heart—all of his life. And like I've often said," added McNair, with a twinkle in his eyes, "if they made the class long enough, he simply couldn't be beat. He never got tired, only better."

*Sakr won more championships—Class A or better—than any other Arabian horse up to that time—regardless of bloodlines— a record he held for nearly 20 years. (His record was finally surpassed by the stallion GS Khochise, mentioned in the Khemosabi chapter.) *Sakr's wins included 13 national titles in native costume, halter, and park. Five were national championships and three of them reserves (the other five being Top Ten awards, including 1972 U.S. National Top Ten Halter Stallion).

He was 24 times a champion stallion in halter, 19 times a Most Classic winner, and 35 times a park champion. Native costume and other championships earned him a total of 123 championships in his lifetime. In addition, he held the Legion of Supreme Merit award, and is the only Arabian to win four successive national championships in the same performance division (native costume).

Foaled in Egypt on January 1, 1968, *Sakr was by the Sameh son *Sultann and out of the *Morafic daughter Enayat. She, in turn, was out of the Hamdan daughter Ameena. In addition to *Sakr, *Sultann sired the flashy stallion *Asadd, who was

Halter and Performance Record: 123 championships in halter and performance; 13 National titles in halter, native costume, and park; Legion of Supreme Merit Award winner.

Progeny Record:

Purebred Foal Crops: 16
Purebred Foals Registered: 105
U.S./Canadian National Winners: 4
Class A Champions: 12
IAHA Legion of Honor Award Winners: 2
IAHA Legion of Supreme Honor Award Winners: 3
IAHA Legion of Merit Award Winners: 1
IAHA Legion of Supreme Honor/Merit Award Winners: 1

Sakr had a beautiful head and very expressive eyes.

Photo by Jerry Sparagowski

123

Sakr as a weanling in Egypt.

Photo by Judith Forbis

both a U.S. National Champion Stallion and a U.S. National English Pleasure Champion. Unlike the white-gray *Sakr, *Asadd inherited *Sultann's coppery chestnut coat and flaxen mane and tail. Like his two famous sons, *Sultann was eventually imported and lived in America well into his 30s. Long considered to be subfertile, *Sultann sired only a handful of horses in North America.

*Sakr was imported into the United States in November 1968 by H.J. Heubner of Silsbee, Texas. McNair had suggested Heubner purchase the young colt.

"I saw *Sakr first as a 6-month-old over in Egypt," said McNair. "Even then, he had an elegance, a look, and that terrific trot—even as a baby. One of the things that impressed us most is that he moved so well. I liked him very much."

"Mr. Heubner was looking for a horse, or horses, for his daughter. He kept calling me for advice—which I was happy to share—and I suggested this young colt, *Sakr. So Mr. Heubner imported him and had him at his farm in Texas. Walter Chapman, a good trainer friend of mine, had *Sakr for a little while at one point, but he was still too young to start, so he couldn't do much with him yet.

"When *Sakr was almost 2 years old, Mr. Heubner called again to tell me about a trainer he had found to train his horses—he was excited that he was so cheap too. He was planning big things for his horse program. Well, I had never heard of the guy, never knew him. The next thing you know, Mr. Heubner calls back and wants to sell all of his horses, and could I help him?"

When McNair asked what the problem was, Heubner replied that things had not worked out. Shortly thereafter, *Sakr and all of his stablemates were purchased by Douglas and Margaret Marshall of the famous Gleannloch Farms (located then at

*Sultann, the sire of *Sakr, was foaled in 1961 and imported from Egypt in 1975. He also sired *Asadd, who won national championships in both English pleasure and halter, and *Manzoura, who won a national championship in sidesaddle.

Photo courtesy of the Pyramid Society; photo by Johnny Johnston

Spring, Tex., near Houston), McNair's long-time employers.

McNair started working with the youngster almost immediately. At his first show, the Texas State Fair, *Sakr won his first halter championship. He was just 2 years old.

"I started him under saddle at age 3," McNair said. "You know, from the first day I sat on him, I realized I had a lot of horse, a lot of power in just 15.1 hands. He was a giant when he came into an arena, a giant."

*Sakr's first show under saddle was at a family-type event in Nacogdoches, Texas. A busy railroad track ran along one side of the ring and rodeo bucking chutes were on the other side. "Lots of scary stuff for any horse," said McNair, "especially for a young one. But he showed just fine and we won."

Later that same year, 1971, *Sakr took home his first national title, a U.S. Top Ten Park award, a rare feat for a 3-year-old. The stallion was off and "trotting."

*The lovely Enayat, a 1961 mare by *Morafic, was the dam of *Sakr. This photo, taken in Egypt, is reproduced with permission of the photographer.*   Photo by Judith Forbis

*Sakr and Tom McNair always wowed the crowds in native costume classes.

Photo by Jerry Sparagowski

In 1992, Douglas Marshall gave the 26-year-old *Sakr to his trainer and lifelong friend Tom McNair.
Photo by Polly Knoll

With *Sakr as their "front man," Tom and Rhita McNair proceeded to lead the large, illustrious Gleannloch show string to international fame in the 1970s. It seemed like they won everything everywhere they went.

(As an aside, it is fascinating to note that 32 Gleannloch-bred horses have been awarded the Legion of Merit. Of the five straight Egyptian-bred horses to receive the Supreme Legion of Merit, all five were Gleannloch-bred. Further, many of these award winners achieved their triumphs in performance divisions, although Egyptian-bred Arabians traditionally do better in halter classes. The McNairs had a lot to do with these achievements.)

"*Sakr crossed the barrier," recalled the former Gleannloch Farms manager, Dr. Bob Dressler. "People loved him, not because he was Egyptian, but because he was a great horse."

Even great horses have idiosyncrasies, and *Sakr was no exception. "But he had

*With the crowd screaming "Sic 'em, *Sakr," the little gray stallion with Tom McNair aboard would sail around the arena. They are pictured here at the 1974 Scottsdale show where they won the park class.*

Photo by Polly Knoll

one that was truly unique in my experience," McNair explained. "I had never run into it before, and I never have since. It took me a year to figure it out, but when I did, we got along great.

"When I got on him, I learned to leave the reins completely loose, just lying on his neck, and let him walk off on his own. After about 7 or 8 minutes, when I saw the hair lie down on his neck , or the veins start to stand out, or a light sweat begin, I knew I could gather up the reins and start to work with him. He was happiest when he could decide when to go to work. He knew when he was ready, and he didn't need me to tell him. If you didn't let him do it his way, you had a fight on your hands for the next 2 hours.

"If you did it his way, he gave you everything, everything, every time. In fact, at horse shows, if there was no time to warm him up his way, there was no way you could show him. Knowing this, of course, you could plan ahead and time things out right. This lasted throughout

his life; it was the same at age 3 and age 12. Nothing changed."

Although *Sakr was best known for his big trot, he loved to run. Recalled McNair, "When Gleannloch was located at Spring, we had an airstrip on the ranch. Once a week, I took *Sakr there and galloped him out. He liked it so much! I never asked him to go, but I didn't hold him back either. He would gradually pick up the pace until he was running full out. We eventually figured out that he would go about 4 miles before he began to back off the least little bit. He'd make your eyes burn!"

McNair believes these excursions helped *Sakr retain a great attitude on the show circuit. He loved to go forward; he loved to show. Over a 9-year period, he was never below a Top Ten at the seven U.S. National Shows he attended.

Nabiel was the best son of *Sakr, and is shown here at the age of 23. He was owned by Bill and Pat Trapp of Arabest Stud Farm in Wisconsin.

Photo by Polly Knoll

"And he wasn't really afraid of anything," said McNair. "I remember once when he was about 6, we were at the airstrip. There were some huge strips of black plastic covering some hay nearby and the wind was blowing hard, right at us. We were galloping along when the plastic blew off and came right towards us. *Sakr saw it coming and slowed way up, then he kind of squatted down like horses do. In that second or two I thought, 'We're about to spin around and leave this place, fast.' But instead, he just watched it, and when it got to us he reached out and struck it with his foot—hard. He was not afraid of the devil himself.

"In the ring he was the same way. There were times he would have gone over the top of someone if I had let him go—which, of course, I would never do. He was one of the boldest horses I ever rode. In fact, he was more fun to ride than you can ever imagine—like riding a cloud. It was a once-in-a-lifetime experience. I'm so glad I had it."

*Sakr sired just 105 registered purebred Arabians, and never managed to reproduce a performance show horse who came anywhere close to himself. Only four won national titles, and many never entered a show ring.

His best was also his firstborn, the stallion Nabiel, out of the mare *Magidaa; she was by Alaa El Din and out of Maysa. A superb halter horse, Nabiel was the 1974 U.S. National Champion Futurity Colt (shown by McNair), and won two U.S. Top Ten open stallion titles (with long-time owner Bill Trapp on the lead).

As a sire, Nabiel did much better than his sire. While alive, Nabiel enjoyed a spot among the top five, living sires of champions of all time for several years.

"I sold Nabiel for Gleannloch to Bill Trapp when the colt was still with his mother," recalled McNair. "Bill decided it was too cold at that time to take him home to Wisconsin, so he left him with us in Texas until the next spring.

"When he came back to get him, Nabiel had grown into an ugly colt, just a gawky little thing—kind of like a teenager, all knees and elbows and awkwardness. Bill didn't like him, didn't really want him," explained McNair. So the men agreed that if things hadn't improved by the time Nabiel was 3, Gleannloch would buy back the horse. Both hoped the ugly duckling would somehow turn into a swan.

Countered Bill Trapp, "Even when he wasn't his best, Nabiel still had a nice top line, an upright head and neck, and he moved with lots of motion, lots of action. There was quality and promise there, but I was kind of looking at another stallion to buy. Anyway, I took Nabiel home and hoped he would live up to his pedigree."

McNair chuckled and said, "I think Bill took him home and hid him for at least a year. A while later, we went up to the IAHA Fair in Wisconsin, and we were stabled right next to Bill. I was in our tack room one day, which was divided from Bill's by a stall curtain or two, and I overheard him laughing off a man who had just offered him $85,000 for the colt. I guess Bill had changed his mind—he was not about to sell Nabiel." The gray had indeed turned into a swan.

The young stallion crossed extremely well with other straight Egyptian mares and also with some Crabbet/American-bred lines, according to Trapp. At the height of his immense popularity, he was breeding about 78 mares each spring—and showing in halter on the weekends. In the early 1980s, when the horse was 13 or so, the Trapps finally syndicated Nabiel and he was shipped to Rinconada Arabians in New Mexico.

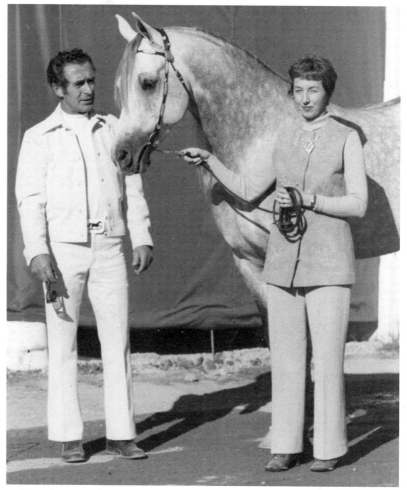

Bill and Pat Trapp with Nabiel just after he had won the 1974 U.S. National Futurity Colt Championship. **Photo courtesy of the Trapps**

All told, Nabiel sired over 125 champions (Class A or better) through 1997. He sired 12 national winners in both halter and performance.

*Sakr's three other national winners include Nabiel's full brother, Sugaa, twice a Canadian English Pleasure Top Ten winner and a Canadian Pleasure Driving Top Ten winner; Ala Ibn Sakr (out of Bint Jubilema), a U.S. National Native Costume Top Ten winner; and Shakr (out of Zeonah), a U.S. National Native Costume Champion. Furthermore, three *Sakr sons went on to sire national winners.

*Sugaa, another
*Sakr son who was
out of *Magidaa, won
Canadian National
Top Tens in English
pleasure and pleasure
driving. He was
also a Class A halter
champion and a
Most Classic Arabian
award winner.*

Photo courtesy of the
Pyramid Society; photo
by Johnny Johnston

*Sakr also had several daughters who were good broodmares, including Zedena Bint Sakr, dam of U.S. Top Ten Stallion and Canadian National Western Pleasure Champion Jaoxs Ishtar.

When the Marshalls moved Gleannloch to its Barksdale, Tex., location in the early 1980s, the McNairs chose not to leave the Houston area. For several years, Tom McNair had little or no contact with *Sakr.

Then in 1991, the Marshalls decided to disperse their Egyptian Arabian horses, and Mr. Marshall called McNair and asked if he wanted *Sakr.

"Of course I said yes," responded McNair. "So I had him for the last years of his life, and that was grand."

McNair was still at his original farm in Pinehurst, Tex., when *Sakr was shipped back. There, an unusual thing happened. "The day after he arrived, I went to work a young horse in an enclosed round pen near one end of *Sakr's paddock," recalled McNair.

"Several people were around and saw what he did next. Now, I couldn't see him and he couldn't see me, but as soon as he heard my voice, he flew to the end of the paddock and stood there, frozen. He stared at the round pen, listening hard, and never moved a muscle. He listened to every word I said, the entire time I was in there, at least 20 minutes, and never moved. Everyone who saw him was astonished. They agreed that it was obviously he knew me, that maybe he was waiting for me to appear, and maybe even that he had missed me. I don't know, but I think he remembered me."

McNair soon took a job at Thistlewood Farm and *Sakr went along. Visitors loved to see the grand old stallion, and McNair

Shakr, sired by *Sakr and out of Zeonah, was a U.S. National Champion in native costume.

Photo by Polly Knoll

often took small children for rides on his old white back, with just a plain halter and lead rope for restraint. "He was perfectly calm," said McNair. "He was one of those who knew the difference."

The veteran trainer cleared his throat and went on. "It was ironic. *Sakr was feeling so good the day before he died. He was pulling the walker around, like usual, and looked good. That afternoon, he started to act sick. I stayed up with him all night, but he didn't get any better. I really didn't want to send him to Texas A&M or try to do surgery that had little chance of helping him . . . he had done too many great things, had been such a good companion. He was old, and he didn't need to die that way. So, in the morning, I made the decision to have him euthanized—at the farm, with me.

"Have you ever seen a grown man cry? Well, I did. . . . It was one of the saddest days of my life."

*Sakr died on June 3, 1997. He was 29 years old.

12   *SANACHT

She was one of the true equine bargains of the 20th century.

AFTER WEEKS aboard an Atlantic cargo ship, the little gray mare was a rather pathetic sight as she came ashore in New York City one day in June 1962. Her new owners, Paul and (the late) Sandi Loeber, hardly knew what to think of the skinny, dirty, disheveled 2-year-old filly they had purchased virtually sight unseen.

Still, there was something innately classic, even elegant, about her, and the

Loebers gamely decided to drive her home to their Plum Grove Farm near Palatine, Illinois. Little did the Loebers ever dream that *Sanacht's purchase price of only $750 would turn out to be among the true equine bargains of the second half of the 20th century.

At the farm, the filly, *Sanacht (SUH-knocked), would grow up to become one of the most respected broodmares in the

*This photograph of *Sanacht was taken in 1982 when she was 22 years old.*

Photo by Bob Reeder

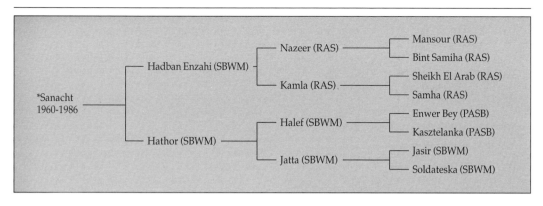

*Sanacht 1960-1986

- Hadban Enzahi (SBWM)
  - Nazeer (RAS)
    - Mansour (RAS)
    - Bint Samiha (RAS)
  - Kamla (RAS)
    - Sheikh El Arab (RAS)
    - Samha (RAS)
- Hathor (SBWM)
  - Halef (SBWM)
    - Enwer Bey (PASB)
    - Kasztelanka (PASB)
  - Jatta (SBWM)
    - Jasir (SBWM)
    - Soldateska (SBWM)

history of the Arabian breed in America. Not only would she become a champion show mare, but she would also produce 15 foals, of which 12 became champions, including a pair of national champions. With those 12 champions, she shares the record (as of this writing) for the most champions from one dam; she's tied with the mare TW Forteyna (*Fortel x Tapiola, by Sur-Grande).

In addition, her offspring produced just as well, and it can therefore be said that *Sanacht founded a dynasty of show champions numbering in the hundreds and extending today well into the fourth and fifth generations. To them all she has given her two most precious gifts: excellent conformation and sweet disposition.

*Sanacht was foaled on February 25, 1960, at the highly-respected Marbach Stud (also known as the Wurttemburg State Stud) in Germany. Her sire was the straight Egyptian stallion Hadban Enzahi, a Nazeer son, who was out of the mare Kamla (Sheikh El Arab x Samha).

*Sanacht's dam, Hathor, was a nice, neat cross of Polish Arabian lines, through her sire Halef (Enwer Bey x *Kasztelanka), and old German (Weil Stud) bloodlines through her dam, Jatta (Jasir x Soldateska, by Souakim).

All in all, *Sanacht's pedigree was one a breeder could trust, one that was solid and widely outcrossed, with no shared ancestors in the family tree. It bespoke stability and the promise of excellent breeding results year after year, time after time. And *Sanacht fulfilled that promise.

The Loebers happened to purchase *Sanacht through Paul's father, Martin. The elder Loeber had traveled to Germany to buy a riding horse, and went to the Marbach Stud to see his old friend Dr. Georg Wenzler, who was the director there.

"She was absolutely correct," Paul

Halter and Performance Record: A multiple halter champion.

Progeny Record:

Purebred Foal Crops: 15
Purebred Foals Registered: 15
U.S./Canadian National Winners: 2
Class A Champions: 12

Loeber told Mary Jane Parkinson in an interview for an article in *Arabian Horse World* magazine, "a product, I think, of all the hundreds of years of breeding and culling at Marbach. In her breeding, she was so genetically clean there was just no way to make a mistake, the kind of mare who makes you look like a brilliant breeder—like you really know what you're doing . . . when it's probably fate as much as anything."

*Sanacht was especially well-known for her exceptional body and straight legs. Her topline was smooth and strong, with excellent tail carriage and good withers and shoulders. When crossed with more exotically "pretty" stallions, she produced incredible, high-quality foals who took Plum Grove Farm to the pinnacle of Arabian horse breeding success.

"She wasn't a spectacularly showy mare, but there just weren't any holes

133

Sanacht as a younger mare, with handler Sandi Loeber at Plum Grove Farm, Palatine, Illinois.

Photo by Gloria DeFillips

in her," said Loeber, recalling her training and subsequent horse show experience, during which she won several halter championships.

"Besides her excellent conformation, *Sanacht had such a great mind," added Loeber. "I can't recall in all the years we owned her that she ever did a dumb thing. She had the most human-like qualities I've ever known, and she was so good with her foals."

*Sanacht produced her foals from 1964 through 1983. Of the 15, all 10 daughters and 5 sons were gray. They in turn begat 229 grandchildren (including 13 national winners) for the venerable old matriarch.

All 15 of *Sanacht's offspring (and many of her descendants) bear the prefix name "Amurath," bestowed on them with respect to one of *Sanacht's significant ancestors, Amurath 1881. Here, a slight digression:

According to one of the best authorities on Arabian horses, (the late) Gladys Brown Edwards, Amurath 1881 and his ancestor Bairactar are important through several noteworthy modern descendants.

As GBE wrote in her book *The Arabian: War Horse to Show Horse:* "Bairactar, a beautiful gray stallion whose descendants prove that his portrait was not idealized, especially in regard to level topline, was imported by the King of Wurtemburg for the Weil Stud in 1817. He was used at stud there for 21 years, which accounts for his being in the pedigree of practically every horse bred there, over and over. The tail male line

is represented through Amurath 1881 and more recently by Amurath Sahib, a singularly successful broodmare sire. . . . Among the mares by Amurath Sahib are the dams of the American champions *Gwalior, *Ardahan, *Arwilga, *Aramus (see the *Naborr chapter), *Bask (refer to the *Bask chapter), and *Dornaba (*Naborr chapter)."

Such illustrious company nearly guaranteed *Sanacht's superior potential as a broodmare.

Offspring

The stallion Fadi was the sire of *Sanacht's first three foals: Amurath Kalahari in 1964, Amurath Kasari in 1965, and Amurath Kashmira in 1966. Fadi was by the "Fabulous Fadjur" (see his chapter) and out of the very good Hall of Fame mare Saki, by Ferseyn.

Kalahari, a 1967 Region VI Top Five Mare, eventually had 16 foals, 8 of them champions, including 2 national winners: five-time National Top Ten Mare Amurath Isis and U.S. National Top Ten Futurity Colt Amurath Freedom, both by the imported Egyptian stallion *Ramses Fayek.

Kasari had 15 foals, like her mother. Three were champions.

Kashmira, a halter champion, also had 15 foals, 10 of them champions and an impressive 4 who were national winners. They included the 1978 U.S. National Champion Stallion Amurath Bandolero and the 1979 U.S. National Champion Futurity Filly Amurath Bali (both by *Ramses Fayek).

*Sanacht next was bred three times to the imported Polish stallion *Czortan

*Sanacht's last two champions were Amurath Santiago (left), foaled in 1982, and Amurath Sandsprite, foaled in 1983. Both were sired by *Ramses Fayek.

Photo by Waltenberry

*Amurath Kalahari (by Fadi) was *Sanacht's first foal. She was as prolific as her dam, producing 16 foals. Eight became champions, and two became national winners.*

Amurath Kashmira, herself a halter champion, produced 15 foals. Ten became champions, an incredible four became national winners, and two, national champions. They were Amurath Bandolero, the 1978 U.S. National Champion Stallion, and Amurath Bali, the 1979 U.S. National Champion Futurity Filly.

*Amurath Spellbound was *Sanacht's only foal by Ramses Ibn Fayek. Foaled in 1979, Spellbound sired just two foals.*

Photo by Polly Knoll

(Czort x *Mortissa, by Trypolis). The mare Amurath Czarina, foaled in 1967, was named 1971 Region VI Top Five Mare. She produced eight foals, of which four are champions and one a national-champion producer.

The stallion Amurath Kashmir (*Sanacht's first colt) was foaled in 1968 and sired 15 foals.

The third *Czortan offspring was the mare Amurath Chamonix, foaled in 1969. She became a junior halter champion and later produced seven foals.

For *Sanacht's next foal, the Loebers went right to the top: *Bask. Since he was out of the Amurath Sahib daughter Balalajka (and by Witraz), *Bask would give another dose of highly regarded Amurath blood to *Sanacht's offspring.

The result was her best daughter, Amurath Bandeira, foaled in 1971. Bandeira first was a superb show mare who earned five national titles, including U.S. National Champion Futurity Filly and U.S. National Reserve Champion Mare. She then went on to produce 12 foals; 5 became champions and 1 became a national winner.

*Sanacht then was bred twice to regional halter champion and national-winner sire *Ramses Fayek. (She would be returned to him near the end of her breeding career.) Foaled in 1958, *Ramses Fayek was a Nazeer son out of the Sid Abouhom daughter Fayza II. Paul Loeber's father, Martin Loeber, had imported *Ramses Fayek from Egypt in 1970.

With *Ramses Fayek, *Sanacht had park reserve champion Amurath Chandar, foaled in 1973, who eventually sired nine foals, and halter champion Amurath Selari, foaled in 1974. Selari had eight foals, including Minotaur (by the Russian stallion *Menes), who, in 1996, was a National Top Ten Stallion in both the United States and Canada.

In 1974, *Sanacht returned to the court of the "emperor," *Bask. Her next two

*The *Sanacht grandson Amurath Bandolero in 1978, when he was named U.S. National Champion Stallion. He is by *Ramses Fayek and out of Amurath Kashmira.*　　　　Photo by Jerry Sparagowski

foals were her best sons: Amurath Bakonur, foaled in 1975, and Amurath Baikal, foaled in 1977.

Bakonur sired 57 foals, 3 of them national winners, including Canadian Top Ten Mare Kamesha, U.S. Top Ten Futurity Gelding Bahraini, and U.S. Top Ten English Pleasure JOTR winner SFA Chippyr.

Baikal steals the show from his full brother, however, first by being a show ring sensation. He excelled in Most Classic classes, and was the 1980 U.S. Reserve National Champion Futurity Colt and 1984 Region 14 Champion Stallion. Baikal has sired more than 60 foals for the Loebers and present owner Janie Greenberg of Rideaufield Farms, Merrickville, Ontario.

"We consistently get good-legged, good-footed horses, with excellent clean, dry bone, beautiful shoulders, and high-set necks," Greenberg told writer Mary Jane Parkinson in her 1997 *Arabian Horse World* article. "The *Sanachts are 'thinking horses' with wonderful temperaments. Our Amurath Baikal sires properly conformed foals; hence, saddle work is easy for them."

A prime example is JK Jedi, one of Baikal's three national winners. JK Jedi (out of Kemahs Josephine, by Ismid) excelled under saddle. He was the 1985 National English Pleasure Champion in both the United States and Canada and was the 1986 U.S. National English Pleasure AOTR Champion.

*Sanacht then was bred in 1978 to a *Ramses Fayek son, Ramses Ibn Fayek (out of *Ramses Wafeya, by Nasralla). That mating produced Amurath Spellbound, a colt who sired just two foals.

*Sanacht's last three foals were all by the Loebers' own *Ramses Fayek. Amurath Sandpiper, a halter champion mare foaled in 1980, had two foals. Next came Amurath Santiago, a halter reserve champion mare foaled in 1982, who also had two foals. And finally, in 1983, *Sanacht had Amurath Sandsprite, a halter reserve champion mare who did not breed on.

Of all these 15 illustrious offspring, only three did not succeed in the show ring: Amurath Kashmire, Amurath Spellbound, and Amurath Kasari. Kasari did win the Illinois State Futurity, but it is not regarded as an official IAHA Class A championship.

The Later Years

Sharon Eider-Orley, who with husband Bill owns several *Sanacht descendants, recalled seeing *Sanacht at the end of her breeding career. "*Sanacht was brought in from the pasture and walked down the barn aisle toward us," she told Mary Jane Parkinson. "I was immediately struck by her beautiful body, even at age 22. A great topline, smooth and flat, and she had good size. After that we'd go back each spring to see the Plum Grove foals and to visit with her. In the pasture, she would always come up to be petted. She just knew all visitors were there to see her."

*Sanacht spend her retirement years at the Plum Grove farm near Ocala, Fla., lounging under the live oak trees.

Recalled Sharon Eider-Orley: "In the fall of 1985, we walked way out in the pasture to see *Sanacht and about 10 of her daughters and granddaughters. There she was, still beautiful, still carrying herself with a regal air, still tightly muscled, and still the kind, intelligent, sweet mare whom everyone loved. Suddenly, the mares realized it was feeding time and all started running across the pasture—pure beauty in motion."

*Sanacht was 26 when she died in 1986. She is buried in front of the Plum Grove stallion barn, her grave marked by a plaque.

In February 1997, the Arabian Horse Trust inducted *Sanacht into its Hall of Fame, along with such mares as Saki, Bint Sahara (see her chapter), *Roda, and *Rifala, as one of the breed's most influential mares.

The Loebers still have a few Arabian horses. Mary, whom Paul married after Sandi died, loves endurance riding, and their children, Christopher and Carrie, both ride. According to Paul, as their *Sanacht descendants mature, they become even more beautiful.

"They are one of the prettiest sights

*Sanacht's best daughter was Amurath Bandeira, foaled in 1979. Sired by *Bask, she earned five national titles, including U.S. National Champion Futurity Filly and U.S. Reserve National Champion Mare. **Photo by Polly Knoll**

you can imagine," Loeber told Parkinson. "I reminded Mary that if you went out looking for a group of mares like this, you could never find them, or ever buy them. . . . She was an absolute treasure of a mare."

13   *RAFFLES

He is considered to be one of the greatest Arabian stallions.

IF NOT FOR the unprecedented efforts and faith of a rural Kentucky couple, *Raffles might never have sired his first foal—let alone a dynasty that would fill chapters in a history of today's Arabian horses.

His breeder, Lady Judith Wentworth of Crabbet Stud in England, considered him little more than a pretty pony, "... ideal for your little son later on when he is old enough to ride," she once wrote to Ohio breeder Roger Selby, his eventual owner. Kentuckians Jimmy and Thelma Dean, however, saw much more. From his large dark eyes, set in a wide brow above a

*This George Ford Morris photo of *Raffles appeared in Roger Selby's book,* **Arabian Horses** *(out of print). A little guy in size but big of heart, *Raffles has been described as standing 13.1 to 13.3 hands and weighing 850 to 875 pounds. However, most of his offspring were taller.*

Photo courtesy Arabian Horse Trust

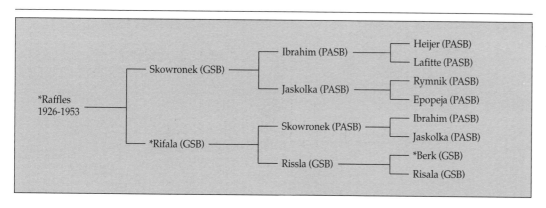

```
                                    ┌─── Heijer (PASB)
                    ┌─ Ibrahim (PASB) ─┤
                    │               └─── Lafitte (PASB)
      ┌─ Skowronek (GSB) ─┤
      │             │               ┌─── Rymnik (PASB)
      │             └─ Jaskolka (PASB) ─┤
*Raffles ─┤                            └─── Epopeja (PASB)
1926-1953 │                          ┌─── Ibrahim (PASB)
      │             ┌─ Skowronek (PASB) ─┤
      │             │               └─── Jaskolka (PASB)
      └─ *Rifala (GSB) ─┤
                    │               ┌─── *Berk (GSB)
                    └─ Rissla (GSB) ─┤
                                    └─── Risala (GSB)
```

refined nose, to the tip of his silvery tail, they saw exquisite Arabian horse type—albeit in miniature at about 13.1 hands and 850 pounds—and a plucky personality. *Raffles had superior bloodlines, was linebred for genetic punch, and seemed a perfect outcross for the mere handful of Arabian mares living in the United States during the 1930s.

Foaled in 1926, *Raffles was the result of a cross between the legendary Polish-bred sire Skowronek (Ibrahim x Jaskolka) and the Skowronek daughter *Rifala (out of Rissla, by Berk). The genetic power of this inbred combination was perhaps best expressed by Bazy Tankersley (a noted breeder of Arabian horses for 60 years and whose Al-Marah horses are famous around the world). She has written: "Skowronek is the horse I now believe to be the greatest Arabian stallion in recorded history."

In the late 1950s Lady Wentworth wrote and published a book titled *The Crabbet Arabian Stud* (now out of print). In several places she talks about Skowronek (pronounced Sko-RONE-ek); here are several excerpts:

"Skowronek, though foaled in Poland, returns by both sire and dam to the old Abbas-Crabbet strains, and his fame rests entirely on his show and stud career at Crabbet, his celebrity being such that I once safely received a cable addressed simply to *Skowronek, England*, without any other name or location.

"Skowronek's dam was Yaskolka (spelled Jaskolka in the Polish Arabian Studbook), out of Epopeja. The latter was described by Lady Anne Blunt as a

Halter and Performance Record: 1933 Nashville National Show Three-Gaited Champion.

Progeny Record:

Purebred Foal Crops: 15
Purebred Foals Registered: 122
U.S./Canadian National Winners: 2
Class A Champions: 28

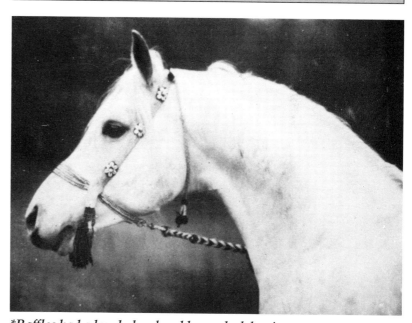

**Raffles had a lovely head and large, dark luminous eyes.*

Photo courtesy Arabian Horse Trust

*Raffles, considered to be sterile, was added as a free bonus by Lady Wentworth to a 1932 package deal she made with Selby.

particularly beautiful gray mare then being driven in a team. Skowronek was mated exclusively to mares of pure Crabbet blood so that the fame of his illustrious progeny is exactly halved by Crabbet mares, from which his blood cannot be divorced. Skowronek himself was of a spotless white seldom seen, and of spectacular pride of carriage."

In his book titled *Arabian Horses* (also out of print), Roger Selby described *Rifala, the dam of *Raffles, this way:

"Arab mare. White. 13.2 hands. Foaled 1922. 875 pounds. Well-broke, good saddler. Sound. Gentle. Register No. 815 Arabian Horse Club. 5465 Jockey Club.

"An outstanding example of the finest type of Arab mare and the only mare who is both an English and American champion. Gold medal, Royal Show, England, 1922. First prize, Horsham, 1923. Winner of a

silver cup at the Sussex County Show in 1923. Winner of the mare championship, National Arabian Show, Nashville, 1923.

"Sired by the celebrated World Champion, Skowronek, an ideal type and now unprocurable in the desert. Lady Anne Blunt, mother of Lady Wentworth and the founder of Crabbet Stud, spent the last 20 years of her life in a vain search for a horse of Skowronek's type. Skowronek was secured by Crabbet from the Antoniny Stud of Poland, which was destroyed by the Bolsheviks during the World War.

"*Rifala's grandsire on the dam's side, Champion Berk, was celebrated for his brilliant trotting action. Her dam, Rissla, won first prize at the Richmond Royal Show, the only time shown. Rissla, also, was remarkable for her wonderful trotting action.

"*Rifala is the dam of our stallions, *Raffles and Image. She is the ideal Arab mare, a proven breeder of the finest foals, bred to any stallion. All her foals have that wonderful expression and alertness combined with a proud way of going that she so aptly demonstrates."

As *Raffles was growing up at Crabbet

Stud in England, a shoe manufacturer named Roger Selby was building the soon-to-be-famous Selby Stud (which now no longer exists) near Portsmouth, Ohio. From that stud came the legendary American Saddlebred stallion King's Genius, as well as a number of other influential Saddlebreds and Arabians—but that is another story.

When on business trips to Europe, Selby often visited Crabbet Stud. From 1928 to 1933, he purchased from Lady Wentworth and imported to the United States 20 Arabian horses, many found in important pedigrees today. *Raffles, considered to be sterile, was added as a free bonus by Lady Wentworth to a 1932 package deal she made with Selby.

In his book, Selby described *Raffles as standing 13.3 hands, weighing 850 pounds, and being "active but gentle." He also wrote:

"*Raffles is highly inbred to the celebrated champion Skowronek, who is ideal type which Abbas Pasha I, Viceroy of Egypt, spent a fortune in collecting from the desert, where it is now unprocurable. *Raffles is a replica, on a smaller scale, of his famous sire, and both his sire and dam

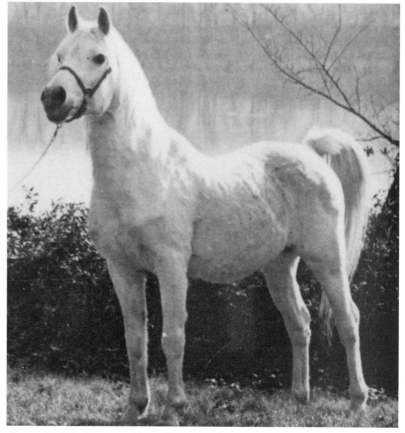

*A wooly *Raffles sporting a heavy winter coat.*

Photo courtesy Arabian Horse Trust

*This is Skowronek, Lady Wentworth's wonderful stallion who sired *Raffles and many other out-standing horses. This photo was repro-duced from Lady Wentworth's book,* **The Crabbet Arabian Stud** *(out of print).*

Photo by Lady Wentworth

Here's a photo of Lady Wentworth with Skowronek which appeared in the April 1951 issue of **Western Horse-man.** *The caption quotes Lady Went-worth as stating, "No more perfect specimen has ever been imported to England." The photo was from the Spide Rathbun Collection.*

This picture of *Rifala, a daughter of Skowronek and the dam of Raffles, appeared in a WH article in March-April 1944 that was titled "Polish Arabians May Have Been Saved." The author was Ben Hur, who wrote: "*Raffles, then, is the inbred son, son, and grandson of Skowronek, and has three-quarters of the blood of his sire rather than the usual one-half. Possibly for this reason the blood of *Raffles has been found unusually potent in passing on the extremely desirable qualities, from the Arabian breeders' point of view, to the offspring." The foal in the picture is unidentified.

Azraff, a top-siring son of *Raffles, is shown here at age 21. He was out of the mare *Azja IV, who was of German and Polish breeding. Photo by Johnny Johnston

being champions, he shows his breeding in marked degree. His natural action is exceptionally high. Under all circumstances, he makes such a perfect picture as to be truly fascinating—a picture Arab if one ever lived. His haughty carriage and vim make him the cynosure of all eyes."

For years, most Arabian horse aficionados have believed *Raffles' sterility to be the primary reason Lady Wentworth gave him to Selby. However, pedigree researcher Arlene Magid, of Louisville, Ky., recently discovered correspondence that seems to indicate that Selby may have misinformed Lady Wentworth concerning *Raffles' dam, *Rifala (whom he had imported in 1928), in an attempt to influence some purchase negotiations.

In Selby's letter he apparently claimed that *Rifala was barren, and had not produced a foal. Lady Wentworth responded with surprise in a letter dated January 15, 1932: ". . . She had no trouble with the foal she had here (in England), and if you care about it, I propose to present him (*Raffles) to you." In fact, *Rifala was in foal

and about to give birth to the colt Rifbo, by the American Saddlebred stallion Four Acres Erskine Bourbon King.

One might speculate that Selby was really after *Raffles, or a lower price on another horse, and that Lady Wentworth's "gift" was due more to the alleged sterility of *Raffles' dam, than to his own.

Whatever the real reason, *Raffles, the "little gift," turned out to be a sire whose strongly prepotent, pretty "look," and his strong, square trot and unusual intelligence survives into the fourth and fifth generations of his descendants—and beyond.

The Fertility Problem

Northern Kentucky native Jimmy Dean, with his wife and constant companion, Thelma, at his side, went to work for Selby in 1934. He served as the farm's manager

Rafaia, by *Raffles and out of *Indaia, was a full sister to the well-known Indraff.

Photo courtesy Arabian Horse Trust

Although *Raffles was trained, he was decidedly difficult. . . .

and trainer for nearly 20 years. It could easily be argued that if not for the Deans, *Raffles' genetic gifts would have been lost to the Arabian breed.

As (the late) Jimmy Dean recounted some years ago, the couple ventured into unexplored territory in their quest to improve *Raffles' fertility.

"He had been declared hopelessly sterile by two of the best veterinary schools back then: the Royal Veterinary College in London and Ohio State University," said Dean. "He would breed the mare, but he had only seminal fluids; there was no sperm."

Dean had read about hypertension and its effects on sexual dysfunction in humans, and he thought that theory might explain the horse's problem as well. Over time, *Raffles had learned to greatly distrust people and often displayed a poor attitude.

So, during the cold winter of 1935, each evening after chores were finished, Jimmy and Thelma worked with the 9-year-old stallion in the indoor arena. "We'd just play with him and feed him apples and carrots," said Jimmy. "It took us 6 weeks just getting to the point where he wasn't on his defensive."

Finally, the Deans decided to try to ride *Raffles. Although he was trained, and, in fact, had won the three-gaited championship with his brilliant trot at the 1933 Nashville National Show, he was decidedly difficult and barely under control. "I led him and told her (Thelma) to walk right behind me and put her hand on his back while she was walking. We got to the point where I put my hand back, she stepped up in it, slid onto his back, and he went straight up in the air. She just put her arms around his neck, patted him, and talked to him. He walked two or three steps on his hind legs. Then he would just come down and go up, come down and go up. She just kept talking and

146

This good-looking horse is Aaraf, by *Raffles and out of Aarah. Owned by the Ben Hur farm in Indiana, he won the Arabian stallion saddle class in both 1949 and 1950 at the National Stallion Show in Waterloo, Iowa. The photo was taken by McClasky and appeared in the April '51 issue of **Western Horseman.**

The legendary Jimmy Dean stands between two grandget of *Raffles. On the left is the mare Azleta, the dam of U.S. National Champion Gai-Parada, and on the right is the stallion Azy.

Photo courtesy Ginger Detterman

*Raffles' foals were almost an instant sensation.

patting him. We went through that rigama-role for a couple weeks," Jimmy recalled (as recorded for the Arabian Horse Trust Heritage Video *Jimmy and Thelma Dean*).

Soon Thelma, whom Jimmy said rode bareback "just like an Indian," began riding the white stallion in a more relaxed manner. The pair sometimes spent entire days roaming trails in the nearby woods. Thelma took her lunch and often returned at dark.

Jimmy built a special paddock for *Raffles. "After we brought him back off of 8 or 9 hours of ridin', we'd turn him loose in there, and then he'd start to running and he'd run even after that much riding. He'd run off 150 pounds before he finally settled down to eat," Jimmy added with a chuckle.

That spring, 1936, came the big test. *Raffles was bred to two pony mares kept for the farm's children to ride. Both settled.

The next spring (1937), Jimmy bred *Raffles to the Arabian mares *Indaia and *Rishafieh; both had foals in 1938. As if by some grand predestination, those first two purebred Arabian youngsters went on to strongly influence the breed. *Rishafieh's filly, Raffieh, became a foundation mare for L.W. "Boss" Van Vleet in Colorado. *Indaia's colt, Indraff, became the foundation stallion for Bazy Tankersley's famous Al-Marah Arabians, now of Tucson.

"After we got *Raffles to breeding again," said Jimmy, "she (Lady Wentworth) wanted to buy him back. And Mr. Selby wouldn't sell . . . so *she* wouldn't sell *him* any more horses."

The Offspring

*Raffles' foals were almost an instant sensation. As Jimmy explained, "Their heads were shorter and wider, and they had more of a dish in them. They had more animation and more presence than the majority of other foals. Seemed like

Here's a picture of Arraff cutting with Harold Brite in the saddle. Brite was the Al-Marah trainer for many years.

every time they started off from standing still, the tail would go up just like it was connected to their feet. Everybody who came noticed and wanted to know if that was a different strain of Arabians. It was the Skowronek influence that made the difference, I think."

*Raffles sired a total of 122 registered foals from 1938 through 1953. Two were national halter winners and 43 percent produced national winners. That's a higher percentage than possibly any other major purebred sire. The names of many are like cornerstones in American foundation bloodlines: Indraff and Raffieh (already mentioned), Imaraff, Rapture, Hanraff, Ibn Raffles, Rafmirz, Bamby, Handeyraff, Mraff, Azraff, Mysteraffles, Rifraff, Joye, Geym, and Gajala, to mention only a few. His best sons, arguably, were Indraff and Azraff.

Indraff, out of the Crabbet-bred mare *Indaia (Raseem x Nisreen), was sold by Selby to Donald Schutz, who then sold the horse to Bazy Tankersley of Al-Marah Arabians. Indraff placed first 15 times out of 27 times shown and, at age 10, was named champion Arabian stallion at the 1948 National Stallion Show in Waterloo, Iowa. In its day, a win there was considered to be the equivalent of a U.S. National

*At Chicago's all-Arabian horse show in 1955, Bazy Tankersley of Al-Marah Arabians won the cutting on Arraff, by *Raffles and out of Arsa, by *Saoud.*
Photo by Norman Grantham

The lovely Rose of Raswan (*Raffles x Zareyna, by *Zarife) was named champion mare at the 1955 Chicago Arabian show. She was bred by John and Alice Payne, Chino, Calif., and was owned by Dr. and Mrs. William Munson, who lived in Cambridge, Ill., at the time. The handler is possibly Carl Raswan.

Photo by Norman Grantham

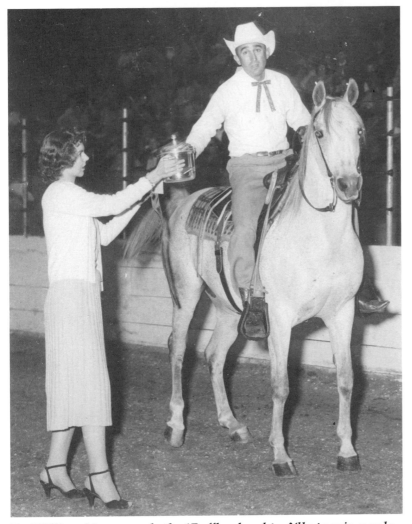

Dr. William Munson rode the *Raffles daughter Ylla to win a pole bending class at the 1955 Chicago Arabian show. Bred by Roger Selby and owned by Albert Ehnle of Cambridge, Ill., the mare was out of Nabima, by Image.   Photo by Norman Grantham

Championship. During the 1940s and 1950s, very few Arabian horse shows were held, yet 48 of Indraff's 254 registered foals won championship titles.

Indraff's descendants are known as much for their athletic ability, especially in cutting, stock horse (reining), and working cow horse, as for their beauty. Indraff stood for all but one year (1954, when he was in California with Howard Marks) at Tankersley's Al-Marah Arabians.

Azraff, bred by Walter Ross of Kansas City, was foaled in 1949, out of the German- and Polish-bred mare *Azja IV (Landsknecht x Asra). He is the top-siring son of *Raffles, with 500 registered get, 87 champions, and 23 national winners, including U.S. National Champion Stallion Galizon and Canadian National Champion Stallion Comar Bay Beau. He is also well known for the popular Ferzon-Azraff cross responsible for numerous champions and for having a significant impact on the famous Gainey Arabians program.

After the Deans left Selby Stud and went out on their own, the Ferzon-Azraff cross became the hallmark of their program as well. Azraff stood for most of his life at Garth Buchanan's Comar Arabians, Story City, Iowa.

The Broken Leg

Nearly every Arabian horse legend has one or, at most, two persons with whom he or she is unfailingly linked. For *Raffles, that connection was with, obviously, Jimmy and Thelma Dean. In 1949 that special bond literally saved the white stallion's life.

Early one morning, while the Deans were still at the Selby Stud, Jimmy's son, Pete, went to feed the stallions before heading off to school. *Raffles lived at one end of the barn and Image (a wonderful *Mirage son) at the other, with seven or eight more stallions in between. Usually *Raffles was fed first.

"For some reason, I never did know why, Pete started at the other end of the barn, and fed Image first," Jimmy recalled. "When Pete got to *Raffles, he sort of hung in the back of his stall, and Pete said, 'Come on and get your feed.' And then he went in and took his mane to lead him up, and *Raffles sort of hopped.

"Pete came screaming back over to the house, 'Raffles broke his leg!' I went over and he was eatin' his meal, but the leg was really broken. When you would take it and maneuver it, it sounded just like you had broken glass in a cloth. You could turn it clear around."

That kind of break just above the hock in a 23-year-old breeding stallion spelled certain death—especially in 1949. Nevertheless, Jimmy placed a telephone call to Dr. Vernon Tharp at Ohio State University. His reply was to the point. "You can't save him, Jim. There's no way," Jimmy remembered Tharp saying.

Thelma was standing next to the phone. Said Jimmy, "She started crying and screaming, 'You're not gonna kill him! You're not gonna kill him!' and I says, 'Well, Doc, I'm either gonna have to shoot the horse and my wife both, or do something. Will you come down and keep him under sedation while I splint him up and give it a try anyway?' Well, he said he'd come down, but that we were just wasting our time and we'd have to destroy him in the end."

*Raffles was sedated at about 9 p.m. the same day. Tharp, two other OSU veteri-

*This photograph from the 1955 Chicago show is of Joan Berman on Rafourid (*Raffles x Ourida, by Ribal). They won a western pleasure class. The breeder and owner of Rafourid: Manion Canyon Arabian Farm, South Bend, Indiana.* Photo by Norman Grantham

narians, and Jimmy worked through the night to splint the leg and build a sling. Jimmy had some lightweight airline tubing that he'd been experimenting with and, together with wire and plaster, an elaborate cast was formed. All four men held down the little horse as he came out of sedation. "He was thrashing around . . . but I just kept talking to him and finally got him to listen," said Jimmy. They got

him into the sling, the vets left for Columbus, and Jimmy went in for breakfast.

Within minutes, one of the hired hands came running to say that *Raffles had escaped from the sling and was hopping around on the new cast. Jimmy realized more work was needed. He built a stouter sling and hoisted the stallion up higher. Every hour, around the clock, the horse was lowered for 10 minutes to stand on his three good legs in order to increase circulation and lessen the chance of colic and pneumonia. The courageous stallion soon figured out the routine and settled into his

convalescence. From January through April, someone was with *Raffles every minute of every day. Jimmy took the night shift. "I slept right in the stall in front of him, where I could put my hand on him while I was lying down."

Finally, X-rays showed that the leg was healed. After a week of hobbling carefully around his stall, *Raffles was allowed outside. "He went runnin' and screamin' and hollerin' and lookin' for a fight with the 2-year-old stallion in the pen next to him. He never had any more trouble," Jimmy recalled.

To California

While *Raffles was laid up, Roger Selby began disbanding the stud farm. The now-famous Selby-bred Arabian horses were

Rafferty, by *Raffles and out of Masrufa, sired two national winners.

Sotep, by *Raffles and out of Zareyna, sired five national winners.

sold to breeders all across the country. Only a few remained.

For years, Alice Payne of Asil Arabians in California, who already owned *Raseyn, had wanted to purchase *Raffles. After weeks of negotiations, Selby agreed to send him to the West Coast. However, there were conditions: Jimmy would have to accompany the horse, and then stay long enough to breed him to one mare.

An agreement was struck, and, in mid-November 1949, *Raffles, his son Raffey, a *Raffles daughter, and several people boarded a Pullman railroad car and set off across the country. In those days, women were not allowed to ride in freight cars, only in passenger compartments. It comes as no surprise, however, that Thelma managed to work around the rules. At departure and during stops, she simply hid in *Raffles' stall, which had hay bales piled around the horse on all sides. Five days later, on Thanksgiving Day, the entourage arrived in California.

Payne and her family, as well as a large crowd of curious neighbors, met the train. "It wasn't far to Alice's barn," said Jimmy,

"so we got *Raffles unloaded and led him over to Alice's place with all these people following along behind him like he was the Pied Piper."

Jimmy and Thelma stayed until a mare was ready to be bred. During the wait Jimmy recalled counseling Mrs. Payne. "'Now, Alice,' I said, 'You oughtta get arrangements with Kellogg or somebody who has *Raseyn daughters while you still got the opportunity to breed the two half-brothers' lines, and you should produce some really nice horses and concentrate the blood.' But she told me she wasn't gonna take any outside mares and there were no mares in California good enough to breed to *Raffles. She never did breed him to those *Raseyn mares, and I always wondered how that would have worked."

*Raffles sired 14 registered foals for Alice Payne and one more for the Deans. He died quietly in California, on May 11, 1953, at age 27.

INDRAFF

Indraff's true legacy is as a sire of superior broodmares.

WHEN Madame Fortune deigned to smile upon the stallion Indraff, surely that good luck came in the form of a determined and spirited young woman named Bazy McCormick Miller, later Bazy Tankersley, of Al-Marah Arabians. Of course, it also helped to have a bit of pedigree "preparation" in place when opportunity came knocking.

Indraff was the first purebred Arabian son born of the famous sire *Raffles (see his chapter), and was out of the excellent mare *Indaia, by Raseem. Both parents were imported from Crabbet Park in England by Roger Selby of the Selby Stud in Ohio. Indraff was bred by Selby and foaled at his stud on May 9, 1938.

In an old book (now out of print) published by Roger Selby in 1937, *Indaia is described as a bay mare, foaled in 1927, standing 14.3 and weighing 1,000 pounds, bred at Crabbet Arabian Stud in England. The description continues with this information:

"Sire: World Champion Raseem, winner of the World Champion Gold

A painting of Indraff by the renowned Elizabeth Bell.

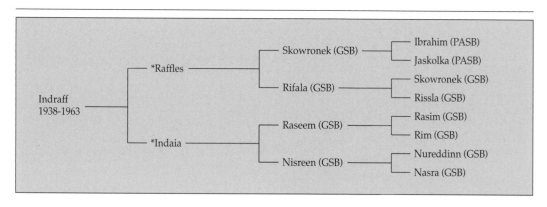

Indraff
1938-1963
├─ *Raffles
│   ├─ Skowronek (GSB)
│   │   ├─ Ibrahim (PASB)
│   │   └─ Jaskolka (PASB)
│   └─ Rifala (GSB)
│   ├─ Skowronek (GSB)
│   └─ Rissla (GSB)
└─ *Indaia
    ├─ Raseem (GSB)
    │   ├─ Rasim (GSB)
    │   └─ Rim (GSB)
    └─ Nisreen (GSB)
        ├─ Nureddinn (GSB)
        └─ Nasra (GSB)

Cup at the Richmond Royal Horse Show (1926). Dam: Nisreen, winner of the Junior Championship at Islington (1922). *Indaia is a most valuable broodmare. She is big and combines the most valuable blood strains. Her sire, the World Champion Raseem, and both grandsires, Ch. Nureddin and Ch. Rasim, as well as her granddam, Champion Nasra, are all champions. Her pedigree shows four crosses to the famous Mesaoud, whose progeny includes 52 champions. Indaia has produced for us an exceptionally fine string of foals of outstanding type."

Selby sold Indraff while he was quite young to Donald Schutz, who bred several nice horses using the gray stallion, as did some other area breeders. While at Schutz's, Indraff was spotted by Bazy, who purchased him in 1946 and proceeded to make him one of the most famous show horses in the country and one of the most influential sires of his day—a true ambassador for the Arabian breed.

"The great wonder was not that I found Indraff, but that I recognized him," said Bazy, who was a rather young woman at the time. In her forthcoming autobiography, *Ride Away Singing* (portions of which have been published in the *Arabian Horse Times* magazine and used, in part, here with its publisher's and the author's permission), she recalls her years with the beautiful white stallion.

"Indraff was my dream without my knowing it and, in the mysterious way of life, he was born the year he took shape in

Halter and Performance Record: 1948 Waterloo, Iowa, National Stallion Show Champion; 15 1st-place wins.

Progeny Record:

Purebred Foal Crops: 22
Purebred Foals Registered: 254
U.S./Canadian National Winners: 10
Class A Champions: 48
IAHA Legion of Merit Award Winners: 3

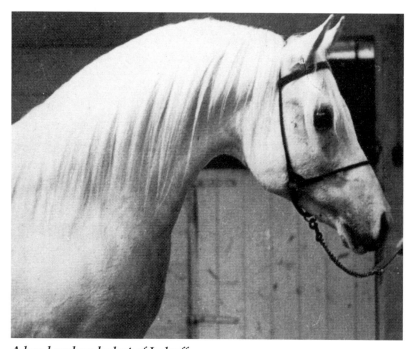

A head and neck shot of Indraff.

Photo courtesy of Arabian Horse Owners Foundation

Bazy and Indraff, circa 1947. Of this photograph, Bazy said it was taken "in the days when I still hoped we would ride hunt seat."

Photo by E.C. Grothman

my imagination, although I did not find him until 8 years later.

"Like so many discoveries, Indraff turned up when I least expected him," she added. Bazy's husband at that time, Peter Miller, and a family friend, Harry Thomas, were the first to actually see Indraff. They were more than impressed; they raved. Although Bazy was pregnant and fighting morning sickness, she decided she had better drive over and take a look. She was living in Peru, Ill., at the time. She had long known that she wanted a *Raffles son, based on a visit she made to Selby's while

still a teenager, and also through the wise counsel of Jimmy Dean, Selby's manager at the time and a man who would become one of Bazy's closest friends.

"Perhaps, since I felt so passionately about these horses, I was remembering my mother's adage about marriage: 'Never marry the man you think you can live with; marry the man you can't live without.' When Donald Shutz led out Indraff, I knew instantly that I had found the horse I couldn't live without." She bought him on the spot.

Bazy was halfway home before reality hit. "We were living in a rented house in the city. I had no barn, much less a stallion run. . . . His first night in the public boarding stable, he reduced most of his stall to kindling by either kicking it or by grabbing sections with his teeth and shaking. At 6 a.m. I got a call to remove him immediately."

She hauled him to a small carriage house on some property she had just purchased. "Why I thought Indraff would be any more content in a carriage barn, I don't know, but I did know he was the whole world to me and I was going to have him no matter what.

"He started in on the carriage barn within minutes of our arrival. I went into the stall and, lip trembling, tears gathering, gazed at my gorgeous problem. Selfra (Bazy's mare) was next door, restless, but ladylike, and Indraff kept trying to squint at her through a crack in the boards. I found something to pry out a board just nuzzling height between the two stalls. Selfra allowed him to breathe on her muzzle. She squealed, he nickered, and peace reigned."

The little two-stall carriage barn was set just off the main street in Peru, without so much as a fence nearby, let alone a paddock. But 8-year-old Indraff needed exercise, ". . . so townsfolk and travelers alike were treated to a very pregnant lady standing in the middle of her lawn holding one end of a long longe line while at the other end a beautiful and delighted white stallion trotted and bucked and occasionally stopped to call to his ladylove in the barn," Bazy said.

Late one night during that time, Bazy found herself gazing out the window, lis-

Offspring of Indraff competed successfully in a variety of events. This is Al-Marah Nautilus (out of Kondi, by Handraff) competing at the 1971 Nationals where he won the open cutting and was second in the novice. The owner-rider was Lee Bolles of Kirtland, Ohio.

Photo by Johnny Johnston

As a mature horse Indraff stood 14.2 and weighed 1,000 pounds.

Photo by Connie Rounds

A photograph of Indraff's dam, Indaia, with the foal named Ragin.

Photo courtesy of Arabian Horse Trust

One of Al-Marah Radames' winning offspring was Radamason, owned and shown by E.D. Shea Jr. of St. Marys, Pa., to the 1960 National Champion Stallion title. The national classes were held at that time at the Colorado All-Arabian Horse Show in Estes Park.

Photo by Alexander

158

Al-Marah Radames, out of the mare Gutne, by Bazleyd, was considered to be Indraff 's best son. He sired 11 national winners and founded the breeding program of Bru-Mar-Ba Arabians.

Photo courtesy of Al-Marah Arabians

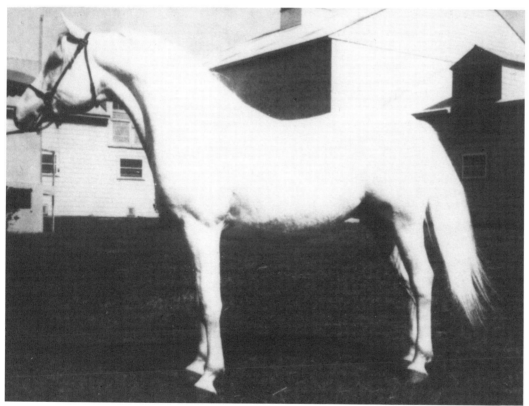

Al-Marah Indraff, out of the *Raffles daughter Rose Marie, was considered to be Indraff's second-best son and the basis of Al-Marah's breeding program. Incidentally, the name Al-Marah means "a garden-like oasis."

*Count Bazy, owned by Al-Marah Arabians, was the 1967 National Champion Stallion. He was by *Count Dorsaz, by Rissalix, and out of Al-Marah Ragtime, by Indraff—the reverse of Bazy's Double R cross.*

Western Horseman
File Photo

The Indraff daughter Georgia, a National Top Ten Mare at halter, shown here with Walter Chapman. Georgia was out of the mare named Egypt.

Photo courtesy of
Al-Marah Arabians

tening to the munching, nickering, horse sounds in the nearby barn. A tiny sliver of moon rode high overhead. "That's like my dream," she said to herself. "I have realized the first sliver and the rest will come, sliver by sliver."

Indraff was put to work in the show ring, and soon, like a full moon at harvest time, he lit up the landscape. Out of 27 times shown, he won first 15 times. At the 1948 National Stallion Show in Waterloo, Iowa (considered by showmen of the day to be the equivalent of a national championship show), he was named the Champion Arabian Stallion. (It is interesting to note that only one horse, Indraff's own son, Aah Abu, bred by Ben-Hur Arabians and out of the mare Hayah, ever defeated his sire in halter competition.)

Although he did exceptionally well, Indraff was, in Bazy's words, "a headache to show," as he was not trained to ride until after Bazy purchased him, and had his own rather hard-headed ideas about it.

Arabian horses were few and far between in the late 1940s—and Arabian horse shows were even fewer—so owners (often led by Bazy) were always looking for an opportunity to get into other horse shows. One such opportunity proved to be far more exciting than originally planned.

Recalled Bazy: "The first year that we managed to get into the Chicago International Show, we did an Arabian costume exhibition. It was to begin with Mike Mervis and Harold Brite each riding a white charger—Harold's was the somewhat-broke Indraff—in sort of Lawrence of Arabia costumes with white britches and voluminous flowing purple and gold capes."

As the gates opened, each of the riders dashed in and each went the opposite direction, hugging the rail at a mad gallop. "It was breathtaking," Bazy continued, "especially so the second lap around when Harold's cinch broke and he and the saddle went flying through the air, landing in a heap, he tangled and smothered by the cape."

Right then, 10 other bearded and costumed riders burst into the ring, and Indraff was loose in the chaos. Bazy, who

An undated picture of Gulastra. When Indraff was bred to Gulastra daughters and granddaughters, it turned out to be a "golden cross."
Photo courtesy of Arabian Horse Owners Foundation

was standing on the rail, realized the danger and vaulted the fence, dashed up to Indraff, grabbed his bridle, leaped on his back, and rode out with the band of "raiders" to thunderous applause.

"Nothing quite like this had ever been seen in the halls of the Chicago International," said Bazy, "and a very excited manager came panting down to me to ask if we would repeat it the next night 'without a single change. It was marvelous!'"

Indraff spent most of his adult life with Tankersley when her Al-Marah Arabians was based near Washington, D.C., and later Barnesville, Maryland. (Al-Marah is now based in Tucson, Arizona.) The only exceptions were prior to age 8, and one other

Tasliya, by Indraff and out of Temag (Fay-El-Dine x Turfada, the latter a Babson-bred mare), won numerous halter championships and was the U.S. Reserve National Champion Mare one year. She was owned by Donoghue Arabians of Goliad, Texas.

Photo by Hellbusch

Overall, Indraff sired 11 sons who, in turn, sired national winners, and 38 daughters who produced national winners.

year, 1954, when he was leased by Howard Marks of California. (Tankersley used Marks' stallion, Gulastra, during that year.)

Offspring

Indraff sired 254 registered purebred Arabian foals, and some good Half-Arabians, as well. Remarkably, those 254 get produced 2,717 foals of their own, making Indraff one of the stallions found most often in pedigrees today.

Of his purebreds, 10 were national winners, while a total of 48 won championships—a difficult feat because there were very few Arabian horse shows during the 1950s and 1960s (about 50, compared to 500 or so today).

Among those national winners were: Al-Marah Gable (x *Zulima), Canadian Top Ten Stallion; Al-Marah Kontiki (x

Kondi), U.S. Native Costume Top Ten; Al-Marah Nautilus (x Kondi), a multiple U.S. National Cutting Champion; Bindaffa (x *Bint Rajwa), Canadian Top Ten Mare; Tasliya (x Temag), U.S. Reserve National Champion Mare; Al-Marah Ruwala (x Rose Marie), U.S. Top Ten Mare; Al-Marah Surindraff (x Sureba), U.S. National Champion Novice Cutting and U.S. Top Ten Open Cutting; Georgia (x Egypt), U.S. Top Ten Mare; Bint Kontessa (x Kontessa Lee), Canadian Top Ten Mare; and Ikhtiyarin (x Imagida), U.S. Top Ten Stallion.

The "golden cross" for Indraff as a sire turned out to be on Gulastra daughters and granddaughters. Bazy claims to have stumbled on this cross only by accident, as she just liked the looks of Gulastra mares and decided to try them with Indraff. (Her old friend Jimmy Dean often told Bazy: "We'll never know if you're a good breeder or not because you're so lucky!") Gulastra (*Astraled x Gulnare) passed on to many of his descendants his fiery red chestnut color, white markings (both of which come from his famous paternal grandsire Mesaoud), exceptional athletic ability, and a distinct personality—best described as one laced with courage and the desire to "move to the front of the pack." Many top endurance horses and working performance horses descend from Gulastra.

Also successful was Indraff on daughters of Rissalix—and the cross also worked in reverse. Bazy bred her Indraff daughters to the Rissalix sons *Ranix and *Count Dorsaz—which produced some of the best-known show horses of their era, including U.S. National Champion Stallion Count Bazy, U.S. National Formal Combination Champion Al-Marah Canadius (who, in turn, sired U.S. National Champion Mare TJs Georgie Girl and U.S. National English Pleasure Champion Canadian Love), three-time performance national champion Seahorse Duke Dorsaz, and Al-Marah Countess Sparkle, dam of seven champions, including U.S. National Champion Mare Heritage Desiree and U.S. National English Pleasure AOTR Champion Heritage Eclat.

Other good matings for Indraff were with daughters and granddaughters of Indraff's own sire, *Raffles. For example, at the first Al-Marah Sale, a ground-breaking auction held in 1956, Al-Marah Ruwala, by Indraff and out of Rose Marie (*Raffles x Rodetta), sold for $10,000—the highest price known to have ever been paid for an Arabian mare at auction at that time.

Another excellent cross was with one of Bazy's first and favorite mares, the aforementioned Selfra, by the Naseem son *Selmian, and out of *Rose of France. A courtship begun in a little carriage barn behind Bazy's Peru, Ill., house, produced Al-Marah Bint Selfra, a reserve halter champion and dam of three champions; Al-Marah Salila, a halter and English pleasure reserve champion and park champion; and Al-Marah Shuayla, whose good daughter Al-Marah Countess Sparkle, was mentioned earlier.

The Double R

Based on the weaving of *Raffles/*Raseyn and Rissalix blood, Bazy today describes her program as "Double R," with taproots sunk deep in the old pedigrees of England's historic Crabbet Stud

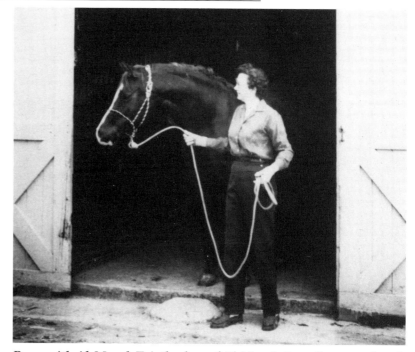

Bazy with Al-Marah Tai, the dam of Al-Marah Canadius, a national champion in formal combination and a good sire in his own right.

Photo courtesy of Al-Marah Arabians

Al-Marah Kontiki, who won a Top Ten in native costume, is shown here with Stanley White in, probably, a horse show grand entry. By Indraff, Kontiki was out of Kondi, by Hanraff. **Photo by Budd**

*The Indraff daughter Al-Marah Ruwala (out of Rose Marie, by *Raffles), sold for $10,000 in 1956 at Al-Marah's first auction. This is a 1958 photo; the rider is Owen McEwen's daughter. Owen was a longtime Arabian breeder in Kansas.*

Photo by Launspach

A 1960 photo of Indy Mac, a Half-Arabian also registered with the American Quarter Horse Association. He was by Indraff and out of the Quarter Horse mare Cotton Girl. The rider is Kristie Miller. Indy Mac's record does not show any AQHA points.

Photo courtesy of Al-Marah Arabians

horses. She wants her horses to have both Rissalix and either (or both) *Raffles and *Raseyn in the pedigree. Additional Rissalix blood tends to produce a more "English" type, high-action horse, and an extra jolt of *Raffles/*Raseyn produces a more "western" type horse. "It's more a state of mind than a strict procedure," explains Bazy, who, in the mid-1990s, added a young Spanish stallion to the brew: Chauncey DB (WN Santana x *Yanifa, by Garbo).

Overall, Indraff sired 11 sons who, in turn, sired national winners, and 38 daughters who produced national winners. His best son, as a sire, is probably Al-Marah Radames, who sired 11 national winners, including Radamason, the 1960 National Champion Arabian Stallion. Radames was out of Gutne, a mare of W.R. Brown's breeding program.

Among Indraff's many famous offspring, one daughter, Sahra Su, perhaps wears the brightest crown. She is the only mare in the breed to produce both a U.S. National Champion Stallion (Synbad, in 1959) and a U.S. National Champion Mare (High Fashion, in 1964).

Bazy's personal favorite Indraff daughter was Al-Marah Thrice Mine. "The minute I looked at her I knew she was going to be my favorite, which was why I named her Thrice Mine. She was by my favorite stallion, out of my favorite of the imported mares (*Thorayya, by Rissalix), and was my favorite color—I try not to think about this—mahogany bay. She justified her name by being one of our best broodmares. Up to my old inbreeding tricks, I bred her three times to *Count Dorsaz (by Rissalix), all with spectacular results."

All in all, Indraff's true legacy is as a sire of superior broodmares. He has more daughters who have produced national winners than even the famous *Serafix. His sons and grandsons—including Al-Marah Indraff, Raffon, Gazon, and others—also have a tendency to be top broodmare sires.

As has historically been the case for Arabians, Indraff favorably influenced at least one other breed. American Quarter Horse Association records show that Indraff sired two Half-Arabians who were registered as American Quarter Horses: Indy Mac and Indy Sue, both out of the Quarter Horse mare Cotton Girl. (In those days, a horse with Arabian breeding could be accepted into the AQHA registry if he/she passed a visual inspection and certain other criteria.)

Indy Sue, foaled in 1953, belonged to Patty Brite, the daughter of Bazy's long-time trainer, Harold Brite. Indy Sue earned numerous AQHA points in six events (including western pleasure, reining, and hunter under saddle). She was also a champion hunter pony of Virginia, and produced three registered Quarter Horse foals. Indy Mac also was a champion on the hunter circuit.

In 1961, Indraff suffered a severe stroke which left his hindquarters paralyzed. But soon he could use his back legs for some support and hop along as he walked with his front legs. "After the first stroke," remembered Bazy, "he never lay down again, as if he remembered how much difficulty he had getting up the first time following the stroke."

Because his libido was unchanged, Bazy decided, after much debate and many

Indy Sue, full sister to Indy Mac, with Patty Brite aboard. This mare earned AQHA points in six events and produced three registered AQHA foals. **Photo courtesy of Al-Marah Arabians**

prayers, to use a block and tackle to lift him up to cover mares. In this fashion he sired several more foals.

In 1963, he suffered another stroke. This time he constantly needed to have a canvas sling under his belly. He was never able to breed again since he could not leave his stall.

"It was very hard to make the decision to put him down," Bazy said, "and the night I made it, he died on his own, as if to save me that awesome decision. I felt that he had not given up the fight so much as he knew he had accomplished his mission on earth." It was August 22, 1963. Indraff was 25. His carefully preserved skeleton is on display at the Arabian Horse Center in Denver.

"I miss these gallant spirits," added Bazy, referring to her three favorite old stallions, Indraff, *Count Dorsaz, and *Sulejman, "although I am surrounded by their descendants. They never asked for pity nor indeed did they display any reluctance to depart. As in so many other ways, horses show us, if we allow them, how to live and how to die."

15 *RASEYN

His breeding legacy is directly responsible for such legends as Khemosabi, Bay-Abi, Ferzon, and much of the Bint Sahara legacy.

ONE WONDERS if the ever-shrewd Lady Wentworth would have so easily let go of the dark gray colt *Raseyn had she even a tiny inkling of the tremendous influence he would have on the Arabian horse breed in America. At the very least, she would most assuredly have demanded a much higher price.

Admittedly, there was nothing extraordinary about *Raseyn as a youngster; he was just a nice horse. Foaled at the Crabbet Park Stud in 1923, he was attractive, had good general conformation, and possessed an excellent pedigree.

His sire, Skowronek (who never came to the United States, or he would definitely have had a chapter of his own in this book), is considered by many to be the greatest recorded Arabian sire of all time.

Skowronek, which means "the Lark," was bred by Count Jozef Potocki and foaled at his Antoniny Stud in the Podolia

Raseyn as a young horse at Kellogg's ranch in Pomona.

Photo courtesy
Arabian Horse Trust

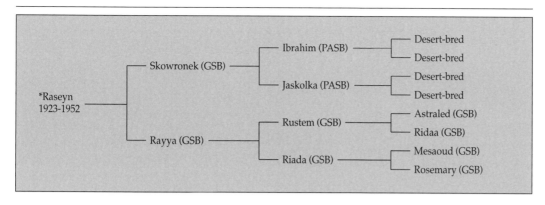

```
                              ┌─ Ibrahim (PASB) ──┬─ Desert-bred
            ┌─ Skowronek (GSB) ┤                  └─ Desert-bred
            │                  └─ Jaskolka (PASB) ─┬─ Desert-bred
*Raseyn ────┤                                      └─ Desert-bred
1923-1952   │                  ┌─ Rustem (GSB) ────┬─ Astraled (GSB)
            └─ Rayya (GSB) ─────┤                  └─ Ridaa (GSB)
                               └─ Riada (GSB) ─────┬─ Mesaoud (GSB)
                                                   └─ Rosemary (GSB)
```

region of Poland in 1908 or 1909 (there is some discrepancy). In 1913 American Walter Winans visited the Count's game park, Pilawin, to hunt. While there, he tried to purchase a pair of beautiful Half-Arabian coach horses. The Potockis refused and instead offered to sell him Skowronek for 150 (English) pounds. Winans took the stallion to England, where he used him for riding, and then sold him the next year to his solicitor, Mr. Webb-Ware, who also used him as a riding horse.

In 1919 H.V. Musgrave Clark bought the stallion and for the first time Skowronek was used at stud. He was, by now, age 11, and Clark took him to some horse shows. There Lady Wentworth noticed him and by the next year had managed to buy him for her program. The method by which she acquired him from her rival, Mr. Clark, remained a bone of contention between them for years afterward.

To his offspring, including *Raseyn, and their descendants, Skowronek gave strong hindquarters, good legs, classic heads, kind dispositions, intelligence, and excellent overall Arabian type. Unfortunately, he also sometimes passed on his flat, muttony withers and short shoulders. Even so, he was most highly valued as an exceptional outcross stallion.

To this day, Skowronek's influence is seen and used in nearly all breeding efforts around the world, with the specific exceptions of straight Egyptian groups, a few Polish lines, and a handful of other programs.

While *Raseyn's sire had everything to recommend him, his dam had nothing. Rayya, unfortunately, was downright ugly. Well-bred—being by Rustem and out of the Mesaoud daughter Riada—she nevertheless was quite poor in both conformation and type. No picture of her

Halter and Performance Record: 1933 Champion Arabian at Los Angeles County Fair; 1933 Champion Arabian at Los Angeles National Horse Show.

Progeny Record:

Purebred Foal Crops: 20
Purebred Foals Registered: 135
U.S./Canadian National Winners: 1
Class A Champions: 11

could be found for this book.

Perhaps that was why Lady Wentworth chose not to incorporate the mare's young colt into her own breeding program. She was very willing, however, to include *Raseyn in a package of 17 horses (three being *en utero*) that she sold to breakfast cereal magnate W.K. (Will Keith) Kellogg in 1926 for about $80,000.

Speculation aside, there is no question that *Raseyn (pronounced Ray-SEEN) was one of the most influential and popular Crabbet-bred stallions to arrive on American shores. Not only did he find fame as an individual, but his breeding legacy is directly responsible for such legends as Khemosabi, Bay-Abi, Ferzon, and much of the Bint Sahara dynasty—a minute number of his illustrious descendants.

Ironically, history shows that *Raseyn was the second choice as a Kellogg herd breeding stallion to another Skowronek son, the ill-fated *Raswan. By 1926 Kellogg

This photo of Skowronek, the sire of *Raseyn, appeared in the May-June 1945 issue of **Western Horseman.** *Skowronek was easily England's most famous Arabian stallion.*

*Raswan was considered to be Skowronek's most beautiful son. Some say that it was only through the untimely death of *Raswan that *Raseyn was ever given the opportunity to shine as a breeding horse.

Photo courtesy Arabian Horse Trust

Alice Payne with *Raseyn after she purchased him in 1948 when he was 25 years old. The name-plate on the door gives *Raseyn's height and weight as 14.2 hands and 940 pounds.

Photo courtesy
Arabian Horse Trust

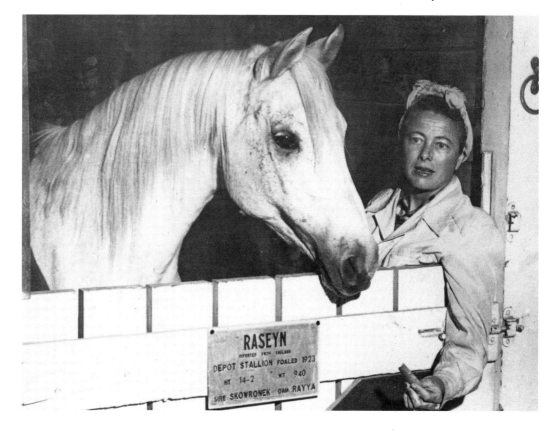

RASEYN
IMPORTED FROM ENGLAND
DEPOT STALLION FOALED 1923
HT 14-2   WT 940
SIRE SKOWRONEK DAM RAYYA

168

had built his ranch in California's Pomona Valley and had purchased the entire Chauncey Clarke herd of Arabian horses, along with a few others. Seeking more of what was a very rare breed in those days, he sent his farm manager, Carl Schmidt (who later changed his last name to Carl Raswan and became a well-known writer), to England to deal with the formidable Lady Wentworth.

On April 10, 1926, Schmidt returned with 14 horses (plus a lovely Welsh pony who was a gift to Mrs. Kellogg from Lady Wentworth). Among them were the aged stallion *Nasik, *Raswan, and the 3-year-old *Raseyn.

Soon after the trip, Schmidt and Kellogg parted ways and therein sealed *Raswan's fate. Schmidt idolized the stallion and rode away on him when he left the ranch. Kellogg, of course, demanded him back, but Schmidt swore he had been promised ownership of the stallion in return for his hard work and counseling. Gladys Brown Edwards wrote in her book *The Arabian Horse: War Horse to Show Horse* that Schmidt claimed Lady Wentworth gave him the colt as a gift.

Before *Raswan had a chance to sire any horses in the United States, he was severely injured and had to be put down. He did sire three horses in England, all of whom—Star of the Hills, *Rose of France, and Ferhan—produced superior offspring.

Kellogg's side of the story is that the horse, while in Schmidt's care, broke away from the fence to which he was tied and ran across a field, where he badly cut his hind foot on a farm implement. Schmidt, on the other hand, claimed for years after that Kellogg secretly had a groom "hamstring" *Raswan's leg, jealously seeking to keep Schmidt from establishing a breeding program and trying to collect on an insurance policy.

The years have proven that Kellogg's version is almost certainly correct. That the multi-millionaire needed $10,000, or wanted to destroy the stallion many consider Skowronek's most beautiful son,

That the multi-millionaire needed $10,000, or wanted to destroy the stallion many consider Skowronek's most beautiful son, is ludicrous.

Although Jadaan was not related to *Raseyn, the two were stable-mates at the Kellogg ranch. Jadaan gained fame as the mount for the movie star Rudolph Valentino in his roles as a desert sheik.

Ferseyn, by *Raseyn and out of *Ferda, launched a dynasty of his own and sired the great mare Fersara. He was owned by H.H. Reese. This photo appeared in **Western Horseman,** *April 1951.*

Photo by Tallant

is ludicrous, according to (the late) Gladys Brown Edwards. Nevertheless, this sad story opened the door for *Raseyn's use as a breeding stallion.

Herbert H. Reese was Kellogg's choice as a new farm manager. In his book, *The Kellogg Arabians,* Reese wrote that *Raseyn was typical of the Skowronek line. He had "... a short, wedge-shaped head with broad forehead and fine muzzle; an arched but not especially long neck; level croup; straight hind legs; and broad, flat bones. He also had the deficiencies of that dynasty, the low withers and a shoulder that could have had a little better slope. . . . (He also) was a trifle low in the back."

Reese noted that *Raseyn offspring, when crossed with high-withered, good-shouldered horses, such as in the *Nasik, *Ferdin, and *Rabiyas lines, made an excellent blend—often with an increase in size, as well.

*Raseyn's color was often mentioned by those who knew him. Born quite black, he retained a dark coat for several years, giving way to white only gradually. Wrote Reese: "*Raseyn's dappled grey color was exceptionally beautiful, as he was nearly black, not the usual rusty color, when young, and the pattern of dapples spread as he gradually lightened in color. At around 6 years of age he showed the same amount of dappling so admired in his granddaughter Fersara (see the Bint Sahara chapter) many years later, keeping the dapple on his croup and neck for a longer period than is usual with such coloring. The fine quality of his coat gave him a silvery sheen, with unusual luster even after he had turned nearly white."

Reese also wrote: "I saw him first as a coming 3-year-old, and at the time he was a little shaky in the forelegs, standing over at the knees. I was told he had been ridden western by a man weighing 200 pounds using a 45-pound saddle and was exercised over the hills, receiving more work than a horse of his size (14.2) and age should have had. On the discontinuance of this saddle work for a time and letting him exercise in a corral, his front legs became normal and the soreness left."

In old age, *Raseyn was again over at

the knees and had some pain, which was attributed to the old abuse.

Following his recovery, *Raseyn was put into training. He turned out to be an enthusiastic jumper and then progressed on to an even more interesting career as a five-gaited show horse.

Kellogg loved to share his Arabians with the public, and started the "Sunday Shows," which continue to this day at the W.K. Kellogg Arabian Horse Center at California State Polytechnic University at Pomona. *Raseyn soon became a featured star at the presentations.

"*Raseyn had the unusual trait, for an Arab, of having a born-in natural amble (which he passed on sparingly to some of his get)," wrote Carol W. Mulder in the September-October 1984 issue of *The Crabbet Influence* magazine. "Later it was therefore a relatively simple task for trainer Charles A. Smith to teach him to convert this amble into two artificial gaits—the slow-gait and the much faster rack."

As such, he was exhibited for years—twice on Sundays—as a five-gaited Arabian. He also was shown at various fairs and exhibitions. At age 10, he was champion Arabian at the Los Angeles County Fair and Champion Arabian Stallion at the Los Angeles National Horse Show.

People flocked to see Kellogg's Arabians, and soon Hollywood came knocking. Stars of the era, such as Tom Mix and Will Rogers, visited the white-arched stables, and often had their photographs taken with *Raseyn or another Kellogg horse. It became traditional for Pasadena's Tournament of Roses Parade Queen to have her portrait taken with one of the ranch horses, often *Raseyn.

Several Kellogg horses, such as the famous Jadaan, starred in films. Two in which *Raseyn had a role were *Beau Ideal*, an adventure depicting French soldiers in the desert, and *The Scarlet Empress*, involving Russia's Catherine the Great.

Offspring

For 20 years, beginning in 1928, *Raseyn was used as a breeding stallion, siring 135 registered purebred foals. Of interest, according to author and artist Gladys Brown Edwards, who was a long-time secretary at the ranch: His foals were

One of *Raseyn's best sons was Courier, who was out of Sheherzade, by Joon. Charles Smith is the rider in this photo taken at Kellogg's.

difficult to sell as babies. As she wrote in *War Horse to Show Horse*: ". . . his foals being either gray, bay, or brown with little or no white, (t)his made them rather hard to sell as foals, compared to the sparkling chestnuts with their satiny coats and white markings. The *Raseyn foals were furry compared to the foals by other stallions until they shed off to the new coat. . . . At that time most of the Kellogg horses were sold as young foals, and the chunky little fluff-balls simply did not compare to the elegant sleekness and cheerful markings of chest-

This photograph, taken at the Kellogg ranch, shows two sons of *Raseyn, Courier (left) and Echo (center), and the 4-year-old Jezayat. Courier and Echo were 3 years old. The handlers are Cal Poly students Frank Illnick, Harold Walker Jr., and Wayne Collins.

WH File Photo

Ibn Hanrah was a descendant of *Raseyn who enjoyed immense popularity and success in the 1950s and '60s. He traced back to *Raseyn through his sire Hanrah, whose dam was Ronara, a great-granddaughter of *Raseyn. Ibn Hanrah was owned by Donoghue Arabians of Goliad, Tex., and his handler here is Walter Chapman. This picture was taken at the 1957 Deseret Arabian Show in Palm Springs, Calif., where Ibn Hanrah was named champion stallion.

Photo by John
H. Williamson

172

nuts and bright bays. But usually they did have pretty heads."

Of *Raseyn's offspring, several grew up to be particularly superior:

Angyl (x *Wierna) was a U.S. Top Ten Mare and the dam of Bay-Abi.

Chloeyn (x *Chloe) was a halter champion and dam of six champions, including U.S. National Champion Mare Chloette.

Courier (x Sheherzade) was a champion stallion and good sire in the Kellogg program.

Pomona Ahmen (x *Nakkla) was an excellent sire.

Ferseyn (x *Ferda) launched a dynasty of his own and sired the great mare Fersara (x Bint Sahra).

Finally, there's Sureyn (x *Crabbet Sura). At the first official IAHA U.S. National Championship Show (in 1958), *both* the national champion stallion, Mujahid, and the national champion mare, Surita, were by Sureyn.

In all, 22 *Raseyn get had national-winning offspring.

Other illustrious names from *Raseyn's direct family, get, and grandget include Ronek, Alyf, Bolero, Ferneyn, Gali Rose, Hassan Pasha, Ibn Hanrah, Ibn Raseyn, Moneyna, Mraff, Nafatez, Nitez, Rakafix, Skorage, Chloette, Galimar, Figaro, and Rose of Raswan, among many, many others.

Surprisingly, at the height of the ranch's success and popularity, Kellogg decided to give away both the stables and the horses. He was determined to improve the Arabian breed in the United States—which he estimated might take 50 years—and then in his late 60s, Kellogg felt the need to ensure the continuance of his breeding program long after his death. (He did not know he would live to be 91.)

Therefore, in 1932, with great ceremony and before a crowd of 25,000 people, he handed over the entire operation to the University of California—and gave them an endowment to pay for running it. Renamed the W.K. Kellogg Institute, students from around the country could learn state-of-the-art horse management practices, while breeding good horses and continuing the popular Sunday Shows.

World War II put an abrupt end to the arrangement. Kellogg convinced the university to donate the ranch and horses to the U.S. Government for use as a remount station and breeding facility. Renamed again as the Pomona Quartermaster

*W.K. Kellogg, the cereal king who imported *Raseyn as part of a 17-horse package. He's holding a horse named Antez.*

WH File Photo

Depot, the ranch was busy during the war. Immediately after peace was declared, horses who were deemed "spoils of war"—such as *Witez II—were shipped into the ranch.

Times had changed, and the Army no longer had any use for horses, so the U.S. Department of Agriculture decided in mid-1948 to move the Kellogg animals to Fort Reno, Okla., to be auctioned off. Concerned, Kellogg and others worked behind the scenes to stop the sale, and it was cancelled.

In late 1948, the ranch and its horses were turned over to the W.K. Kellogg Foundation, and on July 1, 1949, the ranch again became a California education center, this time under the Cal-Poly banner. As before, Kellogg stipulated that the breeding program and the Sunday Shows continue, and so they do up to the present time.

His Later Years

Just before the Kellogg Foundation regained the ranch and its horses, it was discovered during the 1948 breeding

Surprisingly, at the height of the ranch's success and popularity, Kellogg decided to give away both the stables and the horses.

*Raseyn sired these twins, Calsabiyat (a mare), and Calsabi (a gelding). They were out of the mare Rifdah and are shown here on a teeter-totter under the watchful eye of Charles Saherthwaite, a Cal Poly trainer.

Photo courtesy Arabian Horse Trust

Cholette (*Serafix x Choleyn) was a maternal grand-daughter of *Raseyn who achieved notable success in the show ring. Owned by John M. Rogers of Walnut Creek, Calif., she was the 1962 U.S. National Champion Mare. This picture was taken in 1958 when she was named Pacific Coast Reserve Champion Mare. The handler is unidentified.

Photo by
John H. Williamson

season that *Raseyn had become sterile. He was 25 years old and quite arthritic, so the Army decided to have him put down.

Enter Alice Payne. No one is certain how she learned of *Raseyn's plight, but she quickly entered a plea to spare the stallion's life and allow him to live with her at Asil Ranch, her "old stallions' home" in Chino, California. More amazingly, she succeeded, and had him moved to what would be his final abode.

As presented in Mary Jane Parkinson's fine book *The Kellogg Ranch: The First Sixty Years*, Mrs. Payne soon wrote to Kellogg: "Your darling *Raseyn is happy here, I'm sure. Once in a while he puts his head against me as much as to tell me that he loves me. The feeling is mutual. I have been feeding him small pans of chopped carrots, ground hay, ground grain, and added vitamins every three hours and now he puts up his head and speaks to me whenever I get near his corral. . . . and surely, after all the tremendous influence he has had on the breed he is entitled to be spoiled. . . .

"You, or any of your friends, are welcome at any time to pay *Raseyn and Hanad (age 24) a visit. These fellows are funny—they speak casually to each other but do not offer to hurl insults back and forth as most stallions do. *Raseyn sneers at one of our 6-year-old stallions but has too much dignity to insult Hanad."

The conclusion of *Raseyn's story could not be more poetic. Payne, in 1950, acquired another famous Skowronek son, *Raffles, who was *Raseyn's greatest rival in terms of sire lines of American champions. Of the 25,569 entries in the Arabian studbooks from 1950 through 1965, 6,773, or roughly one-fourth, of all foals registered were of the *Raffles and *Raseyn bloodlines, according to Gladys Brown Edwards. Of the sires of 10 or more champions from that era, more than half are of one or the other of these two lines. When you throw in the mares who trace to Skowronek, the Polish-English stallion's tremendous influence on American breeding lines can easily be seen.

The two old Skowronek sons lived out their remaining years in adjoining paddocks at Payne's ranch. Again Payne wrote to Kellogg about *Raseyn: "I fenced in our front yard for him, and he likes it so well that I don't even offer apologies to anybody for having a horse

*Here's another *Raseyn son, Abu Raseyn, who was out of Hawija. The rider is Buzz Wilson.*   Photo by John Douthit Jr.

practically in the house—and no one has made any remarks about it being a sort of unusual place for a horse. . . . Thank you for helping snatch *Raseyn from his unknown fate. It seems ironical that you should be the one who was responsible for his being in this country—and then you have to make an effort to keep the same country from destroying him. I have found that Arabians have given me my greatest happiness and my heaviest heartaches."

*Raseyn died on May 19, 1952, following a stroke at the Payne ranch. He was 29 years old.

16 ABU FARWA

He was known best as a sire of versatile horses.

SURELY Gladys Brown Edwards was touched for a moment with the gift of prophecy when she christened the little red foal "Abu Farwa"—meaning *Father of Chestnuts* in Arabic—for he grew up to sire 220 chestnut offspring in his 277 registered foals. But even such an Arabian horse expert as the indomitable Edwards could not then have predicted the extensive influence Abu Farwa eventually would have on the breed in North America.

Known best as a sire of versatile horses with a "can do" attitude, Abu Farwa sired descendants who excel today in virtually every competitive venue: in halter with Bey Shah and his offspring, in racing with Kontiki and his descendants, in cutting with such horses as Smooth Zee, Demaciado, Overlook Farwa, etc., and in other arena performance divisions with such legends as Oran's Adagio, Infra Red, Ross'Zi, and Fateena.

When Abu Farwa was foaled on May

Abu Farwa at the W.K. Kellogg Ranch stables, where he was foaled in 1940. The chestnut stallion was noted for, among other conformational features, his exceptional strength of loin and sound legs with substantial bone.

Photo courtesy of the archives of Cecil Edwards in the W.K. Kellogg Arabian Horse Library

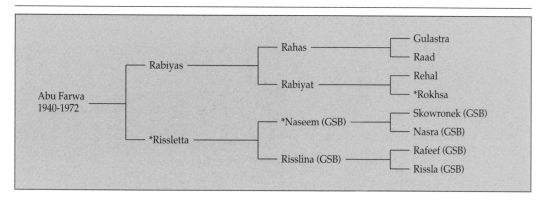

```
                                              ┌─ Gulastra
                                 ┌─ Rahas ─────┤
                                 │            └─ Raad
                  ┌─ Rabiyas ────┤
                  │              │            ┌─ Rehal
                  │              └─ Rabiyat ──┤
Abu Farwa ────────┤                           └─ *Rokhsa
1940-1972         │
                  │                           ┌─ Skowronek (GSB)
                  │              ┌─ *Naseem (GSB) ┤
                  │              │            └─ Nasra (GSB)
                  └─ *Rissletta ─┤
                                 │            ┌─ Rafeef (GSB)
                                 └─ Risslina (GSB) ┤
                                              └─ Rissla (GSB)
```

22, 1940, at the famous W.K. Kellogg Ranch, the late Gladys Brown Edwards was secretary, and it was her job to name all the foals. The institute is located on what is now the campus of California State Polytechnic University in Pomona.

GBE, the "handle" by which she was often referred, later wrote about Abu Farwa in her book, *The Arabian: War Horse to Show Horse*.

"The Abu Farwa dynasty is, of course, the most prolific in its number of champion-siring sons, many of which also have founded many branched lines. A champion at halter and in park, Abu Farwa was magnificent under saddle. He had the beautiful neck of the Naseem line (through his dam) and this relationship also served to give his head more class than his sire's. He, of course, had plenty of action. . . ."

Abu Farwa's sire, Rabiyas, was well-known as Kellogg's flashy five-gaited stallion, popular with the crowds who gathered for the Sunday shows featured at the ranch. Foaled in 1936, he was sold to South Africa in 1954, where he eventually died at age 35. (This sire line, which goes back to *Astraled, is particularly long-lived.) Five-gaited Arabian descendants of Rabiyas still "rack on" in show rings today in that country.

GBE recalled in her book that "Rabiyas had a rather plain head, and a croup on the apple order, but he was an outstanding performance horse." Two of his other sons, Rabab and Rabiycar, were splendid show horses.

As for Abu Farwa's dam, *Rissletta, she became an unwitting participant in one of W.K. Kellogg's little schemes. She is listed as being imported by K.M. Brown, who was, in fact, GBE's mother. Kellogg, who really imported the horse, didn't want Lady Judith Wentworth, the owner of Crabbet Stud in England, to know that he

Halter and Performance Record: Twice a halter champion; Three-Gaited Show Champion.

Progeny Record:

Purebred Foal Crops: 28
Purebred Foals Registered: 277
U.S./Canadian National Winners: 4
Class A Champions: 18
IAHA Legion of Merit Award Winners: 2

Another photograph of Abu Farwa taken at the W.K. Kellogg Ranch, which is now the campus of California State Polytechnic University, better known as Cal Poly.

Photo courtesy of the Arabian Horse Trust

Abu Farwa being used to check cattle by an unidentified rider. Photo courtesy of the archives of Cecil Edwards in the W.K. Kellogg Arabian Horse Library.

Here's Abu Farwa, with Karl Reese in the saddle, possibly decked out for a parade class. Photo by Williamson

was the actual buyer of *Rissletta and two other mares because he thought she might charge him more for them. Lady Wentworth herself used such a ruse when she obtained the stallion Skowronek from H.V.M. Clark.

Although Lady Wentworth was suspicious from the start, a deal was struck and *Rissletta and two other mares, *Incoronata and *Crabbet Sura, were shipped to California. Recalled GBE in a 1984 article in *Arabian Horse World*, "My mother was very much against doing this in the first place . . . (however) the whole farce was rigidly followed to the end," she wrote. "But how Lady Wentworth must have laughed and said 'I knew it!' when she saw that the mares' foals were registered as 'bred by W.K. Kellogg!'"

*Rissletta was by the Skowronek son Naseem, and out of Risslina, a maternal half-sister to *Rifala, the mother of *Raffles. From Naseem, she inherited his superb head and neck, but, unfortunately, also his long back and poor hocks. *Rissletta also had somewhat short legs; but always her overall beauty prevailed.

Luckily, she nicked extremely well with muscular, athletic stallions, such as Abu Farwa's sire, Rabiyas, to produce outstanding individuals with her lovely head

178

This is Rabiyas, the sire of Abu Farwa. During the 1940s, Rabiyas was a popular and flashy five-gaited horse at the Kellogg Ranch Sunday shows.

Photo courtesy of the Arabian Horse Trust

Abu Farwa, as an individual, exhibited traits much sought after at the time and even today.

and neck and the sire's better body and leg conformation. In addition to Abu Farwa, *Rissletta produced Rifnetta, dam of Rifseyn, a U.S. National Top Ten English Pleasure winner.

*Rissletta also produced two full sisters to Abu Farwa. Joanna, foaled in 1943, was a fine broodmare with an exceptionally pretty head, whose offspring did well in the show ring and then produced champions. The second full sister, Rossletta, a roan, was registered and then had her registration rescinded at Cal Poly's request as her color was considered by someone there to be a detriment to the Arabian breed. A typey, correct individual, she then produced lovely purebred foals (for Anna Best Joder of Colorado) who could only be registered as Half-Arabians. Ironically, none of her foals were roan.

Pedigree analysts, such as GBE and Arlene Magid, surmise that Abu Farwa's exceptional ability to sire horses noted for their superb performance ability comes from the presence, several times, in the stallion's pedigree of the horses *Nasik and *Berk, both noted for their talent at the trot. Stepping farther back, GBE credits the desert horse Azrek, imported from the Middle East to England by Lady Wentworth's parents, Lady Anne and Wilfrid Blunt, as introducing flash and speed at the trot to the Crabbet program.

Pedigree aside, Abu Farwa, as an individual, exhibited traits much sought after at the time and even today. He was "robust, correct, and typey," according to Magid.

W.K. Kellogg imported *Rissletta, Abu Farwa's dam, from the Crabbet Stud in England. She's shown here in the Kellogg Ranch pasture.

Photo courtesy of Arabian Horse Trust

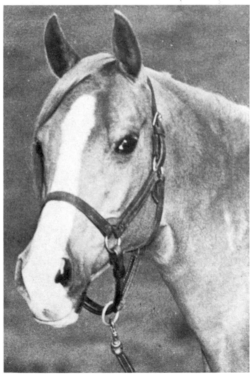

A close-up of *Rissletta, who inherited the superb head and neck of her sire, Naseem.

"(His) conformation included exceptional strength of loin, a well-shaped neck properly set on, correct shoulder angle, and sound legs with substantial bone. He was very prepotent at passing these attributes to his descendants, many of whom show exceptional athletic prowess."

And not only did most of his offspring carry his chestnut color, but they also had his distinctive head and neck. To many Arabian horse enthusiasts, Abu Farwa was and is regarded as the quintessential "Crabbet stallion." Technically, though, he was only 90 percent Crabbet, as he carried lines to the Randolph Huntington and Ethelred Dillon breeding programs, which were not founded on Crabbet-bred stock.

Abu Farwa spent his entire life in southern California. As a yearling, he was sold to Paul Paul, a fruit grower from Fresno. Arabians had few chances to compete in all-Arabian horse shows in those days, but Abu Farwa did win at halter as a young colt.

When Mr. Paul dispersed his Arabian herd, Abu Farwa was sold to another farmer in the Central Valley, Herman Dreyer. There he was trained to ride and drive. Mrs. Dreyer recalled the horse for writer Mary Jane Parkinson in 1984 in *Arabian Horse World* magazine.

"Abu was a wonderful individual, but he was a handful. He was a real sweetheart except that he was like one of these 250-pound football players. You know he's there. He . . . had no vices, but he was noisy, and if you had him around, everybody in the neighborhood knew he was there. He would bellow at everyone who came here. . . . We began to feel we were imposing on the neighbors. Since we had another stallion who was a little easier to live with, we decided Abu should go to a home where he would be used extensively for breeding. He deserved the chance. Mr. Reese seemed like the logical person to contact."

The Abu Farwa son Farlowa, out of Farlouma, by Farana, was a rare bay who became an important sire at the Kellogg Ranch. He sired five national winners, who had multiple wins in several divisions.

Photo courtesy of Arabian Horse Trust

Herbert H. Reese, who was Kellogg's manager for many years and now had his own ranch in Covina, eagerly purchased Abu Farwa in 1944 for $2,000. He would own the red stallion for most of his life.

Reese took Abu Farwa to just a handful of shows, and the horse was twice named champion stallion and was a champion in the three-gaited division, now known as park.

Gordon Lemons was a trainer at Reese's ranch, and he shared some memories of Abu Farwa with Parkinson in her 1984 *Arabian Horse World* article.

"He wasn't particularly tall, probably a little bit taller than the average Arabian at the time, but there was something to his massiveness and musculature that made him very imposing. I rode him occasionally (for exercise and my pleasure), always with a flat saddle. He was definitely a park horse. He was always kind of a restless, fiery sort, a dynamic horse, and many times the only thing that would settle him down—no matter what he was fretting about—was to put a young foal in the adjoining paddock. You could just watch him being transposed from the fiery charger image to a baby-sitter role. That always amazed me. I remember his stud fee was $100 when I went to work there. I was impressed . . . I thought I'd hit the big time!"

Abu was first offered at public stud for $50. Reese bred the horse to any mare whose owner had the money to pay the stud fee. No mare was refused. Although this reduced the chances that top-quality

Ga'Zi was, by far, Abu Farwa's best son, with 21 national winners to his credit. He was out of the mare Ghazna, by Chepe Noyon.

Photo courtesy Woody Madsen

foals would be produced in a consistent manner, Abu Farwa always managed to significantly improve on the mare. Such was his genetic prepotency.

Offspring

The first national classes for Arabians weren't held until Abu Farwa was 18 years old, so that venue was not available for his older offspring to demonstrate their abilities. However, Abu Farwa still managed to sire four national winners: Abu Ahwa, first registered as "Red Deer," 1973 U.S. National Top Ten Western Pleasure winner; Shahzada, 1959 Canadian Top Ten Stallion; Galan, 1963 U.S. National Top Ten Stallion

and 1964 Canadian Top Ten Stallion (also an English Pleasure champion); and Overlook Farwa, 1974 U.S. Reserve National Cutting Futurity Champion.

In addition, 13 sons and 20 daughters produced national winners, for a total of 78 national-winning grandget, according to statistics provided by Arlene Magid.

Abu Farwa's best son, by far, was Ga'Zi. A brilliant chestnut with a full blaze, Ga'Zi sired 21 national winners who won 52 U.S. and Canadian Top Ten or better awards in halter, western pleasure, native costume, English pleasure, and trail. An amazing 45 percent of his 266 offspring won championships.

Ga'Zi was foaled in 1949 on the Leland Mekeel Ranch in California and was out of the mare Ghazna, by Chepe Noyon, a dam of nine Class A champions. In the early 1950s, Dr. Eugene LaCroix, then living in Lake Terrace, Wash., spotted him. So enamored of Ga'Zi was LaCroix that he formed a partnership with his stepfather, Peter Smith, and his neighbor, Woody Madsen, in order to purchase the young stallion. Thus, was born "Lasma" (La-S-Ma) Arabians, which would grow to become an internationally renowned Arabian horse breeding and showing business that virtually reigned supreme in the industry during the 1970s and 1980s.

With Madsen as his trainer, Ga'Zi won 18 western pleasure and halter championships. The stallion had a wonderful disposition. Madsen's children often rode the horse, and he did a long list of tricks by voice command alone. Rarely advertised at stud, Ga'Zi sired only 16 foals by the time he was 10, but he then made up for lost time.

When LaCroix purchased *Bask and moved to Scottsdale, it was decided to leave Ga'Zi with Madsen in Washington state. This probably proved a good choice, as he may have been overshadowed in Arizona by *Bask (history's leading sire of national winners). By staying put, Ga'Zi retained his extreme popularity in the

Awad was another of Abu Farwa's very few bays. Out of the mare Shamrah, by Balastra, Awad was a park champion who sired only 23 off-spring, of which 2 sons—Afari and Ibn Awad—were exceptional. In this 1955 photo, Awad was ridden by Earl Wilson to the grand championship in the English Performance Stake, at the Chicago Arabian show, for owners Mr. and Mrs. Stanton Speer of Barrington, Illinois.

Photo by
Norman E. Grantham

Ghezala, a full sister to Ga'Zi, was an incredibly beautiful mare who won 35 halter championships. Foaled in 1948, she was 18 months old in this picture.

Overlook Farwa, by Abu Farwa and out of Al-Marah Zaibaq, by Indraff, was the 1974 Reserve National Cutting Futurity Champion.

Photo by Polly Knoll

Pacific Northwest, and continued to sire high-quality show horses. Ga'Zi died just 44 days before his 30th birthday, and was buried in Madsen's yard in Spanaway, Washington.

Ga'Zi also had an incredibly beautiful full sister, Ghezala, who won 35 halter championships for the Mekeel Ranch. She is considered one of Abu Farwa's best daughters, along with Alla Farwa (out of Maryam Amal, by Alla Amarward), who is his best producing daughter.

Alla Farwa produced a trio of national winners, including El Hermano, 18-time national winner Demaciado (in cutting and trail), and 5-time national winner TuRiff (in halter, trail, and cutting). Of Abu Farwa's 144 daughters, only 9 did not breed on.

Two other Abu Farwa sons worth mentioning are Farlowa (out of Farlouma, by Farana), a rare bay who sired five national winners; and Abu Baha, out of Surrab, by *Latif. Abu Baha was a full brother to U.S. Top Ten Stallion Shahzada and was himself a multiple halter champion. He sired six national winners.

Reese leased Abu Farwa back to his birthplace, now more commonly known as Cal Poly, in 1952 and 1953. There, he was used in the breeding program and as a star attraction in the Sunday shows, where his strong, reaching, flashy trot highlighted his charismatic presence.

In 1959, Reese sold Abu Farwa to Dr. Harold West of Green Acres Ranch. There, he sired 10 foals. Two years later, however, when the stallion was 21, Reese bought him back in partnership with Charles Doner of Elsinore Stud. The following year, in August 1962, Charles and Inez Doner became the sole owners of the red stallion.

Although he had not been shown for many years, Abu Farwa went back into the show ring at age 22 to win the aged stallion class at the prestigious Del Mar Arabian Horse Show in California. He was third at the same show the next year, and then won against stiff competition at the grand old age of 24.

"That's ample testimony," said writer-researcher Magid, "to his basic

184

Abu Baha was another successful Abu Farwa son. He was a multiple halter champion, and he sired six national winners. He was out of Surrab, by *Latif.

correctness and overall quality."

At the Doners' Elsinore Stud, Abu Farwa continued to sire superb foals and to live like the king he truly was.

As he got older, however, arthritis began to take its toll, and it became very painful for him to get around. Finally, the Doners decided to put him down. As Inez Doner told Parkinson, "His health was marvelous, just marvelous. His teeth were just wonderful. He ate well, and he was in good flesh. Old horses generally go down, especially when they're crippled up as he was, but he didn't lose flesh. He was in wonderful spirits. But those old legs. . . . When he got down, he couldn't get up. We winched him up a number of times, but it was just cruelty to let him go on. A terrible thing to have to put him down because, except for his legs, he was fine."

The red stallion's last foal was born in 1971. Abu Farwa died on July 27, 1972. He was 32 years old.

A head shot of the photogenic Abu Baha.   Photo by Martin Charlop

17   *SERAFIX

His greatest legacy lies in his daughters, but he also sired some important sons.

"EVERYTHING about him set me on fire," the late John Rogers once said about the first time he saw the bright red stallion *Serafix. The yearling colt had just won his class at a 1950 horse show in London, England. For Rogers, an internationally renowned mining engineer, the conflagration ignited that day became a flame that burned steady and true in his heart for the rest of his life.

So impressed was Rogers that he fol-

lowed the horse from the show ring back to his stall and immediately asked Cecil Covey (manager of Lady Judith Wentworth's Crabbet Park Arabian Stud) about the horse's pedigree and particulars. Rogers thought the colt's price was too high, so he went home to California without him. But he couldn't get the chestnut horse out of his mind.

"In 1951, I again saw *Serafix in a big win at the Red Hills show where Grand Royal was grand champion of the

Serafix as a 6-year-old when he was named Grand Champion Stallion at the Pomona (Calif.) Arabian show in 1955.

WH File Photo

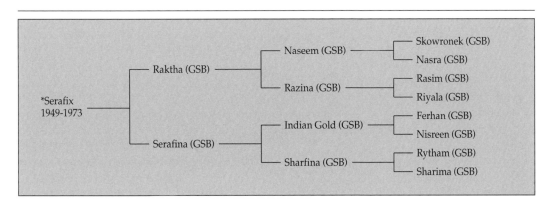

```
                                                    ┌─── Skowronek (GSB)
                                 ┌─── Naseem (GSB) ──┤
                                 │                   └─── Nasra (GSB)
             ┌─── Raktha (GSB) ──┤
             │                   │                   ┌─── Rasim (GSB)
             │                   └─── Razina (GSB) ──┤
 *Serafix ───┤                                       └─── Riyala (GSB)
 1949-1973   │
             │                   ┌─── Indian Gold (GSB) ──┬─── Ferhan (GSB)
             │                   │                        └─── Nisreen (GSB)
             └─── Serafina (GSB)─┤
                                 │                        ┌─── Rytham (GSB)
                                 └─── Sharfina (GSB) ─────┤
                                                          └─── Sharima (GSB)
```

show, later to become supreme horse of the year (in Great Britain)," Rogers told the *Arabian Horse Journal* in 1976. *Serafix was reserve champion to Grand Royal at age 2. "Again, I wanted to buy the horse, but the price was beyond my reach. At least, I thought from the standpoint of common sense he was priced utterly too high for a young colt and an unproven one."

Meanwhile, Rogers purchased from Lady Wentworth the mares *Silver Crystal (Rangoon x Somara) and *Serafire (Indian Magic x Grey Royal). Back in California, he bought several other mares and the 2-year-old *Witez II son Natez, who would later be a Pacific Coast champion. Rogers knew his fledgling breeding program would benefit immeasurably with the addition of *Serafix.

"On a trip to England in 1954, I (again) priced *Serafix and said I would take him," recalled Rogers. "The price jumped 30 percent overnight on account of a bid from Australia. By this time, my neck was bowed and I decided to buy the horse. I closed the deal on *Serafix for what at the time was the largest price paid for any stallion brought to America—at least that also was the opinion of Lady Wentworth."

Rogers didn't want the 5-year-old stallion (who had never been ridden) shipped by sea, and he also wanted him better conditioned for the long trip, so he arranged for the horse's groom to start him under saddle and improve his condition for a month or two.

*Serafix eventually flew to California with two horses owned by cowboy actor Roy Rogers (no relation). "After the 7,000-mile trip, I was delighted for *Serafix to arrive in Walnut Creek in all his glory, looking fit and without injury," said Rogers. "The horse looked around, was turned out to run on grass,

Halter and Performance Record: 3 halter show championships in Great Britain; 3 Class A halter championships, 2 reserves; 1954 Cow Palace Reserve Champion Stallion; 1955 Pomona Show Grand Champion.

Progeny Record:

Purebred Foal Crops: 21
Purebred Foals Registered: 259
U.S./Canadian National Winners: 41
Class A Champions: 128
IAHA Legion of Honor Award Winners: 5
IAHA Legion of Supreme Honor Award Winners: 1
IAHA Legion of Merit Award Winners: 33
IAHA Legion of Supreme Honor/Merit Award Winners: 1
IAHA Legion of Supreme Merit Award Winners: 3

*A classic head shot of *Serafix.*

Photo by
Johnny Johnston

*John Rogers with his
beloved *Serafix.*

*John Rogers with his
beloved *Serafix.*

**His color and
white markings
possibly came
from the leg-
endary and loudly
marked chestnut
Mesaoud.**

and seemed to take over the ranch then and there."

Pedigree

That *Serafix became such an exceptional sire is hardly a surprise when one considers the illustrious horses scattered throughout his pedigree. His color and white markings possibly came from the legendary and loudly marked chestnut Mesaoud (imported to England from Egypt by Lady Wentworth's parents, Wilfrid and Lady Ann Blunt), whose name appears far back in the family tree.

Raktha, *Serafix's sire, was a gray bred by Lady Yule at the Hanstead Stud, but who was of Crabbet bloodlines. He had a superb head and great presence, according to Rosemary Archer, long one of England's better authorities on Arabian horses. Lady Wentworth purchased him at age 5, and he was used in her program until his sale to South Africa at age 16.

Raktha also sired, among others, the popular British National Champion Stal-

lion Indian Magic, sire of U.S National Western Pleasure Champion *Lewisfield Magic; the noted sire *Electric Storm; U.S. Top Ten Mare *Serafire; and halter champion *Silwa, dam of four champions, including U.S. Top Ten Mare *Silwara.

But it is Naseem, Raktha's sire, who, along with his sire, the famous Skowronek, enjoys international acclaim. Lady Wentworth once described Naseem as "a perfect horse," and he was used a great deal at Crabbet, siring such horses there as Silver Fire, Irex, and *Rissletta, dam of Abu Farwa (see his chapter). In 1936, Naseem was sold to the Tersk Stud in Russia where he had an enormous impact. His best-known son, Negatiw, the sire of *Naborr (see his chapter) and others, was foaled there.

*Serafix's dam, *Serafina, was no slouch either. A rangey, long-necked chestnut with an attractive but straight face, *Serafina produced foals who would soon travel around the globe. In addition to her firstborn, *Serafix, she produced his full brother, the gray *Silver Drift, a well-known sire in the United States whose offspring included 17 U.S. and Canadian national winners.

*Serafina also produced *Oran Van Crabbet (by Oran), three-times U.S. National Champion in performance (park, formal driving, and formal combination); *Royal Constellation (by Grand Royal), who was purchased by American breeder Bazy Tankersley; Sherif (by Royal Diamond), who went to Tasmania; and Super

Serafina, the dam of *Serafix, pictured on the lawn at Crabbet Park.

Naseem, who was sired by the renowned Skowronek, was the paternal grandsire of *Serafix. Naseem is considered by many to be one of the best Arabian stallions ever in terms of both conformation and Arabian type.

Lady Wentworth is pictured here at Crabbet Park holding a mother-daughter pair. The chestnut mare is Sharima (Shareer x Nashisha), the great-grand-mother of *Serafix in his maternal line. The gray mare, Grey Royal (out of Sharima), was a half-sister to *Serafix, as they were both by the same sire, Raktha.

Grand (also by Oran), who went to Nassau in the Bahamas.

*Serafina's sire, Indian Gold, was a superb dark chestnut of superior quality and magnificent bearing and was one of England's best horses, according to Archer. *Serafina traces in tail female line to Nasra, one of the Blunts' foundation mares.

John Rogers had high hopes that, over the years, the red stallion would continue to sire the quality for which his ancestors were known. A few days after his arrival in California, however, future plans for *Serafix were set on the back burner as a more pressing issue arose. *Serafix stopped eating.

"When he arrived in California, his coat was shiny, his tail almost touched the ground, and the horse was full of action and animation," recalled Rogers in *The Arabian Horse* magazine. "This was not to

last, however, because across the hay mound from *Serafix was stabled Natez. They immediately took a dislike to each other, and *Serafix went off his feed."

Natez was moved to a different barn, but *Serafix continued to be uneasy and nervous, and only picked at his feed. "It was only after some weeks that I learned that the man who was in charge of my horses was trying to dominate *Serafix and . . . whipped him in the stall. This resulted in a quick change of handlers," Rogers continued.

"I got in touch with Lady Wentworth to see what she thought put *Serafix so far off his feed. Her conclusion was that he missed his groom, who had always fed him, always handled him, and he was lonesome for human companionship. As a result, I took on this job myself."

A routine soon developed. Rogers returned home from work at 7 p.m., ate a hasty supper, and, without changing clothes, camped out in *Serafix's stall. "I'd talk to him, scratch him, pet him, and then groom him thoroughly. Then, I'd

The legendary Mesaoud appears 11 times far back in the pedigree of *Serafix.

take out the feed he'd refused and put in identically the same feed and try to feed him by hand," said Rogers.

After 2 hours or so, Rogers would curl up under the horse's manger and sleep until the wee hours of the morning, get up and go home, crawl in bed and sleep a little more, then shower and rush off to work. *Serafix loved the attention.

On weekends, the pair took long walks, followed by a wild 30-minute romp. "His favorite form of exercise," said Rogers, "was to take an automobile tire and throw it in the air and catch it or take it over and splash it in the water trough and try to knock the water out. It wasn't long until he was himself again. Our friendship grew to be a lifetime affair after the first few nights in his stall."

*Serafix seemed always to want to be with Rogers—even if that meant a climb to the hayloft. As Rogers told the story, "That fall, when we put up a year's supply of hay, I went over to see *Serafix and also see how the hay was stacked in his barn. To my utter amazement, this hay pile was just about to tumble down into *Serafix's stall. I immediately called my wife and asked her to come over and help me and I climbed up on this pile of hay and started tying the corner together with baling wire."

The outside door to the stallion's stall was open so that he could go in and out to his paddock as Rogers worked above his head. "In no time at all, down came the pile of hay, and me! I rode it down coming out on top, half filling *Serafix's stall. I scrambled back up the pile then to try to stop other hay from caving in, and here came *Serafix right behind me, jumping from bale to bale and scrambling just as fast as he could, and he wouldn't leave me. I had to lead that horse down off of that pile of hay about 12 feet above his head and walk him back out the door and shut it so he would stay out. He wanted to be where I was."

Show Record

*Serafix had won championships in England as a yearling, 2-year-old, and

Four *Serafix daughters dominated the 1962 U.S. National Champion Mare class, held at Estes Park, Colorado. Left to right are Cholette (out of Choleyn), the National Champion Mare; Fixette (also out of Choleyn), the Reserve National Champion Mare; Silver Dawn (out of *Silver Crystal), a Top Ten mare; and Starfire (out of *Serafire), also a Top Ten mare.   **Photo by Alexander**

Carinosa, out of *Caliope (by Witraz), was the best-producing daughter of *Serafix, with seven national champion offspring to her credit.

Photo by Fallaw; courtesy of Ruth Husband

3-year-old, and was shown on a very limited—but highly successful—basis in the United States. In 1954, he was reserve champion at the Cow Palace and the Pomona shows in California. In 1955, he stood as champion stallion and show grand champion at Pomona, with Bob Smith on the lead. He was unshown in 1956, due to an injury suffered in the trailer. *Serafix was shown once each in 1957 and 1958, and was named champion stallion each time. He was never shown again.

Well-known Arabian horse breeder and judge Jim Panek recalled seeing *Serafix at one of the horse's last shows. "Shortly after we arrived at the showgrounds (in Antioch, Calif.), the unmistakable noise of a horse very upset in a trailer was heard. Into the middle of a vacant field drove the Rogers Arabians rig," Panek wrote in an issue of *The Crabbet Influence* magazine published in 1986. "The driver and his assistant leaped out of the truck, opened the trailer, and out jumped *Serafix.

"For me it was like an apparition, to see this gleaming chestnut stallion emerge from his trailer, hold his head up, survey all that surrounded him, and let out a scream that penetrated for miles. It is 30 years since that incident occurred, but I remember it as though it was yesterday."

He continued, "That was an exciting weekend for me—my first Arabian horse

show, the opportunity to see *Serafix named champion stallion, his young son Nafix win his halter class, and the decision made to breed Arabian horses to look as much like *Serafix as possible." (Panek eventually used the *Serafix son Rakafix and several *Serafix daughters in his breeding program.)

What Panek saw that day, and John Rogers saw in England, was a horse of excellent conformation, balance, and substance. His skin was like tissue paper, his veins close to the surface. He was tall, typey, and refined, but thoroughly masculine. Add to that a certain aura Panek described as "... his magic, his charisma, his bloom, his attitude, his indescribable *noblesse oblige*. . . ." and you have a champion.

In truth, however, *Serafix won far more acclaim for the show ring triumphs of his offspring than for any of his own accomplishments. Rogers had studied long and thought hard about exactly the kind of breeding program he wanted. Then he carefully set out to accomplish it.

He was committed to quality and accepted only approved mares to be bred to *Serafix. Bloodlines were important, but not limited, as success was achieved with a wide variety of lines, ranging from Crabbet and Davenport to pure Polish. Of more importance were individual quality and the ability to reproduce

that quality. Rogers did not charge a stud fee. Instead, he leased mares on an every-other-foal basis—and only if he thought the mare good enough.

Offspring

Of *Serafix's 259 registered foals, 128 were champions in halter and/or performance, with 41 winning U.S. National Top Tens or better, according to Arabian horse researcher Arlene Magid.

The most exciting year of *Serafix's career was probably 1962. At the U.S. National Championship Arabian classes, held in Estes Park, Colo., his four gray daughters dominated the show ring. Chloette (out of Chloeyn, by *Raseyn) was named National Champion Mare. Fixette (Chloette's full sister) was the Reserve

*Silver Dawn (*Serafix x *Silver Crystal) was named the 1963 U.S. Reserve National Champion Mare, with John Rogers showing her. The national classes that year were held at the Texas Fall Arabian Show.*

SX Conquistador (*Serafix x *Yamina) won three national titles and sired four national winners.

Photo by
Johnny Johnston

Champion. Starfire (out of *Serafire) and Silver Dawn (out of *Silver Crystal) were both named Top Ten. (Silver Dawn would later be a U.S. Reserve National Champion Mare. Fixette also was 1963 Scottsdale champion mare.) All four were bred and owned by Rogers.

In addition, the *Serafix son Royal Magic (out of *Royal Silver, many times a halter and performance champion), who was bred by Rogers and owned by Conley Horse Farms, Bradbury, Calif., won a Top Ten Stallion award.

Incidentally, Chloeyn produced nine foals by *Serafix, of which seven were champions. Included was the stallion Fixeyn, who was extremely successful as both a halter and performance horse.

Looking back, it becomes apparent that *Serafix's greatest legacy lies in his daughters. Not only did they do well in the show ring, but their offspring also won a wide variety of prizes, in the purebred show ring as well as in other

competitive venues, from cattle events to endurance rides.

Of his 127 daughters, 120 produced at least 1 registered foal, and 80 of those have produced at least 1 champion—often more. In addition, 34 had produced national winners through 1996.

And they crossed well with almost every bloodline imaginable, producing champions with Egyptian Arabians such as El Hilal, Nabiel, *Ansata Ibn Halima, Ibn Morafic, and Dalul; American-breds such as Khemosabi, Bey Shah, Gai Parada, Fadjur, etc.; Russian horses like *Muscat, *Naborr, and *Padron; and Polish Arabians such as *Bask, *Essaul, and *Aramus.

The best-producing daughter of *Serafix is U.S. Top Ten English Pleasure winner Carinosa (out of *Caliope, by Witraz, the sire of *Bask). Her offspring include 10 champions, 7 of them national winners themselves.

*Serafix was more than just a premier broodmare sire, however. Statistics indicate his sons did well also. Of his 132 sons, 97 have at least 1 registered foal, and, of those, 66 have sired at least 1 champion, and 29 had sired national winners through

Nafix, 18 years old in this picture, was another outstanding son of *Serafix. Out of the mare Nabiya, he sired eight national winners.

Photo by Foucher

1996. *Serafix's better known sons include:

• Nafix (out of Nabiya, by Abu Farwa), who sired eight national winners.

• SX Conquistador (out of *Yamina), who won three national awards himself and sired four national winners.

• Seraj (out of *Silver Crystal), a U.S. national Top Ten winner in halter and performance and the sire of three national winners.

• SX Saladin (out of Cobah, by Pomona Ahmen), a Canadian National Reserve Champion Stallion and the sire of three national winners.

Transitions

When *Serafix was 15, Rogers hired Murrel Lacey as horse manager at the Rogers Ranch. Lacey soon developed a special rapport with the horse and spent hours with the stallion. Lacey described that time in a 1976 issue of the *Arabian Horse Journal:*

"He started each day as dynamic and powerful as he ended the day before. I never once saw the horse let down or ill in any manner in the 8 years I handled him. He was always bright, demanding, happy, and ambitious, and gave you the feeling of being in the presence of royalty when you were with him.

"He continuously watched over the entire ranch and was better than any watchman you could ever hire. Many nights I would run to the barn, hearing his restlessness in his stall, only to find a horse cast or someone out of a stall who should not be. . . . John M. Rogers and *Serafix made some beautiful years for me—and words cannot thank either one of them enough," Lacey concluded.

Rogers had a dispersal sale in 1971, and *Serafix died in 1973 at age 24.

In 1976, shortly before he died, Rogers summarized *Serafix, the horse, and John Rogers, the man, for Peg Johnson, editor of the *Arabian Horse Journal.* He said, "In addition to being a great individual, a beautiful Arabian, and, I think, the best-balanced Arabian I know or have seen, *Serafix had the proper pedigree . . . that made the difference.

"Life is hard to squeeze up into focus, but I have always said and still say, I don't want to live without a lovely lady, without a good dog, or without a good Arabian."

18 SKORAGE

Skorage was a superb ambassador for the entire Arabian breed.

WHEN THE highly-touted imported Polish Arabian stallion *Gwiazdor died just 2 days before the big 1965 Scottsdale All-Arabian Horse Show, owner Edwin J. Tweed of the nearby Brusally Ranch did a most unusual thing. He pulled an 18-year-old stallion out of the pasture, "dusted him off, and entered him in *Gwiazdor's place," recalled Tweed's granddaughter, Shelley Groom Trevor.

With absolutely no preparation, and after years of retirement, the flashy chestnut with the four white stockings and blaze face proceeded to prove that old campaigners never really stop campaigning—or winning. The horse won three of his four classes, including the English Pleasure Championship Stake with 44 entries.

His two other wins were in English pleasure stallions and informal pleasure

The flashy Skorage was one of the most famous Arabian show horses in the 1950s, winning numerous halter and performance championships.

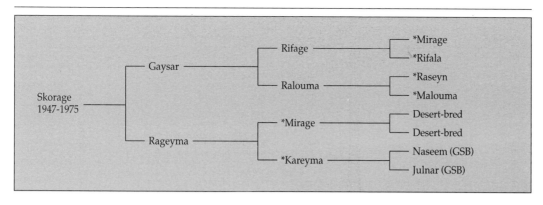

```
                                        ┌─── *Mirage
                        ┌─── Rifage ─────┤
                        │                └─── *Rifala
          ┌─── Gaysar ──┤
          │             │                ┌─── *Raseyn
          │             └─── Ralouma ─────┤
Skorage ──┤                              └─── *Malouma
1947-1975 │
          │                              ┌─── Desert-bred
          │             ┌─── *Mirage ─────┤
          │             │                └─── Desert-bred
          └─── Rageyma ─┤
                        │                ┌─── Naseem (GSB)
                        └─── *Kareyma ────┤
                                         └─── Julnar (GSB)
```

driving, and he placed second in the large native costume class.

"And there were my grandparents, Ed and Ruth Tweed, standing on the sidelines, with tears in their eyes," recalled Trevor, who now lives in Cave Creek, Arizona. "He won so easily, so effortlessly. It was a wonderful day."

The stallion's fans, including his biggest—Ed Tweed—may have been thrilled, but they were hardly surprised. After all, this was just business as usual for the winningest Arabian show horse of the 1950s, "Mr. Versatility" himself—Skorage.

Tweed had quite a simple explanation for the 1965 Scottsdale Show wins in a May 1965 *Arabian Horse News* article: "He keeps himself fit by playing in his corral—chasing birds!"

Skorage (rhymes with mirage) was one of the first Arabians purchased by the Tweed family and was the base upon which their ranch was built. As Trevor recalled in her memoir *A Light In The Stable,* there was hardly an Arabian in the entire state of Arizona in the early 1950s. And the little town of Scottsdale boasted only about 200 hardy souls!

"My grandfather was a dynamic man of many talents—an architect, musical and artistic, with a feeling for animals and eyes to the future. No one needed to pave his way," she wrote. Despite the small number of Arabians, "he built a stable, founded a club (the Arabian Horse Association of Arizona), and sponsored a horse show (with the assistance of Philip Wrigley and Anne McCormick); all of which, as time passed, grew to grand proportions. (He) would help lead the way as an importer of Polish and Russian horses in the 1960s, hold the first Arabian auction in Scottsdale, pioneer Arabian racing, and finally, hold fast to his ways when the horse show and auc-

tions, originally staged with quiet western elegance, took on shades of Hollywood—big dollars, big names, glitter, and rock 'n' roll."

Brusally Ranch was a place of breathtaking beauty, with Spanish-style stables, a lake, aviary, lush pastures, and even an Ayrshire dairy. It was called Brusally for Tweed's children, Bruce and Sally, and truly was a family venture. Tweed loved to have visitors, and "his crackling sense of humor and sincere love of people touched many," wrote his granddaughter.

Although the ranch was eventually known as "Little Poland" for its high-quality Polish Arabian imports and breeding stock, the decidedly non-Polish Skorage remained Tweed's favorite horse.

"Skorage was Brusally," Trevor firmly stated. "He launched the ranch. My grandfather never really rode very much; he and my grandmother were occasional pleasure riders only. I can't actually say if he ever rode Skorage—but he loved him very much, probably better than any other horse he ever owned. Skorage was the horse of his life."

An undated photo of Skorage when he was owned by Gainey Arabian Farms of Owatonna, Minnesota. The handler accepting the trophy is Bob Powers, who worked for Gainey.   Photo by W. Sam Stochl

Gaysar, the sire of Skorage, clearing a fence. Gaysar was bred by the Van Vleet Arabian Stud in Colorado.   Photo courtesy Arabian Horse Trust

Bred by Daniel Gainey of Owatonna, Minn., Skorage was foaled May 11, 1947, at Gainey Farms. Interestingly enough, he is by a *Mirage grandson and out of a *Mirage daughter, making Skorage closely linebred to that little white-grey stallion imported by Roger Selby of Ohio. Selby had purchased *Mirage from Judith Blunt, Baroness Wentworth, of the Crabbet Stud in England. Instead of being grey like *Mirage, however, Skorage was chestnut like his parents and was the spitting image—both in color and markings—of his dam's great-great grandsire, the famous Egyptian horse Mesaoud.

Skorage's dam, the *Mirage daughter Rageyma, was a wonderful mare who made immense contributions to the Gainey program. Rageyma's dam, *Kareyma, was sired by one of the prettiest stallions Crabbet ever had, Naseem, who later was sold to Russia where he had a major impact on the Tersk Stud's breeding program.

Rageyma stood less than 14 hands, yet she often won five-gaited classes. In addition to Skorage, she produced U.S. National Top Ten Trail winner Gallant,

198

national winner producers Gageyma and Galimar (full siblings to Skorage), and Geym and Gajala, both by *Raffles; the latter is his top-producing daughter.

Gaysar, Skorage's sire, was bred by the famous Van Vleet Arabian Stud in Colorado. In his pedigree are such illustrious ancestors as *Raseyn and *Rifala, the dam of *Raffles.

Skorage was shown extensively as a youngster by the Gaineys. He won often and was reputed from the very beginning to be quite a ham in the show ring. Crowds loved him and he loved them.

In 1950 Ed Tweed was scanning some show results when he read about a 3-year-old youngster named Skorage, who had just beaten out the big boys to be named grand champion stallion at the annual Waterloo, Iowa, show, which, at the time, was considered to be the equivalent of a national event.

Tweed quickly checked out the colt's pedigree and became even more excited. In minutes, he was on the phone with Dan Gainey.

*Skorage was closely line-bred to *Mirage, shown here in a photograph from Roger Selby's book,* **Arabian Horses** *(out of print). In the book, *Mirage is described as follows: "Pure white. 14.2 hands. Foaled 1909. 1,000 lbs. Three-gaited. Sound. Most gentle and lovable." This photo was taken at Crabbet Park in England.*

Earl Craig and Skorage in native costume regalia loping across the Arizona desert.

Ever alert, Skorage was acutely aware of his surroundings.

It wasn't long before the Arizona ranchman found himself in Minnesota on a frigid, windy day, wrapped in horse blankets and trying to keep warm as he watched both Skorage and his full brother, Galimar, being presented. While Tweed liked both horses, he chose Skorage—and, by so doing, turned another page in the annals of Arabian horse history.

Skorage went to Arizona and the lime-light grew even brighter. Tweed believed in promoting Arabian horses at every opportunity—and the Tweed horses in particular. With Harold and Florence Daugherty as his trainers—and later Earl Craig, Charlie Carter, and Steve Spalding—Tweed sent the spunky chestnut stallion on the road. He became the star attraction at horse shows, parades, and special exhibitions all over the country for well over a decade. The stallion became well-known to horse lovers across the nation, no matter what their breed affiliation, and influenced scores of people to purchase purebred and Half-Arabian horses. Skorage was simply a superb ambassador for the entire Arabian breed.

All-Arabian horse shows were few and far between in those days, so Skorage often found himself engaged in all-breed competitions. Even in breeding (halter) classes he several times was named grand champion over all breeds presented.

It was not unusual for Skorage to come home from a show with wins in western pleasure (both ladies' and men's), English stakes, native costume, pairs, parade, driving, and halter divisions. The trophy room at Brusally Ranch soon was packed with his ribbons, silver trays, and trophies.

In all, he won 22 championships and 112 first-place awards, many against all breeds. In 1956 he also achieved the American Horse Show Association's High Score Award.

Said Trevor, "I remember showing him when I was 15 years old. I spent that summer with my grandparents, and I showed him at the (1961) Estes Park (Colo.) show in amateur English pleasure. That was the same show where his daughter, Skorata (out of Rasata, by *Raseyn), was named a U.S. National Top Ten Mare.

"I didn't know very much, but he was a push-button horse, and he knew his job. We won second place easily.

Earl Craig and Skorage (right) with Earl's daughter on Donita (Mahabba x Mlecha) after winning a parade pairs class.

Photo by Ed Ellinger

"Skorage was charismatic," Trevor continued, "and a true professional. His disposition couldn't have been better; he was easy to handle, a true gentleman."

Trevor also wrote in her memoir: "Skorage had what it takes to make a name for himself: charisma, balance, heart, and, as he soon proved, potency as a sire."

Because of his show schedule, and Tweed's later interest in Polish-bred horses, Skorage was only lightly used as a breeding stallion. Explained Trevor, "The original plan was to cross Skorage on the Polish mares that my grandfather imported. The first importation was in 1964 and the second in 1967—26 horses all together.

"By the way, my grandfather was one of the first to fly Arabians over here, rather than ship them by sea. He had planned to buy only a few Polish horses, but when he found out the airplane would hold 14 horses, he decided it was more economical to fill it up!

"The cross (with Skorage) worked very well," added Trevor, "but it was soon apparent that the marketplace wanted pure Polish horses, and so Skorage wasn't used as much on them as originally planned."

Skorage sired just 69 registered purebred foals over 20 years from a small band of mares that included daughters of *Raseyn, Zarife, Asif, Hanraff, and *Rifage. Nevertheless, his contributions to succeeding generations are significant. Those 69 horses produced 784 grandget who have had a commendable impact on North American show rings and breeding programs.

Among his 69 offspring, 5 were national winners. Skorata (out of Rasata, by *Raseyn) was a 1961 U.S. National Top Ten Mare, as previously mentioned. Skor-Enne

Skorage was a pioneer in promoting Arabian horses, such as in this advertising photograph for Porters, a renowned western store in Scottsdale.

Shelley Groom Trevor, the Tweeds' granddaughter, and Skorage in a 1961 photograph taken at the Tweeds' mountain ranch in Arizona. Regarding this picture, Shelley says, "It's so typical of Skorage's expression, and a tribute to his temperament that he was so safe for a 15-year-old to ride."

(out of Chi-Enne, by Hanraff) was a 1964 Canadian Top Ten Mare. Brusally Skorage (out of Latsemah, by Latseyn) was a 1974 U.S. Top Ten Formal Combination winner and considered by Tweed to be Skorage's most look-alike, act-alike son. Skordonas (out of Donata, by Mahabba) won seven national titles, including a U.S. Reserve National Stock Horse Championship and four U.S. Top Ten Trail placings.

Pulque was Skorage's best and best-known son. Out of the mare Rohanna, by Hanrah, Pulque won six national titles, including four as a U.S. National Top Ten Stallion, a U.S. Reserve National English Pleasure Championship, and a U.S. Top Ten Western Pleasure win. In 1961 and 1962 he was the reserve AHSA high-point winner in the country (over all breeds) and won his IAHA Legion of Merit Award. He was owned and shown by Carol Chapman.

"The Skorage horses were very athletic, and often had his wonderful neck," said Trevor. "There were quite a few chestnuts with white markings—always very popular—and quite a few liver chestnuts, as well. You know his best son, Pulque, was so liver in color that he was practically purple! Carol Chapman did everything with him, everything. They were quite a team, a joy to watch."

Pulque was also the only stallion at the time to have sired three AHSA high-score winners: Que Mira, Que Hama, and Kawliga. He produced several Arabian national winners as well. Ironically, he died in a freak accident at about the same time Skorage died in 1975.

Pulque is acknowledged as the best son of Skorage. Owned and shown by Carol Chapman, this flashy stallion won six national titles. This photograph was taken in 1962 at the Houston Livestock Show where Pulque stood reserve grand champion Arabian stallion.

Even when not in the show ring or on parade, Skorage loved his fans. Visitors to Brusally Ranch were always treated to a show by the cocky chestnut. As guests approached his paddock, Skorage would begin to trot up and down, dance around, and generally strut his stuff.

"Even in his later years, when he was so terribly crippled from arthritis, that special spirit of his wouldn't give up," said Trevor. "I remember if you walked toward his paddock and he was lying down, he would force himself to jump right up and run to your end of the paddock as if to say, 'I'm okay! Really! Here I am!' He wouldn't allow himself to be downhearted. He was truly a shining spirit.

"You know, my grandfather really loved that horse," Trevor added. "He had so many drawings made of Skorage, commissioned paintings of him. The famous painting of my grandfather—with Skorage and Tex, his favorite collie, in the background—still hangs at the old ranch house to this day. When Skorage died, my grandfather had a bronze made as a headstone for his grave."

On June 3, 1975, at age 28, the old master show horse died. He was gently laid to rest at Brusally Ranch, the special bronze monument placed on his grave by a sorrowful Ed Tweed.

Ed Tweed with his wife, Ruth.

203

19   BAY-ABI

Bay-Abi launched the incredibly influential Varian breeding program.

FOR BAY-ABI, life was a lark and he its star merrymaker. All he needed to make his world complete was the perfect side-kick. He found her in 1959 at the first Arabian horse sale to be held at San Francisco's Cow Palace. Her name was Sheila Varian, she lived near Arroyo Grande, Calif., and she was just 19 years old.

"Bay-Abi turned his head and looked at me with his small, tipped ears and quizzical expression. It was a look I grew to know intimately for the next 25 years of his life," Varian said, recalling the first time she saw the then 2-year-old colt. "Whatever the instinctive connection between the two of us was, I don't know, but if I ever felt the pull towards something, I felt it towards Bay-Abi."

Bay-Abi, the 1962 U.S. National Champion Arabian Stallion, became a legendary sire whose descendants are still dominant in today's show ring.

Photo by
Jerry Sparagowski

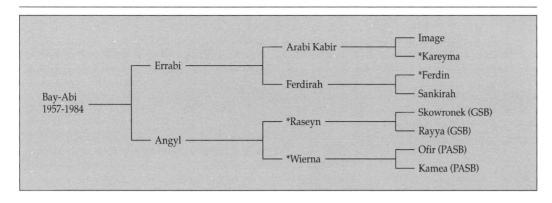

```
                                          ┌─── Image
                      ┌─── Arabi Kabir ───┤
                      │                   └─── *Kareyma
        ┌─── Errabi ──┤
        │             │                   ┌─── *Ferdin
        │             └─── Ferdirah ──────┤
Bay-Abi ┤                                 └─── Sankirah
1957-1984│
        │                                 ┌─── Skowronek (GSB)
        │             ┌─── *Raseyn ───────┤
        │             │                   └─── Rayya (GSB)
        └─── Angyl ───┤
                      │                   ┌─── Ofir (PASB)
                      └─── *Wierna ───────┤
                                          └─── Kamea (PASB)
```

There were other wonderful stallions in the sale, including Rakafix (by *Serafix) and Nikitez (by *Witez II), who was a paternal half-brother to Varian's mare Ronteza (who would become the first Arabian ever to win the Cow Palace's tough reined cow horse championship against all breeds in November 1961—with Varian aboard). Well-respected horseman Jeff Wonnell had spent hours walking with Varian and examining the various horses offered for sale. "No matter," said Varian, "there was only one horse I was interested in and that was the bay stallion with the gay tail.

"The bidding commenced and somewhere along the way I looked at my mom (Wenonah Varian) and she nodded and I bid. At $1,000 I could hear Mom murmuring something about 'as high as we could go' . . . another bid came in at $1,050. Before my mom had a chance to comment, I bid $1,100. It seems as though there was no sound until I heard the words, 'Sold to the blonde girl in the front row!' I can't recall a time when I was so incapable of anything as I was in those moments following being told Bay-Abi was mine.

"I would give anything to see the sale agreement today, because one thing I do remember clearly was trying to sign my name with a hand shaking so violently. . . . What an incredible mother and father (Eric Varian) I had to trust a youngster's knowledge and intuition, although I best not give myself too much credit. Don't ever believe that my mom didn't do her pedigree research!"

For the next 24 hours, Varian checked on her new horse every 20 minutes only to find him always lying down, sleeping flat out. "He didn't look sick, but just how long can a horse sleep?" Varian wrote in her memoirs, which she plans, eventually, to publish. "When I took him out of his

Halter and Performance Record: 1962 U.S. National Champion Stallion; 1964 U.S. National Top Ten wins in English pleasure and western pleasure; Legion of Merit Award winner.

Progeny Record:

Purebred Foal Crops: 24
Purebred Foals Registered: 275
U.S./Canadian National Winners: 24
Class A Champions: 65
IAHA Legion of Honor Award Winners: 4
IAHA Legion of Supreme Honor Award Winners: 1
IAHA Legion of Merit Award Winners: 16
IAHA Legion of Supreme Honor/Merit Award Winners: 1
IAHA Legion of Supreme Merit Award Winners: 1

stall, he played and pranced and I loved everything about him. When I put him away, he lay down and slept like a drugged zombie until I showed up to admire him all over again. Bay-Abi's ability to sleep was a trait that stood him in good stead all of his life."

Bay-Abi was the horse who started it all, who launched the incredibly influential Varian Arabians breeding program—a program now known around the world for its unique "V" horses, supreme athletes who exhibit breathtaking beauty.

Bred by Loyd and Mary Silva of Oregon, Bay-Abi was foaled on April 22, 1957. His sire, Errabi, was a champion who was killed at age 7. In his pedigree, Errabi carried the lines of *Mirage through Image, Skowronek through *Kareyma (by

A three-quarter front view of the well-balanced Bay-Abi.

Photo by Jerry Sparagowski

Naseem), *Nureddin II through *Ferdin, and the desert-bred *Hamrah, through Sankirah.

Bay-Abi was his dam's first foal. Angyl, a U.S. Top Ten halter mare, was 10 years old when bred to Errabi. A *Raseyn daughter, Angyl was out of the Polish mare *Wierna, who was by Ofir, and out of Kamea, a Farys daughter. This "melting pot" of bloodlines gave Bay-Abi the best each had to offer, resulting in a superior individual.

Bay-Abi and the tall, slight schoolteacher formed an incredible bond based on loving devotion and a delicious sense of humor.

Said Varian, "Since I am lazy by nature, early in our 25 years together I taught Bay-Abi to come when called. Bay added his own enthusiasm and soon galloped to me when I called. I did make one small mistake in the training process, however. I insisted that Bay-Abi not only come to me, but come as close as he could physically without trampling me. He decided galloping to me was the fun part and arrived in a cloud of dust, snorting, bouncing, with his tail over his back, his 15 hands looking like 16. Anyone walking into Bay-Abi's field with me was filled with terror . . . as the head-throwing stallion charged up, not stopping until he was towering over you."

Varian would put her arms around his neck and Bay-Abi would rest his head on her shoulder, almost sleeping in her arms. Then, Varian would clap her hands, and off he would dash to start over again. Once Bay-Abi was trained to ride, new features were added to the game.

Explained Varian, "I'm of the school of riding, not walking. If horses have four legs, and I have two, they should carry me at least half the time. Early on, I taught Bay to side-pass over to the fence when I snapped my fingers so I could hop on from the top rail. I had to jump on his back in a hurry because this train didn't stop long at the station. Down the hill we would roar—fast—with me lying on his back with my fingers laced in his mane." The pair circled the pasture, and if Varian bailed off at the starting point, Bay-Abi would simply circle around again to see if the game could be played once more.

"Bay-Abi was a clown," Varian stated. "But he was also a very sensitive horse whose good spirits were easily wilted with a slap or yell, although it was easy to restimulate him with a voice filled with excitement. It got to be the method of correction that when Bay-Abi was naughty I picked a flower and gave him a gentle little smack with it; he always looked at me like I had just shot him, so I didn't play around with the flower smacking that much. It hurt his feelings."

Raised with California ranch horse traditions, Varian chose not to breed Bay-Abi until he was trained. He, therefore, had no foals ready to be shown until he was 7,

Bay-Abi and Sheila, with Mingo trotting alongside, set out to ride the pastures.

The good-looking Bay-Abi was 5 years old when, shown by Sheila, he was named U.S. National Champion Arabian Stallion in 1962 at Estes Park, Colorado. He was a unanimous first on the cards of all three judges.

Photo by Alexander

Even though he was a national champion, Bay-Abi knew how to put in a day's work on a ranch. This picture was taken at Sid Spencer's ranch where, Sheila says, "I learned most of the things I knew about schooling and taking care of horses." Flanking the calf is Margaret Courtis.

Photo by
Jeanne Thwaites

and he was 10 before his first nationally competitive performance horses entered the ring. "That is one bit of information I followed for the first and last time," Varian offered.

Meanwhile, she began showing him at halter. The fashion of the times called for beefy horses, but Varian chose to show Bay-Abi "lean and hard and healthy, to protect his young growing bones from the effects of too much weight." Her decision kept him out of first place, but usually in

the ribbons. Nevertheless, he won a championship at the Cow Palace at age 3, qualifying him for the national championship class to be held in Colorado.

"My childhood years with Sid Spencer (a neighboring rancher and superb horsewoman) taught me to recognize a correct, good-legged, well-balanced horse with all the romantic features the Arabian horse is noted for, even if no one in the Arabian horse world agreed with me. It did bother me a little that Bay was given so little attention for his many good qualities, but what can you do except never admit you noticed and plan your strategy for success."

That strategy included a run for the most-sought-after award in the Arabian horse industry: the U.S. National Arabian Stallion Halter Championship.

To say that Varian ate, drank, smelled, listened, and felt her way to Estes Park,

Errabi, the sire of Bay-Abi, was a chestnut.

Photo by Loyd Silva

Errabi was shown in this Loyd Silva ad in the September 1954 issue of Western Horseman.

Colo., in the summer of 1962 would be an understatement. She lived, dreamed, and breathed the national championship every moment, both waking and sleeping.

(Note: At that time, only two Arabian national championships were offered, one for stallions at halter and one for mares at halter. The classes were held in conjunction with the Colorado All-Arabian Horse Show in Estes Park.)

Each day after school she dashed home and worked with Bay-Abi. "The best stallions in the United States would be there," Varian said. "I had watched Paul Polk show the Tones' stallion, Fadjur, many times, and was always entranced. With Fadjur as my model, I encouraged Bay-Abi to believe he was the handsomest, most beautiful, smartest, happiest horse in the world. He learned this game with the same enthusiasm as he had learned the others. He listened to me saying, 'Happy

boy. Pretty boy, Bay.' And we would bounce around the barn with Bay dancing at my side, eyes bright, ears up.

"The stallion class would be large and long . . . a very taxing class," she continued. "So, I added, 'Go to sleep, Bay,' in a soft, melodic tone, and Bay-Abi would drop his head and almost start snoring. He had spent plenty of time tied to a tree when we were through gathering cattle, and he knew well the value of rest.

"So, we rode for conditioning, brushed and curried that shining hide, and each day convinced Bay he was more wonderful than the day before."

Varian and her mother set off for Colorado pulling their old Miley trailer behind the family station wagon. At the

Sheila and her bay stallion were a charismatic team.

Photo by Jerry Sparagowski

Estes Park showgrounds, no one took much notice of the unknown girl with the pretty bay stallion. Varian walked a lot and slept little, studying the other classes, and rehearsing her game plan over and over.

July fourth dawned bright and clear at 7,500 feet above sea level, and 45 of the nation's top stallions entered the ring for the grueling 4-hour class. When it was all over, Bay-Abi—showing just as Varian had envisioned—took the crown over such horses as Fadjur, Azrahand, Bolero, Yatez, Gaizon, Murzada, Royal Magic, Sur-Knight, Sur Neet, and Saneyn.

Varian should have been elated. Instead, she was devastated.

"I was an unknown. The professional

trainers were shocked; I saw their faces. We slunk back to the barn positive we had stolen something that didn't belong to us."

Gossip said it was a mistake, or that Bay-Abi won only by default, by placing third on all three judges' cards. "I believed the gossip," Varian admitted. Consequently she did little to promote him, and booked no outside mares to the reigning national champion.

Two years later when more national classes were offered, Varian showed Bay-Abi to U.S. National Top Ten awards in both English and western pleasure.

Shortly thereafter, at another show, Bill Higgins, who was one of the three judges at Estes Park in 1962, came up to Varian and said, "I loved that bay horse of yours the minute he trotted into the ring. Did you know that Bob Armstrong and Bill Burns (the other two judges) placed him first on their cards as well?" (At that time, judges' cards were not posted after the classes, as they are now.)

Bay-Abi had won the national halter championship unanimously!

Said Varian, "I slipped back to Bay-Abi's stall and gave deep thought to never again letting others convince me what was and was not quality in my horses."

A Sire of Champions

In all, Bay-Abi sired 275 registered Arabians, of which 65 are champions and 24 are national winners. Four were national champions or reserves in halter: Bay El Bey (Canadian National Champion and twice U.S. Reserve); Baytar (U.S. National Champion Gelding); Kloi Sinay (U.S. National Champion Futurity Colt); and Four Winds Flyte (U.S. Reserve National Champion Futurity Filly).

Six became national performance champions: Mikado (U.S. National Park Horse Champion); Bay Kinra (U.S. Reserve National Western Pleasure Champion); Bay Event, out of the famous Ronteza (twice U.S. National Stock Horse Champion); Baytar (U.S. National Western Pleasure AOTR Champion); Contessa Bay (U.S. Reserve National Western Side-saddle Champion); and Bay Shadow (U.S. National Open Cutting and Novice Cut-

ting Champion). Further, Varian never showed a Bay-Abi horse at the Nationals who didn't win a Top Ten or better award.

As Varian told this author in a 1986 *Arabian Horse Times* article: "Bay-Abi was a very powerfully strong breeding horse who seemed able to take the best from the mares and make it better. He was a very correct horse and always produced athletes. We were very lucky to have him. He never let me down." To say the least.

Although he crossed well on a wide variety of bloodlines, Bay-Abi made breeding history when bred to three special Polish mares—mares who would establish the fertile fields from which more than nine generations of Varian Arabians would flourish. The Varians imported the trio in 1961 with the assistance of Englishwoman Patricia Lindsay.

*Bachantka (Wielki Szlem x Balalajka, by Amurath Sahib), produced exceptional females such as Bayanka, dam of Kaiyoum, and Baychatka, dam of Moska.

*Ostroga (Duch x Orda, by Omar) produced horses of action, including Bay Image, Dartanee, and Genyya.

*Naganka (Bad Afas x Najada, by Fetysz), founded a dynasty that continues to influence show ring competition across the continent. When bred to Bay-Abi, *Naganka produced the incredible Mikado, a U.S. National Park Horse Champion, and Bay El Bey, also known as "The Kingmaker."

Bay El Bey has his own chapter in this book, so suffice to say that he is best known for his own wins and as a sire of

*Bay Event (Bay-Abi x Ronteza, by *Witez II), with Sheila in the saddle, heads a cow at Santa Maria, Calif., in 1971.*

Photo by Fallaw

Bay Event, ridden by Sheila, was twice the unanimous U.S. National Champion Arabian Stock Horse in the early 1970s.

Photo by Jerry Sparagowski

superior breeding stallions—the three most famous being Huckleberry Bey, Bey Shah, and Barbary. Their offspring and descendants dominate both halter and performance competition at the highest levels.

It is painful for Varian to recall the year 1984. "The last of my family passed away, or so it seemed to me," she said at a 1990 presentation. "Ronteza died at age 28 . . . she had raised me. Now I could see the inevitable happening. My wonderful

mares and Bay-Abi were getting old. They made it to old age, bless their hearts, but it was a terrible year . . . the loss of *Ostroga at 28, *Bachantka at 27, and the start of my program, Bay-Abi, at 27. All my roots, it seemed, were gone. Marnie Sperry cried with me, and Don (Severa) whispered in my ear, trying to cheer me up, 'They can knock us down, Sheila, but they can't eat us.' It was very difficult."

On a lighter note, Varian also recalled: "The most fun etched in my memory—probably because Bay-Abi and I did it together for a lot of years—was the daily teasing ritual we had. Our ranch is up and down (hilly) and quite spread out, so I've never walked if there was a horse to

Sheila, a multi-talented trainer and rider, showed the Bay-Abi son, Mikado, to the 1971 U.S. National Park Horse Championship.

Photo by Johnny Johnston

ride. Consequently, for most of Bay-Abi's life, I teased the mares for breeding on him bareback, out in the pastures," she told writer Linda White in a 1989 *Arabian Horse Times* article.

"We raced from pasture to pasture, sliding into the gates. Bay would give me so many seconds to bend over and get the latch unhooked. He would side-pass through, slip around the end of the gate and side-pass back for me to close it, faster than you could say, 'Boo!' Then, as soon as I had the gate closed, off we would dash again. When we got to the mares (who were used to this daily occurrence of a bay express train with flying mane and tail with a girl on his back singing at the top of her lungs, racing up to them), Bay-Abi would be all business, walking through the mares, determining who was in heat, coming in, or going out. When we would

finish one group, we would whiz off to the next pasture, often with funny crow-hops thrown in for good measure."

Today, Varian has only to gaze out over her pastures or scan the pages of popular breed journals to see the boundless beauty resulting from her labor—years of joys and sorrows, dreams and memories woven into equine masterpieces that preen and prance across four continents.

And, if one looks close enough, one can almost see Bay-Abi's puckish spirit dancing close behind—ears pricked, gay tail over his back, and mischief twinkling in his eyes.

BAY EL BEY

He is perhaps the Arabian breed's finest sire of breeding stallions.

WELL-KNOWN in Arabian horse circles as "The Kingmaker," Bay El Bey earned the title through both demeanor and deed.

By nature, he was more regal, refined, and elegant than his puckish sire, Bay-Abi.

As his breeder and lifelong owner Sheila Varian explained, he had a more serious spirit that was, at the same time, thoughtful, gentle, generous, and "quite endearing."

His show ring accomplishments were

The regal Bay El Bey won the Canadian National Champion Stallion title and twice garnered the U.S. Reserve National Champion Stallion award.

Photo by Judith

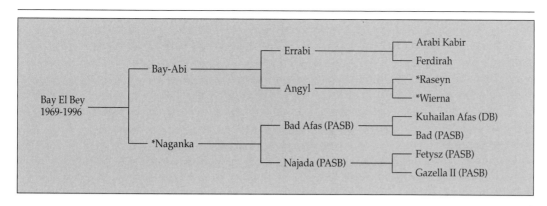

```
                                        ┌─── Arabi Kabir
                         ┌─── Errabi ───┤
                         │              └─── Ferdirah
         ┌─── Bay-Abi ───┤
         │               │              ┌─── *Raseyn
         │               └─── Angyl ────┤
Bay El Bey               │              └─── *Wierna
1969-1996 ───┤
         │                              ┌─── Kuhailan Afas (DB)
         │               ┌─ Bad Afas (PASB) ┤
         │               │              └─── Bad (PASB)
         └─── *Naganka ──┤
                         │              ┌─── Fetysz (PASB)
                         └─ Najada (PASB) ─┤
                                        └─── Gazella II (PASB)
```

impressive, by any measure, and those of his descendants were and are absolutely amazing. However, Bay El Bey's influence extended well beyond the immediacy of the show ring. Few stallions, while kings themselves, sire other kings as good or better than themselves, time after time, foal after foal. Bay El Bey did just that, and, over the years, quietly and confidently became perhaps the Arabian breed's finest sire of breeding stallions.

"My mind knew the bay horse I was looking for," said Varian as she reminisced about her life and horses during one of the open house presentations she regularly hosts at her Arroyo Grande, Calif., ranch.

"He would be taller than his sire, Bay-Abi, longer in the neck, stretchier, but with Bay-Abi's smoothness and spirit and the strength to breed on. On April 25, 1969, 3 days later than the birthdate of both his sire and dam, Bay El Bey gave his first nicker and I had my dream horse."

Dream horse or no, Varian soon found herself engulfed in the pain and stress of dealing with her beloved mother's terminal illness. Daily horse chores were done mechanically, and Varian spent only limited time with her equine friends. So, when Gene Turner of Sagamore Park Arabians called about possibly buying a Bay-Abi son, Varian told him about Bay El Bey, then 2 years old. "It was winter, the horses were all shaggy, and I was feeding

Halter and Performance Record: 1977 Canadian National Champion Stallion; 1974, 1976 U.S. Reserve National Champion Stallion; Region II English Pleasure Champion; 1976, 1977 Scottsdale Reserve English Pleasure Champion; Legion of Merit Award winner.

Progeny Record:

Purebred Foal Crops: 17
Purebred Foals Registered: 441
U.S./Canadian National Winners: 34
Class A Champions: 96
IAHA Legion of Honor Award Winners: 13
IAHA Legion of Supreme Honor Award Winners: 5
IAHA Legion of Merit Award Winners: 3
IAHA Legion of Supreme Merit Award Winners: 1
Race Starters: 5
Race Money Earned: $105,707

them, but I hadn't even really looked at them in months," she admitted. "I was in somewhat of a fog during that time."

Turner and his farm manager, Victor Kerr, came to look, did indeed like what they saw, and quickly struck a deal for Bay El Bey's purchase. Varian was to deliver him, sound, to Arizona's big Scottsdale show in February.

As fate would have it, just a few days before the show, Bay El Bey punctured

215

his tendon sheath and came up lame. Varian recalled that she and her veterinarian did all they could to speed the healing process. "I really tried, but in my heart I kept thinking that if he stayed lame, it was meant to be that Bay El Bey stay here," said Varian. "It was obvious to me, finally, that he was an exceptional colt. I began to realize that I wanted to keep this horse in my life."

Travel day arrived, but a veterinarian check that morning brought the firm pronouncement, "Not sound." The colt wasn't going anywhere. Varian went on to Scottsdale with her other horses and gave Turner his check back. Within a week, Bay El Bey was perfectly sound. "And so," Varian stated firmly, "that was the first and the only time Bay El Bey was ever for sale."

As Varian explained: "When I looked at Bay El Bey, I saw how all the parts fit together, how every muscle layer was defined. . . . So, it came down to three things: the physical look, the personality, and the ability to perform as an athlete. When I looked at Bay El Bey, I saw the picture I had in my head so many years ago."

So many years ago began with Varian's vision of the perfect Arabian, gleaned, she surmises, from Walter Farley's *Black Stallion* books and her personal fascination

In addition to his eight national halter titles, Bay El Bey was a superb English pleasure horse, here with Sheila Varian up, early in his career.

Photo by Jerry Sparagowski

with the wonderful old California spade-bit horses. Her first purebred Arabian was the mare Farlotta, and her first Arabians of note were the mare Ronteza, who, in 1961, was the first Arabian ever to win the tough reined cow horse championship at the Cow Palace, and the popular U.S. National Champion Stallion Bay-Abi, who was Bay El Bey's sire.

Bay El Bey's dam, *Naganka, was one of three mares the Varian family imported from Poland in 1961. A lovely flea-bitten gray, by Bad Afas and out of Najada, by Fetysz, *Naganka also produced Bay El Bey's talented full brother, Mikado, a U.S. National Park Champion and the sire of national performance champions in English pleasure and park. A grand total

of four of *Naganka's offspring were Legion of Merit winners, and three won national titles.

As Varian likes to say, however, "If *Naganka's dam, Najada, hadn't refused to go to Russia, I wouldn't have had Bay El Bey or any of his wonderful offspring." Nor would the world.

The story of Najada begins in the fall of 1939, when the area around the Janow Podlaski stud farm in Poland became a battleground as Nazi and Russian forces

One of Bay El Bey's best sons, Barbary, out of Balalinka.

Photo by Judith Wagner

"To Bey El Bay, I wasn't there; it was just he and the boy."

clashed early in World War II. As the Russian troops pulled back, they took with them 180 of Janow's best Arabian horses. One mare, however, fought the soldier attempting to put on her halter and seriously injured him. That mare, Najada, was left behind.

"She became a national heroine in Poland," said Varian, with a soft chuckle, "and the story grew until she got credit for killing off several Russian soldiers." But when the breeding program was re-established in Poland after the war, there was Najada. At age 19, she was bred to Bad

Afas at the Nowy Dwor Stud (while Janow was being rebuilt) and in 1960 she produced *Naganka, Bay El Bey's dam.

Varian knew from the start that Bay El Bey was special, and bred him as a 2-year-old to a few mares in an effort to determine his potential as a sire. At age 5 he was leased to Lasma Arabians in exchange for Varian's use of the *Bask son Hask. Again, at age 15, Bey El Bey was leased for 1 year to Rohara Arabians in Florida, but he was always owned by Varian and lived most of his life on her ranch.

For roughly the first decade of his life, Bay El Bey managed to combine a busy breeding schedule with a career as an English pleasure and halter horse. Upright and powerful, truly magnificent to behold, he garnered eight national halter titles, including 1977 Canadian National Champion Stallion, and 1974 and 1976 U.S. Reserve National Champion Stallion. Under saddle, he was a Region II English Pleasure Champion, the Scottsdale Reserve English Pleasure Champion in 1976 and 1977, and was awarded his Legion of Merit (++) in 1976.

The Blind Man

One of Bay El Bey's gifts was his ability always to balance his electric show ring presence with a certain gentle good sense. Of all the hours Varian spent in the show ring with him, one moment stands out as if bathed in heaven's own golden light.

The year Bay El Bey was named 1974 U.S. National Reserve Champion Stallion, show officials invited the audience into the ring to see the champions and all the Top Ten stallions up close. Hundreds of people were milling about, stallions were fussing and snorting, and it was very noisy.

Said Varian, "Bay El Bey was standing with his head way up and showing beautifully when—and I'll never forget this—a young man came up and asked to touch my horse. I looked at the man, and he had the most beautiful face, so sensitive and distinctive. Extraordinary, really. I said, 'Certainly,' and he reached out his hands. When his fingers met Bay El Bey's face, Bay dropped his head and just froze. Right then I realized the boy was blind.

"He felt the horse's face completely, moving his fingers around and into his ears, mouth, and nostrils and over his eyes. This went on for 3 or 4 minutes and Bay El Bey never moved, he seemed not even to breathe, and his eyes became like limpid pools. He knew. To Bay El Bey, I wasn't there; it was just he and the boy. All the people standing round—probably about a hundred or so—were totally hushed. We were transfixed, mesmerized by this almost sacred moment.

"Then, the young man thanked us

Bey Shah, a leading sire of U.S. and Canadian National halter winners. He was by Bay El Bey and out of Star of Ofir.

Photo by Jerry Sparagowski

profusely and stepped away. Just that fast, Bay El Bey became electric again and went back to his show stance. Even now," Varian added, "so many years later, someone will occasionally tell me, 'I was there when the blind boy touched Bay El Bey, and I'll never ever forget it.' It was eerie and magical and wonderful."

Bay El Bey's record as a sire is exceptional. Of his 441 registered foals, 96 are champions. On a national level, as this is written, 34 offspring have won more than 90 national titles in every division offered: halter, park, driving, English and western pleasure, native costume, trail, and stock horse classes. (As an aside, Varian claims that Bay El Bey had one of the best sliding stops she's ever experienced. She chose not to train him as a western horse mainly because Arabian breeding stallions of the day were expected to be English performance horses.)

Many Bay El Bey offspring combined a halter title with one in performance. Of the above 34, 24 have been sons (10 geldings and 14 stallions), and 10 are daughters. Although Bay El Bey was a good sire overall, he had more high quality male offspring than he did female.

Found among those exceptional sons are such national winners as Moonstone Bey V (x Moska), Chez El Bey (x Night Wind), Dubonnet (x Ray Dor Girada), El Bey Moon (x Pico Moon), Shamsilah (x Tashana), El Rio Bey (x *Edessa), Bey Contender (x Virginia Reel), and Woodwind V (x Halali Windkite)—to list only some.

The Greatest Sons

The greatest of Bay El Bey's sons, however, formed the famous triumvirate: Barbary, Bey Shah, and Huckleberry Bey. Each, as an individual, had a tremendous presence, enjoyed a stellar show career, and found incomparable success as a sire. Each has sired at least 50 national winners apiece, and more than 650 champions all together. To sire even one such son would be a grand accomplishment; to produce three is absolutely remarkable.

"Barbary, out of the *Bask daughter Balalinka, was foaled in 1973. He was the prettiest, cockiest colt anyone had ever seen. That year, the rest of the colts didn't have a chance," recalled Varian. "In fact, the first time he came out of the barn where he was born, he trotted off like a mature, finished, bridled horse competing at the national championship level, except that he was only a day and a half old and had no rider. He didn't need a rider." Barbary continued to trot "big and square" throughout his life.

Balalinka is unique in that she is the only daughter of the great *Bask crossed on his own five-sixteenths "sister" *Bachantka. Balalinka produced seven champions and four regional and/or national winners.

Barbary was sold as a yearling to well-known film director and producer Mike Nichols. Trainer Don DeLongpre soon became a partner with Nichols on the young colt, and, although Barbary was fully syndicated in 1982, DeLongpre remained his manager and trainer.

No stallion in the last 2 decades has won as many national titles in five divisions as has Barbary. They include: two Top Tens in halter; one Top Ten each in English pleasure, pleasure driving, formal driving, and park, and a reserve national championship in park; for a total of seven national titles. He is also an IAHA Legion of Supreme Merit winner, thus allowing him to carry three pluses after his name (Barbary+++).

Barbary's career as a sire is also impressive. Of his 130 purebred Arabian champions, 51 are national winners. In addition, he has sired 15 national champion partbred Arabians.

The second stallion of Bay El Bey's incredible trio is Bey Shah. During the late 1980s and for much of the 1990s, Bey Shah's offspring dominated halter competition in a way never before seen. For

No stallion in the last 2 decades has won as many titles in five divisions as has Barbary.

A 1985 photograph of Marigold V, with Sheila aboard. By Bay El Bey and out of Moska, Marigold V was successful in the show ring—and the first junior western pleasure champion at Scottsdale. She is now a leading producer of champions.

Photo by Rick Thorson

starters, he himself was named the U.S. Reserve National Champion Stallion in 1980. In 1987, he was the sire of both the U.S. National Champion Mare (Shahteyna) and U.S. National Champion Stallion (Fame VF)—at the time, the only living horse ever to accomplish this feat in the same year.

As of the late '90s, Bey Shah was the leading sire of U.S. and Canadian National halter winners. He sired well over 300 champions (Class A show or better). In addition, he was the Scottsdale show leading sire of halter winners every year from 1988 through 1995, with

the exception of 1991, when his own son, Fame VF, won that honor. Further, more than 40 Bey Shah offspring have gone on to sire or produce national winners—proof that the line remains strong.

That Bey Shah existed at all is serendipitous, to say the least, and a testimony to Bay El Bey's appeal. His breeders, Jenny and Lester Walton of Bend, Ore., in 1975 were hauling their *Bask daughter, Star of Ofir, to a different stallion when they took a wrong turn—or a right turn, depending on how you look at it. They stopped to ask for directions at Sheila Varian's ranch and, while there, took a look at Bay El Bey. So impressed were the Waltons that they decided immediately to breed their mare to Varian's stallion. Bey Shah was foaled in 1976.

For a few years, Bey Shah was owned by the Waltons in partnership with George Dexter and then solely by Dexter until 1990. The horse went through a couple of owners until finding a home with Dan and Maureen Grossman of Indiana. Bey Shah died Oct. 11, 1999.

The third, and perhaps best, member of the illustrious trio was the delightful Huckleberry Bey. As Varian recounted at one of her weekend gatherings, Huckleberry Bey was foaled the same year as Bey Shah—1976. "He was the third generation of the stallion line (but) he was different than the others; he fooled me. I didn't know until his seventh month what we had—but when that seventh month hit, we all knew a major star had been born."

His dam, the bay Taffona, had a pedigree as all-American as could be found. Through her sire, Raffon, she traced to Ferzon, Indraff, and *Raffles. Taffona's dam, Waneta, claimed ancestors such as *Mirage and the Polish mare *Azja IV.

Explained Varian: "From his dam line, Huckleberry Bey received a pedigree that carried beauty, and from his sire a wonderful neckset. . . . (He) was the loftiest, airiest, paper-thin-skinned stallion. . . . He looked like a horse from a Schreyer painting."

Huckleberry Bey had the athletic con-trol of a ballet dancer and the attitude of Mark Twain's famous character, Huck Finn (hence his name), according to Varian. In 1979, he was the U.S. Reserve National Champion Futurity Colt, was a U.S. Top Ten Stallion in 1981, and won the 1984 U.S. Reserve National English Pleasure Champion title, among others.

Huckleberry Bey was syndicated in 1983, but Varian remained his manager and best friend. In one year, 1988, four offspring won national championships. As of 1997, 85 sons and daughters had won more than 200 national Top Tens or better, and 214 offspring are Class A or better champions. One son, Hucklebey Berry, has been named (unanimously by the judging panel) the U.S. National English Pleasure Champion three times, an achievement still unduplicated. Huckleberry Bey has even sired a number of race winners.

The Fruitful Years

Varian happily recalled the many fruitful years spent with Bay El Bey, the horse who would not be sold. "Even during breeding season Bay El Bey was all business and took his job quite seriously. He moved quietly through the broodmare herd while our breeding manager, Angela Alvarez, held the leadline. We didn't ride him then, as I did Bay-Abi, but he was the perfect gentleman as he sorted out who was ready to be bred and who was not," offered Varian. "I have videotapes of the mares bounding down the hill to meet him, and allowing their babies to gather around close. Bay El Bey would thoughtfully tease the mares and gently sniff the babies.

"He would also let us know if something wasn't right with him, or if he was unhappy. Although he was a quiet horse, he would get much quieter. We learned to look for those clues, as he would always tell us how he was feeling. As he got older, for example, he let us know that he was no longer happy in the stallion barn. Maybe it was because he knew he wasn't the strongest anymore. So we moved him to

*One of the famous
Bay El Bey triumvi-
rate, Huckleberry
Bey, out of Taffona,
with Sheila Varian
up. This exceptional
stallion was named
after Mark Twain's
character, Huck Finn,
because of his plucky
personality.*

Photo by Rob Hess

another location, away from the other stallions, and he told us by his expression that
he was much happier there."

When Varian wanted to show Bay El
Bey to visitors, she simply opened his stall
door and asked him to step out. He did so
with a certain regal grace, stepping back
inside when Varian touched him with one
finger. "We communicated on a vibration
level," she explained.

Varian also credits Bay El Bey with
being a major reason why her ranch has
remained self-sufficient over the years.
"Along with Bay-Abi and Huckleberry
Bey, Bay El Bey 'built' the barns and kept
the ranch going."

One of Varian's favorite memories from
her 40 years of breeding good Arabian
horses also includes Bay El Bey. "I believe
Mike Nichols is an astute observer of

horses and really does his homework,"
she said. "One day he came to my ranch
and I got out Bay El Bey and stood him up
for Mike. He looked him over very carefully, and then he walked over and he
shook my hand and congratulated me.
That was a highlight, a really warm thrill.
It brought home to me what I had done.
Nobody had ever walked up to me and
congratulated me for breeding a good
horse. I felt like all the hard work and
lonely times were finally worth it."

The Kingmaker, Bay El Bey, died on
November 25, 1996, at age 27. He was
buried on the ranch where he was born.

21 BINT SAHARA

This gray mare was one of the all-time great producers in the breed.

HER NAME translates from the Arabic as "Daughter of the Desert," but Bint Sahara might just as well have been named "Daughter of the McCoys." The gray mare's relationship with Frank and Helen McCoy of Chino, Calif., was the base upon which the couple built a dynasty of championship-winning

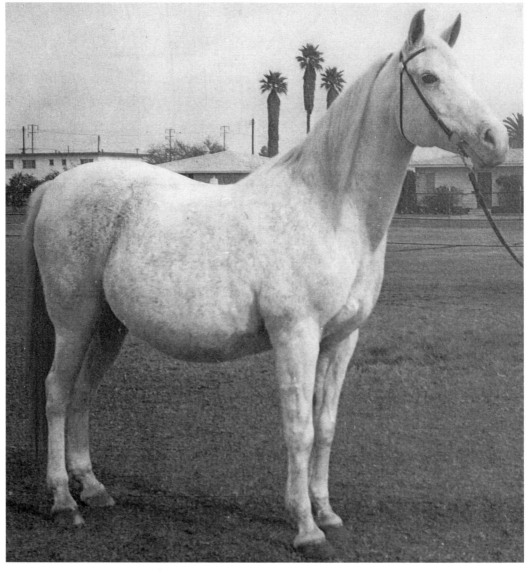

Bint Sahara, the **grande dame** *of American-born Arabian broodmares, and one of the few mares to establish a dynasty of her own.*

Photo courtesy of Helen McCoy

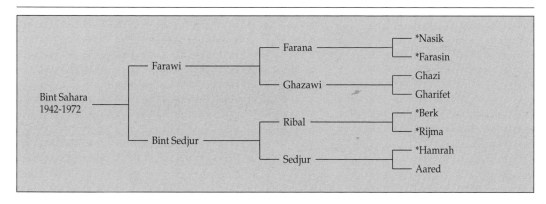

```
                                    ┌─────── Farana ──────┬─── *Nasik
                    ┌─── Farawi ────┤                     └─── *Farasin
                    │               │                     ┌─── Ghazi
  Bint Sahara ──────┤               └─────── Ghazawi ─────┤
  1942-1972         │                                     └─── Gharifet
                    │               ┌─────── Ribal ───────┬─── *Berk
                    └─── Bint Sedjur┤                     └─── *Rijma
                                    │                     ┌─── *Hamrah
                                    └─────── Sedjur ──────┤
                                                          └─── Aared
```

show horses—for themselves, and for several other major breeding programs in the United States.

Such sagas are usually about a stallion. After all, the male begets far more offspring and therefore has a more far-reaching effect than the female, who is limited to one foal per year for maybe 10 to 15 years.

Bint Sahara produced 11 champions from her 18 foals, and 9 of them sired or produced national champions themselves. Furthermore, she produced two horses in particular who went on to become superior in their own right.

Her son Fadjur, by Fadheilan, became the foundation stallion at the Jack Tone Ranch and won so much and sired so well that he has his own chapter in this book.

Her daughter Fersara, by Ferseyn, was one of the best show mares in California in her time and then went on to produce two outstanding offspring herself. They were the stallion Ferzon, by Ferneyn, who "made" the famous Gainey horses, and The Real McCoy, by Aarief, a halter and park champion who sired 21 national winners. Ferzon also has a chapter in this book.

Bint Sahara was foaled on May 21, 1942. Bred by John C. Silva of Cottonwood, Calif., she was mainly of Crabbet lineage, with some old Davenport blood thrown in for good measure.

Her sire, Farawi, was by the noted California stock horse Farana, who also sired the mares Faradina and Yatana. Both of the latter produced national winners. Bint Sahara's dam, Bint Sedjur, was by the *Berk son, Ribal, who was known as a good sire of high-action horses.

But Frank McCoy knew little of this in 1946 when he went looking for an Arabian horse. McCoy was an intelligent, amiable man who had gone West during the Great Depression and eventually made a little

Halter and Performance Record: 1st place mare class 1946 California All-Arabian Show.

Progeny Record:

Purebred Foal Crops: 18
Purebred Foals Registered: 18
U.S./Canadian National Winners: 3
Class A Champions: 11

Although this photo distorts Bint Sahara's very good conformation, it does show her classic head very well.

Photo courtesy of Helen McCoy

Helen and Frank McCoy with Bint Sahara just before her death in 1972 at age 30.

Photo by
Johnny Johnston

Everybody in the horse business thought Frank was crazy the first time he bred Bint Sahara to Ferseyn.

money in the real estate business.

By the mid-1940s, fewer than 4,000 Arabian horses had been bred and duly registered in the Arabian Horse Registry of America since its establishment in 1908. They were quite rare and rather expensive. Still, Frank was determined to have one.

At the recommendation of Mrs. O.H. Vicars, who owned Bint Sahara's sire, Farawi, Frank and his brother, both of whom had always been interested in horses, went to look at two of the stallion's daughters. They bought them.

As Frank recalled in the video *McCoys' Arabians*, produced by the Arabian Horse

Trust just a few years before his death in 1995 at the age of 100, "My brother took the one-eyed mare, Bint Sahara's 2-year-old full sister, Sedi Sedjur, for $500 and I took Bint Sahara for $2,000."

It is of interest to note that Sedi Sedjur went on to produce U.S. National Top Ten Mare Virginia Belle and Canadian Top Ten Mare Virginia Dare, both of whom also produced national winners themselves. This was an incredibly strong female line.

Bint Sahara was in foal to Nusik, by *Nasik and out of Nusara, when Frank McCoy purchased her as a 4-year-old. On the second of May, Bint Sahara had her first foal, a bay named El Shiek, later known as "Herman." The McCoys at that time were not in the breeding business, and had no plans to be, but they were delighted.

A few weeks later, Frank decided to take Bint Sahara and El Shiek to a horse show and chose the second all-Arabian horse show ever held in California, this one at Flintridge. Bint Sahara, with Frank holding the lead shank, won first in her mare class and El Shiek placed fourth in his class. "And that's what got me hooked," confessed Frank.

Herman, by the way, was gelded, and

Frank McCoy with Bint Sahara and five of her nine daughters. From left: Bint Sahara, Sahara Rose, Sahara Dawn, Sahara Queen, Sahara Star, and Sahara Lady. Photo by Johnny Johnston

then was shown successfully in performance classes for many years.

Also around foaling time, Frank went in search of a stallion to breed to Bint Sahara after she foaled. He drove up to Herbert H. Reese's ranch near Pomona and looked at three stallions.

"I fell in love with old Ferseyn (*Raseyn x *Ferda)," Frank said on the Trust videotape. "He came out prancin' with his head up and his tail high and I made up my mind right there. That was a show horse.

"Bint Sahara to Ferseyn. . . . Everybody in the horse business at that time thought I was crazy. People were just getting interested in Arabians and everybody wanted a chestnut with flaxen mane and tail."

But Frank wanted a gray. And what a gray he got! On April 24, 1947, the filly Fersara was born, and the entire Arabian breed in America took an exquisitely beautiful step forward.

For the rest of Bint Sahara's life, whenever Frank McCoy had the opportunity, he bred the mare to Ferseyn—a total of nine times. The exception was the period

We could not find photographs of Bint Sahara's sire and dam, but here is her paternal grandsire, Farana, with Mark Smith up. Farana, owned by the Kellogg Arabian ranch in Pomona, Calif., was renowned as an excellent stock horse in the 1930s.

Frank McCoy all set to ride in the Rose Bowl Parade on El Shiek (also known as Herman), Bint Sahara's first-born. A bay gelding by Nusik, Herman was a successful performance horse.

Photo courtesy of Arabian Horse Trust

W.K. Kellogg "Perpetual" Trophy. She then went on to become a broodmare of the same high caliber as her dam—but more on Fersara later.

As soon as the foal Fersara was weaned, Frank and Helen sold Bint Sahara, in foal to El Amir (Alla Amarward x Joontafa), to Harry Linden of Spokane, Washington.

"The reason I sold her," Frank said in the Trust video, "is that I didn't aim to go in the horse business or anything like that. And I had a foal, Fersara, so. . . . Then, after I'd sold her, I saw that I'd made a mistake."

While Bint Sahara was at Linden's she first had the El Amir son, a chestnut named Sahalla, who was gelded. Then she was bred four times to the bay stallion Fadheilan (*Fadl x *Kasztelanka), an Egyptian-Polish cross.

The first two offspring from that cross did not breed on. The filly Fadhara, foaled in 1949, soon died, and the colt Fadfara, foaled in 1950, was gelded.

The next two did much better, to say the least. Bint Fadhara, foaled in 1951, produced five champions, including two national winners. When crossed with her half-brother Royal Son (Ferseyn x Bint Sahara), who was foaled in 1953, she produced the Canadian National Champion Mare Joana. Joana later became the maternal grandam of the 1974 U.S. National Champion Mare, Jon-San Judizon.

Last, but certainly not least, was the "Fabulous Fadjur," as he came to be known, who was foaled in 1952. Fadjur was twice named U.S. Reserve National Champion Stallion and four times a Top Ten. He also sired 118 champions and 17 national winners.

Back to the McCoys

Just before Fadjur was foaled, the McCoys convinced Linden to allow them to lease back Bint Sahara. The two parties agreed to split her foals 50-50, while Linden retained ownership and the McCoys boarded the mare.

Also in early 1952, Bint Sahara's first daughter, Fersara, was heavily in foal. She had been bred to Ferneyn (Ferseyn x Moneyna). She was, of course, closely related to Ferneyn on both sides of the tree. Her own sire also was Ferseyn,

from 1948 through 1951, when the decision was not McCoy's and the mare was bred to Fadheilan.

Fersara was many times a champion mare at halter. She was one of the first winners of the Pacific Coast Championship (twice) and three times in a row was named the grand champion mare at the large Southern California All-Arabian Show, resulting in the retirement of the

228

Fersara, by Ferseyn and out of Bint Sahara, was foaled in 1947 and became almost as famous as her dam. Frank McCoy is holding her after she was named grand champion mare at the 1950 all-Arabian show in San Francisco.

Photo by Larry Kenney

Fersara with her 1952 colt, Ferzon (by Ferneyn), who was purchased by Daniel Gainey for $10,000, an unheard-of price in those days. But as a sire, he returned Gainey's investment many times over.

Photo by Engleman

229

Royal Son, a chestnut by Ferseyn and out of Bint Sahara, won his class as a 2-year-old at the 1955 Kellogg Spring Show. Mrs. H.H. Reese is presenting the trophy to Frank McCoy.

Photo courtesy of Arabian Horse Trust

Royal Storm, a full brother to Royal Son, was named reserve champion stallion at the 1961 Scottsdale show.

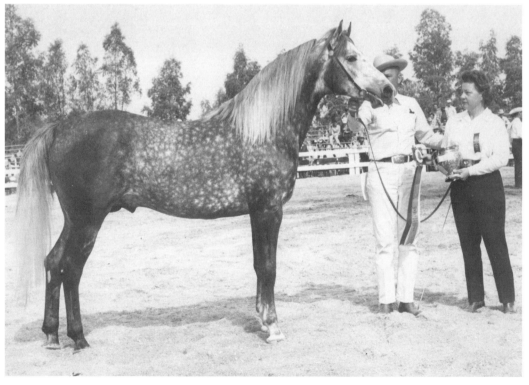

230

McCoy's Count was Bint Sahara's last foal, and was sired by her grandson, The Real McCoy. He was a park horse and halter champion, and a 1972 U.S. National Top Ten Stallion. This picture was taken in 1980 when he was 15 years old.

Photo by Polly Knoll

Fadjur would put the Tone family and their ranch on the map.

who was by *Raseyn, and Moneyna was also by *Raseyn.

Why did Frank choose this heavily in-bred match? "Ferneyn had a beautiful head and a beautiful tailset and a beautiful neck, but most people thought he was a little light in the body," he explained on the Trust tape. "And when I told around that I was going to breed Fersara to Ferneyn, a lot of people said, 'Oh! I wouldn't do that! He doesn't have body enough!'

"I said, 'It doesn't make any difference. My old mare will take care of the body. Put those two together and we'll have a body and a head and a tailset and a neck.' And it turned out I was right."

That spring of 1952, Bint Sahara and her daughter Fersara foaled at the McCoys' place just 46 days apart. Their two colts would grow up to change the face of the Arabian breed: Ferzon, from Fersara, on

February 26, and Fadjur, from Bint Sahara, on April 12.

Jackie Tone Polk and her husband, Paul, while on their honeymoon, just happened to stop to visit the McCoys. They took one look at Fadjur and bought him. He would put their family and their ranch on the map.

Daniel Gainey first saw Ferzon when he was a weanling. A few months later he sent his agent, Preston Dyer, to try to buy the colt. Frank didn't want to sell him, so he priced him extremely high: $10,000 (roughly equivalent to $100,000-plus in the 1990s), which was unheard-of for

The Real McCoy was sired by Aarief (who was by *Raffles) and was out of Fersara, Bint Sahara's famous daughter. Among the offspring of The Real McCoy were 17 sons and 27 daughters who each sired or produced 1 or more national winners.

In 1958, Bint Sahara began producing gray fillies— six in a row.

an unproven colt. Most colts then sold for around $500.

But Gainey paid the asking price, and Ferzon proved to be an excellent sire who, over the next 30 years, established the popular "Gainey look" in Arabians.

Fersara was bred four more times to Ferneyn. She produced the following:

1/ Bint Fersara, foaled in 1953, who was a western pleasure champion and who produced three champions, including national top ten winners in park and stock horse divisions.

2/ Sara Jean, foaled in 1954, also a performance and halter champion, who produced three champions.

3/ The stallion Sands, foaled in 1955, was a halter champion and sired a western pleasure champion. But he died after siring just one foal crop.

4/ The stallion Dunes, foaled in 1956, became a halter champion and also sired eight champions, two of which were national winners.

In 1958, the McCoys decided to breed Fersara to Aarief (*Raffles x Aarah), who was owned by Dr. Eugene LaCroix of Scottsdale. This mating was quite unusual by modern standards. As Helen McCoy recalled on the Trust videotape, "Between Frank and Gene they agreed to meet halfway, which was Indio (California). So, out there in the desert we parked our trailers, bred the mare, went to lunch, came back, and bred the mare again. Gene took the stud and we took the mare and went on home."

The result? Fersara's seventh foal, a lovely filly named Sara Lyn, who was foaled in 1959 and later produced four champions.

So, the next year, Frank and Dr. LaCroix repeated the breeding. This time the result was of history-making proportions. The Real McCoy, Fersara's last foal, was foaled on May 6, 1960. He would become both a champion and a sire of champions.

Originally called Silky Rief, The Real McCoy was given his special name, in part, because of the unexpected death of his dam, Fersara, at 13. Among The Real McCoy's offspring were 17 sons who sired 1 or more national winners and 27 daughters who produced 1 or more national winners.

Added Helen, addressing the uncommonly successful results of the two desert breedings, "I don't know whether we were stupid or just lucky."

Answered Frank, "Both!"

More Breedings to Ferseyn

In 1952, the McCoys again bred Bint Sahara to Ferseyn and would do so eight times in a row until Ferseyn's death. Here are the results of those breedings.

1/ Royal Son, a chestnut colt foaled in 1953. He would be her last foal of that color, as the next 10 would all be gray. Royal Son was a halter champion and a good sire, with 10 champions, including the national champion mare Joana, as mentioned earlier. Joana was out of Bint Fadara, Royal Son's half-sister.

2/ Royal Grey, a colt foaled in 1954, who became a halter champion and also sired a champion.

3/ Royal Turk, foaled in 1955, was a gelding who became a Scottsdale halter champion (when still a stallion) and a performance champion in four divisions: English pleasure, western pleasure, park, and formal driving.

4/ Royal Storm was a colt foaled in 1957 (Bint Sahara did not foal in 1956). Royal Storm was a halter and performance champion who sired 14 champions, 3 of whom were national winners. One was U.S. National Champion Futurity Colt and Legion of Merit winner Mister Storm. Royal Storm was the first of several significant McCoy-bred stallions used in the Ha Ja Hall Arabians breeding program in Michigan.

After Royal Grey was foaled, the McCoys asked to buy back Bint Sahara in full, trading half-ownership in Royal

The well-known Classy McCoy was many times a halter and western pleasure champion. He was sired by The Real McCoy and was out of the Bint Sahara daughter, Sahara Star.

Photo by Potter, courtesy of Arabian Horse Trust

Son for the privilege. Bint Sahara was now home to stay.

Beginning in 1958, Bint Sahara began producing gray fillies—six in a row—who, both individually and as a group, became well-known. The first four were by Ferseyn: Sahara Rose in 1958, Sahara Dawn in 1959, Sahara Queen in 1960, and Sahara Star in 1961.

By her grandson Dunes, Bint Sahara produced Sahara Sue in 1962; and by another grandson, The Real McCoy, she produced Sahara Lady.

"That's when we got all those daughters that we've used as our logo on our letterhead and that you've seen so many times in the magazines," said Helen.

Sahara Rose was a halter champion and produced five champions, three by The Real McCoy. Sahara Dawn also was a halter champion and then produced four cham-

Dunes (Ferneyn x Fersara) was a maternal grandson of Bint Sahara. Shown here at a 1959 California show, he was a halter champion who sired several champions and national winners.

Photo by John
H. Williamson

pions, all by The Real McCoy. Both Rose and Dawn produced national winners.

Sahara Queen was a terrific halter horse who won several top awards, including Pacific Coast Champion Mare and 1968 U.S. Top Ten Mare titles. She then produced three champions—one a national winner—all by The Real McCoy.

Sahara Star was a halter champion who produced two champion offspring, including the well-known stallion Classy McCoy,

by The Real McCoy. Classy was many times a U.S. and Canadian Top Ten halter and western pleasure champion.

Sahara Sue, the Bint Sahara daughter foaled in 1963 and sired by Bint Sahara's grandson Dunes, died of septicemia before being shown or bred.

Bint Sahara's last daughter, Sahara Lady, was by The Real McCoy and was not shown. But she did produce four champions, including the Canadian Top Ten Gelding and U.S. National Western Sidesaddle Top Ten winner Irish Mac and the Scottsdale Top Ten Mare Lady Sahara.

Bint Sahara was 23 years old when she produced her last foal, a colt foaled on July 5, 1965. Sired by The Real McCoy, the foal

Authenticity was a popular and well-known grandson of Bint Sahara, being by The Real McCoy and out of Bint Neyseyn. He's shown here performing a freestyle routine with owner Jack Teague at the Crabbet Symposium in Denver in 1983. For several years at the U.S. Nationals, Jack and Authenticity thrilled the crowds by carrying the American flag at high speed during the grand entry. Photo by Louise Serpa

was named McCoy's Count. This lovely gray stallion was both a park and halter champion and a 1972 U.S. National Top Ten Stallion. He sired national winners, including U.S. Reserve National Dressage Champions Bay Count and JD Counts Shadow, and the three-time U.S. National Top Ten Mare Cover Gal.

Frank McCoy had once claimed he was planning on a nice, quiet retirement. Instead he spent the last 40 years of his life breeding and showing beautiful Arabian horses and participating in many organizations and activities within the Arabian industry.

Frank and Helen were active in the Southern California Arabian Horse Association and Arabian Horse Trust and attended the annual Scottsdale Arabian Horse Show every year since its inception in 1954. And it all started with a little gray mare.

Said Helen, "She had 18 foals for us, 9 colts and 9 fillies. You couldn't help but love the old gal." Bint Sahara lived with the McCoys until her death in 1972 at the grand old age of 30.

235

22 FERZON

His remarkable legacy has bred on for generations.

AS MUCH AS this story is about a horse, it is also about a man—a brilliant, passionate, outspoken man with tremendous drive and extraordinary vision, a man who bred incredibly beautiful horses and changed both the breed and its breeders.

This is the story of Daniel C. Gainey and his Gainey Arabians, whose standard-bearers included a collection of absolutely exquisite mares and an exceptional white stallion produced from the improbable mating of a half-brother to a half-sister. His name was Ferzon.

The tale really begins, however, 12 years before Ferzon was foaled. On August 23, 1940, in a little office in Owatonna, Minn., Daniel C. Gainey had gathered together the small sales force of the company he founded: Josten's. (It would grow to become the nation's largest manufacturer of class rings and other school items.)

His 15-year-old son, Daniel J. Gainey,

This profile photograph of Ferzon was taken in 1975 when he was 23 years old.

Photo by Jerry Sparagowski

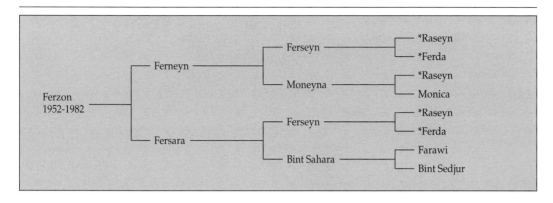

					*Raseyn
		Ferseyn			*Ferda
	Ferneyn				
		Moneyna			*Raseyn
Ferzon					Monica
1952-1982					
		Ferseyn			*Raseyn
	Fersara				*Ferda
		Bint Sahara			Farawi
					Bint Sedjur

was there on that hot summer day to sell cold soda pop to the employees. The younger Gainey recounted what happened next in an interview given for the Arabian Horse Trust's *Gainey Arabians* historical video, its script written by this author.

"My Dad had given his traditional *bon voyage* speech to the salesmen, and the group gave him a great hand because he was, indeed, a fabulous speaker. (Then) the oldest salesman got up and started reading this citation, and the sales force gave Dad a little Arabian stud colt by the name of Kaniht," said Daniel J.

Daniel C. had kept a few Saddlebred horses around just for fun, but, with this gift, he would become deeply enamored of Arabian horses—and never look back.

Within days, Albert W. Harris, the Arabian Horse Registry's president and the colt's breeder, contacted the elder Gainey. "They became lifelong friends," Daniel J. continued, "and Harris ultimately arranged for my dad to get on the Arabian Horse Registry board, and, subsequently, Dad replaced him as its president." Gainey held that post from 1958 until 1972.

When Daniel C. Gainey believed in something, he pursued it with an uncommon zeal. Never one to settle for mediocrity, he demanded the best in himself and in his horses.

"I don't think he actually started out intending to become such an influential factor in the Arabian business," mused Daniel J. "He raised good horses. And he

Halter and Performance Record: Halter Champion.

Progeny Record:
Purebred Foal Crops: 25
Purebred Foals Registered: 227
U.S./Canadian National Winners: 23
Class A Champions: 81
IAHA Legion of Honor Award Winners: 4
IAHA Legion of Supreme Honor Award Winners: 2
IAHA Legion of Merit Award Winners: 12
IAHA Legion of Supreme Honor/Merit Award Winners: 1
IAHA Legion of Supreme Merit Award Winners: 2

acquired good horses. He reveled in his successes. . . . I think he was a man who just loved his horses."

Gainey's first Arabian of note was the mare Rageyma, a *Mirage daughter bred and owned by Roger Selby. But it took a near-death experience to get her.

In 1942, Gainey was in a hospital bed critically ill with pneumonia. Later he told friends that while he lay there, he decided to buy Rageyma—if he survived. The minute the oxygen tent was removed, Gainey telephoned Jimmy Dean, Selby's farm manager (see the *Raffles chapter),

Ferneyn, the sire of Ferzon, winning a halter class at a California show in the 1950s, with Frank McCoy showing him.

Photo courtesy Arabian Horse Trust

Ferzon with his longtime owner and biggest fan, Daniel C. Gainey.

Photo by Johnny Johnston

and claimed the mare. He mailed a check out that same afternoon.

With the purchase of Rageyma, good fortune hopped into the saddle with Gainey and rode there for the next 30 years, as he bred scores of Arabian champions and champion producers.

Rageyma soon foaled Gajala (by *Raffles), who in turn produced 10 champions and became one of the two most valuable female taproots of the magnificent Gainey Arabian family tree. (The other was Bride Rose, by Ronek and out of *Rose of France, who was the grandam of Gay Rose, who produced four national winners, including Galizon.)

Rageyma also produced the champions Galimar and Skorage, both by Gaysar. Gaysar was by Rifage, a *Mirage son, and was out of Ralouma, by *Raseyn. Gainey sold Skorage to Ed Tweed and kept Galimar for himself.

When Galimar was bred to the aforementioned Bride Rose, they produced Gali-Rose, a filly so lovely that Gainey ordered her image made into a *bas relief* medallion. Copies were given to friends and many Arabian horse enthusiasts today treasure these rare mementos.

As lovely as Gali-Rose and his other mares were, Gainey still thought he could do better. By the early 1950s, he knew exactly how he envisioned the perfect

A 1952 photo of Ferzon and his dam, Fersara, romping in a pasture at McCoy's Arabians in California.

Photo courtesy Arabian Horse Trust

Ferzon winning a halter class as a yearling, one of the few times he was shown. Breeder Frank McCoy is at the halter.

Photo by Williamson, courtesy Arabian Horse Trust

Ferzon as a 3-year-old at Gainey's Minnesota farm in 1955.

At age 28, Ferzon still looked and felt terrific.

Photo by Jerry Sparagowski

Arabian to be. In order to achieve that goal, he knew he needed an extraordinary stallion, one both genetically powerful and physically impressive. Gainey found such a sire in Ferzon.

"He heard from some people on the West Coast about a young colt that Frank McCoy had bred (see Bint Sahara's chapter), and so he flew out to take a look," recalled Daniel J. "I happened to be going to Cal-Tech at the time and so he called and asked me if I would like to go along with him to see this colt. We got to Frank's and they very proudly showed us this stud colt by the name of Ferzon, and Frank quite unabashedly put a $10,000 price on the youngster."

This was tremendously high for a weanling in 1952, and, although he knew Ferzon was the stallion he needed, Gainey went home empty-handed. In November 1953, Gainey sent Preston Dyer to examine the colt. Dyer called Gainey and encouraged him to buy the gray yearling. The price was still $10,000.

Daniel C. Gainey sighed and wrote the check. He never regretted it.

"My Dad loved Ferzon probably more than any horse he ever had," said Daniel J. "He loved to go in the stall with him and nuzzle with him—it was a real love affair."

Ferzon's dam, Fersara, was one of the best mares of her generation. She was by the stallion Ferseyn (*Raseyn x *Ferda) and out of the wonderful old mare Bint Sahara. Fersara was twice the Pacific Coast Champion Mare and three times grand champion mare at the Southern California All-Arabian Show, retiring the W.K. Kellogg "Perpetual" Trophy.

In 1951, Frank McCoy, her breeder, owner, and trainer, decided to cross her with Ferneyn. That would result in a highly inbred foal, as Ferneyn's sire was also Ferseyn, who was by *Raseyn. Ferneyn's dam, Moneyna, was also sired by *Raseyn.

Although his friends were skeptical, Frank McCoy believed the cross would work wonderfully. He was convinced Ferneyn's pretty head, neck, and tail carriage

When Ferzon matured he had exquisite beauty. He passed on his short, finely chiseled face, large eyes, and shapely ears to many of his sons and daughters. Photo by Polly Knoll

and Fersara's excellent body conformation and legs would combine to create a truly superior individual. McCoy was right.

On February 26, 1952, Ferzon was foaled at McCoy's Arabians near Chino, California. McCoy showed the yearling to one reserve championship (against a large group of aged stallions) and one other halter champion-

At his 30th birthday party, Ferzon checks out his cake with his breeders Frank McCoy (left) and Helen McCoy (far right), and Robin Gainey, wife of Daniel J. Gainey.

Photo by Polly Knoll

Ferzon was still classically handsome at age 30. He's shown here with Robin Gainey at his big 30th birthday bash.   Photo by Polly Knoll

ship. He was never shown again as, for some reason, Gainey chose not to do so. Perhaps he just didn't need to.

Offspring

Ferzon proved to be the key to the embodiment of Gainey's vision. In all, he sired 24 national winners and 81 show champions. Even more importantly, his remarkable legacy bred on for generations—and continues to have an impact in the pedigrees of many of the best horses of the 1990s.

Gainey immediately started Ferzon's career as a breeding stallion. At the tender age of 2 he was bred to four mares. From one of them, the Indraff daughter Scheraff, Ferzon sired Gazon. He is best known as the sire of Raffon, the 1965 U.S. National Champion Stallion and 1973 U.S. National English Pleasure Champion. From another, Gadina (Fay-El-Dine, by *Fadl, and out of Gajala), Ferzon sired Guzon, a 1965 U.S. Top Ten Stallion.

Beginning in 1955, Ferzon was crossed several times with Gajala (*Raffles x Rageyma), and a small, but significant, dynasty was born. Among its exclusive members were 1962 U.S. Top Ten Stallion Gaizon and his famous

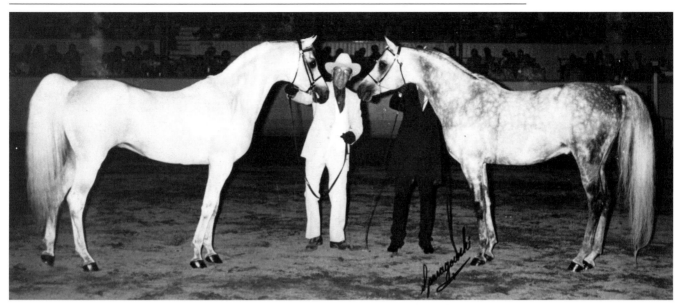

Ferzon stands in center ring at the Canadian Nationals with his son Gai-Parada, who won three national champion-ships during his show career. One was the 1977 U.S. National Champion Stallion title. Frank McCoy is holding Ferzon.

Photo by Jerry Sparagowski

"Four Sisters:" Gavrelle, Ga-Rageyma, Gafferra, and Ga-Gajala.

Gavrelle was a show champion known for her beautiful head and was the dam of 1974 U.S. National Champion Stallion Gai Adventure.

Ga-Rageyma was the best known of the quartet, as she was a 1962 U.S. Top Ten Mare and then the 1970 Canadian National Champion Mare at age 12, as well as being an excellent broodmare.

Gafferra was a good producer and for years was Gainey's favorite riding mare.

The fourth sister, Ga-Gajala, produced three national winners:

• 1975 Canadian National Champion Stallion, Gai Champion (by Gay Rouge).

• 1978 Canadian Top Ten Gelding and Top Ten English Pleasure winner, Gai Supreme (also by Gay Rouge).

• 1976 Canadian English Pleasure Top Ten winner, Gai Ibn Warsaw (by Gai Warsaw).

But the most exciting cross of all was discovered when Mrs. Garth Buchanan, an Arabian horse breeder from Iowa, bred her Azraff daughter, Rafeymaz, to Ferzon three times in a row. (Azraff was by *Raffles and out of *Azja IV, by Landsknecht. Rafeymaz was out of Rafeyma, by *Raffles). That cross produced the lovely gray mares Comar Raferzona in 1964, Comar Ferzona in 1965, and Comar Feymazona in 1966.

Gainey, in turn, bred the Ferzon daughter Ga-Rageyma (another *Raffles grand-daughter) to Azraff. Since then, the "Golden Azraff-Ferzon Cross" has been used in every conceivable way for several generations. It has proven to be magic.

For example, when the Ferzon daughter Gay Rose was bred to Azraff, she produced three foals. One was Galizon, the 1969 U.S. National Champion Stallion. Another was Gay Rouge, twice Canadian National Top Ten Stallion and Canadian

The "Golden Azraff-Ferzon Cross" has been used in every conceivable way for several generations. It has proven to be magic.

The Ferzon son Gazon (out of Scheraff) was a wonderful sire of top broodmares, and also the sire of the national winner Raffon. This photo was taken in 1969. During the last few years of his life, Gazon was completely blind.

Photo by Polly Knoll

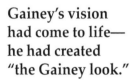

Gainey's vision had come to life—he had created "the Gainey look."

National English Pleasure Top Ten winner. And the third was Gai Gay Rose, twice a U.S. National Top Ten Mare.

Some of the other champions from the Azraff-Ferzon cross include: Gai Apache, 1971 U.S. Pleasure Driving Top Ten winner; and champions Gajala Beauty, Comar Azraffzon, and Azraff Tu. Also from this cross came Gai-Louise, dam of Canadian National Reserve Champion Mare Gai Ballerina.

The Gainey Look

The next step was to breed mares by Azraff and out of Ferzon daughters back to Ferzon. Although criticized by some, Gainey believed in his beloved stallion

and believed it would work. Results soon hushed the critics. Gainey's vision had come to life—he had created "the Gainey look."

Horses who possessed "the look" came to be known for their large eyes, extremely dished faces with wide foreheads, tiny muzzles, and tippy little ears. Their necks were nicely arched, and they had short backs and thick tails carried high even at the walk. They were most often gray, but there were a number of bays too. Sometimes smaller than what is currently popular, they nevertheless made excellent saddle horses, with athletic prowess and quiet, sweet dispositions.

While Gainey's main objective with Arabian horses certainly remained the creation and/or maintenance of ethereal beauty, he never forgot what a horse is really for. He spent hours riding himself, and insisted that all of his Arabians be trained to ride.

As time went on, Gainey began using outcross stallions on his little mares, with

Raffon was a popular and famous son of Gazon and grandson of Ferzon. Out of Vadraff, by Indraff, Raffon was the 1965 U.S. National Champion Stallion and 1973 U.S. National English Pleasure Champion. This photo was taken in 1965.

Photo by Polly Knoll

A 1972 photograph of Gallant Forever and her dam, Gai-Ga-Rageyma, both excellent examples of the class and quality of the Gainey breeding program. Gallant Forever was by Gay Rouge, who was by Azraff (by *Raffles) and out of the Ferzon daughter Gay-Rose—the "golden cross." Gai-Ga-Rageyma was by *Naborr and out of Ga-Rageyma, who was by Ferzon and out of Gajala, a *Raffles daughter.

Photo by Polly Knoll

Gallant Fashion, a typey son of Ferzon and Ala-Arabi Tirzah. Circa 1974.

excellent results. The Crabbet (English) stallions *Nizzam and *Royal Diamond added a better trot and more size, as evidenced by twice Canadian Top Ten Gelding Ganam, U.S. National Hunter Champion GE Sullivan, and multiregional halter and performance winner Gai Rainbow.

The LaCroix family's famous *Bask, when bred to a Gainey mare, sired Gali-Croix who, in turn, produced three champions. One was Gai Marquis, a multiregional performance winner and sire of a national winner.

The breeding of the Polish-Russian *Naborr to Ferzon daughters produced U.S. National Champion Stallion Gai Adventure (already mentioned) and halter and western pleasure champion Gai Ga-Rageyma. The latter was a terrific producer and the grandam of BF Cimmeron, a U.S. National Champion Futurity Colt.

Gainey's highly successful formula through the years followed roughly a 25/75 ratio: 25 percent outcross and 75 percent Gainey blood.

Daniel J. Takes Over

As he grew older, Gainey knew someone had to continue his work, and he looked to his son to do it.

"I think a lot of people viewed Dad as a dynamic, strong-willed autocrat," said Daniel J. "But he was more than that. He had an excellent mind. A very high energy level. He had a strength of personality that could take over an entire room or audience. He had a great sense of humor, and while he was tough-minded, he was also compassionate.

"He was a giant. And a hard act to follow."

But follow, he did. With Daniel J. Gainey at the helm, at one time the Gaineys had farms in Owatonna, Scottsdale, and Santa Ynez. Now after 60 years in the Arabian horse breeding business, Gainey Fountainhead Arabians is based exclusively in Santa Ynez, California.

Further, as Ferzon was for Daniel C. Gainey,

so was Gai Parada—Ferzon's greatest son—for Gainey's son, Daniel J. Gainey. This tremendous gray son of the Azraff daughter Azleta (who was owned by Jimmie Dean) enabled the whole operation to move forward in a grand, dynamic way.

Gai Parada became a Legion of Supreme Merit (+++) Award winner, a U.S. and Canadian National Pleasure Driving Champion in 1974, and the U.S. National Champion Stallion in 1977. He is, by far, the best example of the pure gold in the Ferzon-Azraff cross.

"One of the biggest thrills that I've had during my time in the Arabian horse business came when I decided that we were going to campaign Gai Parada to his national halter championship—and indeed we did," offered Daniel J. "That was a total thrill for me. Almost as thrilling as that was to bring him back home and ride him on the trails of our ranch and, once in a while, chase a few cows, and thoroughly get to know this great horse."

Gai Parada sired many champions, including 20 national winners. Among them: Gai Fawn, Gai Brial, Gaimoniet, Gali Cassandra, Gai Tapada, Gai Madera, A-Gin Gemfire, Gai Odyssey, Gai Seance, Gai Argosy, Phonda, Gai Monarch, and Gai Radiant.

Daniel J. Gainey took over the breeding operation from his father in 1976. The elder Gainey died in 1979, after nearly 40 years of service to the Arabian horse and the Arabian horse community—both here and abroad.

That same year, in March, Ferzon's last foal was born. In 1982, a grand 30th birthday bash was held in Ferzon's honor at the Gaineys' Scottsdale ranch. Looking elegant and fit, Ferzon ran free in a paddock for a most appreciative crowd.

The venerable white stallion died on July 19, 1982. He is buried in California on the Gainey ranch.

Over the years, many breeders looked to Daniel C. Gainey and to his horses for help in their endeavors. Often they were met with understanding and good advice— and, in turn, achieved their own success.

Gai-Parada (out of Azleta, by Azraff), was Ferzon's greatest and winningest son. He also became a tremendous sire and continued the Gainey dynasty. **Photo by Polly Knoll**

Perhaps this often-quoted statement from Mr. Gainey best sums up his life—and that of Ferzon and his other wonderful horses:

"I have always tried to build, as nearly as possible, what I think is the ideal Arabian. I have not rushed to accept fads. I have not hurried. In business, I counted the time by decades. In breeding elegant Arabians, for today and forever, a little longer is necessary."

FADJUR

He was one of the most popular stallions of his era.

Fadjur at age 23 winning the stallion championship at the Santa Barbara All-Arabian Horse Show in May 1975, shown by Paul Polk. Here, he is the epitome of Arabian horse type and demeanor. Note especially the dished face, arched neck, and tail carriage.

Photo by Foucher

THEY CALLED him the "Fabulous Fadjur"—and still do. Indeed, the "F" section of the dictionary is stuffed with adjectives frequently applied to the fiery bay stallion: fabled, fantastic, famous, fair, fancy, fortunate, fun, and so on.

But perhaps the one word best suited to this multiple champion show horse and exceptional sire is "family"—in particular, the Jack "Bud" and Marjory Tone family of Stockton, California.

(Their Jack Tone Ranch—named after Jack's grandfather—is a California histori-

cal landmark, as it is the oldest, continuously operated, family-owned horse farm in the state. In 1999, the ranch celebrates its 150th anniversary.)

"The first time I saw Fadjur," Marge said, "we had gone to the McCoys' to visit. There were a lot of horses around, beautifully groomed to be shown, and he was out in a nearby pasture with little Ferzon; both of those babies were bouncing all around.

"Every time Frank and Helen McCoy would try to show us a horse, Fadjur

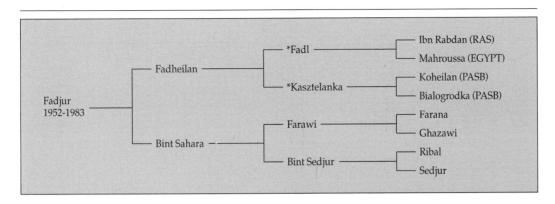

			*Fadl	Ibn Rabdan (RAS)
				Mahroussa (EGYPT)
	Fadheilan		*Kasztelanka	Koheilan (PASB)
				Bialogrodka (PASB)
Fadjur 1952-1983			Farawi	Farana
				Ghazawi
	Bint Sahara		Bint Sedjur	Ribal
				Sedjur

would show off and strut around and pose as if to say he was the best and we should all be looking at him! He was just a pot-bellied, fuzzy little darling, but he acted like he knew he was the best horse on the ranch. The king! I knew then that I had to have him. He was just what we were looking for." The price was $600—a bargain now, but a fortune to Jack. He finally agreed to buy him as a birthday gift for Marge.

The McCoys' California pasture was probably one of the most fruitful little fields in North American Arabian horse breeding history. The two broodmares there, Fersara and her mother, Bint Sahara, were wonderful show horses and incredible broodmares. Fadjur's little buddy, Fersara's foal Ferzon, would grow up to found a dynasty for Gainey Arabians, then located in Minnesota.

Fadjur's dam, Bint Sahara, was the leading living female producer of champions for several years. His sire, Fadheilan, was the result of an unusual—for the times—cross of Henry Babson's straight Egyptian stallion *Fadl (Ibn Rabdan x Mahroussa) on the pure Polish mare *Kasztelanka (Koheilan I x Bialogrodka).

Born at the McCoys' ranch on April 12, 1952, Fadjur was actually bred by Harry Linden of Spokane, Washington. Frank McCoy had sold Bint Sahara to Linden a few years previously, but bought her back (in partnership) when she was carrying Fadjur.

But from the time he was 10 months old until his death in 1983 just before his 31st birthday, Fadjur was wholly Marge Tone's kindred spirit and loyal partner.

In fact, a Tone family joke revolved around a Valentine card Jack would give Marge every year showing a tear

Halter and Performance Record: Twice U.S. Reserve National Champion Stallion; Four times U.S. Top Ten Stallion.

Progeny Record:

Purebred Foal Crops: 29
Purebred Foals Registered: 820
U.S./Canadian National Winners: 18
Class A Champions: 118
IAHA Legion of Honor Award Winners: 3
IAHA Legion of Supreme Honor Award Winners: 2
IAHA Legion of Merit Award Winners: 11
IAHA Legion of Supreme Honor/Merit Award Winners: 1

Fadjur with his lifelong show-ring companion, Paul Polk, the son-in-law of owners Jack and Marjory Tone. Photo by Foucher

Marge Tone's favorite photo of her beloved Fadjur, taken at home while playing.   **Courtesy of Jack Tone Ranch**

corral, and I'd look out and he would be watching me in that window, knowing he was about to be fed first."

Marge Tone is justifiably proud that she rarely had to discipline Fadjur. "He didn't have a mean bone in his body," she explained. "I just believe we had a great communication between us. I would ask him to do something, and he seemed to understand and just do it.

"For instance, when a mare came to be bred, we would call Fadjur to the door and he would watch us prepare the mare. He did not have on a halter, or anything else on his head; he was a perfect gentleman. When we wrapped her tail, he knew it was time to get to business, and I would say, 'Go to your corner' and he would stand there while we washed him and removed his blanket. Then I told him to breed the mare. He would do so and then go right back to his corner to be cleaned up.

"I never trained him to do this, exactly—he just seemed to understand what I wanted him to do," she said. "I guess it just comes from being a special Arabian horse."

Fadjur successfully bred all his mares via live cover through age 30—his entire career—resulting in an impressive 820 purebred Arabian foals registered (and over 1,000 foals in total, counting his Half-Arabian offspring).

The only place Marge was not at Fadjur's side was in the show ring. The first to show him was V.F. Stull. Stull trained Fadjur for halter, winning his first reserve championship at age 3, and also showed the young horse in formal driving classes.

When Fadjur turned 4, the second most important human partnership in his life was formed. Marge's son-in-law, Paul Polk (daughter Jackie's husband), began to show Fadjur. Together, the two brought new excitement to arenas across the country as they used the stallion's innate desire to show off to claim the

running down his cheek as he played "second fiddle" to Fadjur. (Not much harm seems to have occurred, as the Tones were married for over 65 years and had five lovely daughters.)

Marge was involved in virtually every aspect of Fadjur's life, from breeding shed activities, to feeding, and then foaling out his sons and daughters.

"One of my fondest memories is of the early mornings on the ranch," she said. "I always got up first to grain the horses. I had a big window overlooking Fadjur's

Jack "Bud" Tone and Marjory F. Tone with Fadjur and his favorite mare, the wonderful broodmare Saki.
Courtesy of Jack Tone Ranch

judges' attention and press their advantage. The crowds loved it.

Fadjur's first big win came in 1956 with the Cow Palace and Pacific Coast Championship (the first of four). His last win was in 1975, when at age 23 he was named the 1975 Santa Barbara Show Champion Stallion, still with Polk at his head.

In between, Fadjur's accomplishments were extraordinary. He was twice named the U.S. Reserve National Champion Stallion, the second time at age 16 against 60 competitors. He was four times a U.S. Top Ten Stallion, and had twenty-eight halter championships. He was twice Region I Champion Stallion and was the Great Plains Champion Stallion at age 18. Twice, in 1967 and 1971, he won an IAHA popularity poll involving stallions from across the continent.

"One of my favorite memories of Fadjur is that he got a standing ovation wherever he went," said Kathleen Tone Hammer, another of Marge's daughters and the current manager (with husband Jerry) of the Jack Tone Ranch. "Even when people had

Marge Tone was responsible for virtually every aspect of Fadjur's daily life, from handling him in the breeding barn to delivering his sons and daughters.
Courtesy of Jack Tone Ranch

251

Fadjur gobbles up his traditional carrot cake on the occasion of his 19th birthday, April 12, 1971. Marge Tone is joined by just some of her grandchildren.

Courtesy of
Jack Tone Ranch

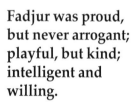

Fadjur was proud, but never arrogant; playful, but kind; intelligent and willing.

other stallions competing against him, they would find themselves standing and clapping for Fadjur! And they have often told us so. . . .

"Fadjur loved crowds," Kathleen continued. "He would prance and dance and arch that neck of his. . . ."

That "neck of his" and several other characteristics made Fadjur, well, Fadjur. His extremely arched neck carried a won-

derfully chiseled head, wide between large eyes, with prominent tear bones, a dished profile, fine skin, a small muzzle and a deep jowl. His legs were strong and true, his back was short, his full black tail was carried high, and his muscles rippled under a glowing bronzed coat.

Impossible to accurately describe, yet a characteristic nonetheless (and one often passed to his descendants) was his super disposition. Fadjur was proud, but never arrogant; playful, yet kind; intelligent and

252

This picture of Fadjur was taken when he was named the reserve national champion stallion at Estes Park, Colo., in 1960. Handler Paul Polk received the trophy from Burr Betts, a long-time Arabian breeder in Parker, Colorado.

Photo by Alexander

willing; and beloved and doted upon by both adults and children. Fadjur gave back as much love as was ever given to him.

"Marge's favorite picture is Fadjur at age 4, with a fuzzy winter coat," offered Kathleen. "You can almost see his big heart in the picture. It was always there, but you never could quite describe what it was really like. You had to experience it."

Marge Tone never planned to use Fadjur to launch a family of pretty, athletic horses who would—and still are—taking the horse show world by storm. But as if it was predestined, that is exactly what he and his descendants have done.

Up until his death, Fadjur enjoyed the title of one of the Leading Living Sires of Show Champions. And when he did die, his grandson, the famous Khemosabi (out of Jurneeka, by Fadjur), inherited and was still holding that title in his 30s.

In all, Fadjur sired 118 Class A or better champions, and 18 U.S. and Canadian National winners. But, as is often the case, he didn't do it alone, for he had Saki.

Saki (Ferseyn x Ferdia) was a little gray mare who became the equine love of Fadjur's life. Together, they had 14 foals, 12 of

Saki (Fersyn x Ferdia), a U.S. National Top Ten Halter Mare, is one of the best Arabian broodmares ever, and was inducted into the Arabian Horse Trust Hall of Fame in 1997. More than 100 Class A halter and performance championships were won by her 14 foals. All were by Fadjur, the last born when the gray mare was 26. Here she is ridden at age 7 in 1957 by Kathleen Tone Hammer.

Photo by
Carolyn Frisbey

whom were champions. She was never bred to any other stallion.

Until her death, Saki was the Leading Living Dam of Champions. Ironically, that title then eventually passed to her granddaughter, Amurath Kashmira, who was by Fadi (Fadjur x Saki). Kashmira's dam, incidentally, was the famous *Sanacht, who also rates a chapter in this book. (The

current titleholder, as of 1998, is TW Forteyna, who also claims a line to Fadjur.)

Marge spoke lovingly of Saki. "We didn't have much money and we were looking for a little horse for Kathleen. She had a big Quarter Horse who was hard to handle. I wanted a little mare for her.

"We found Saki in a little field close to our house. We fell so in love with her. She was the perfect little girl's horse," Marge recalled.

"Kathleen wanted a foal, so we bred her to Fadjur. But she was a working horse first. We did everything with her—gymkhana, pleasure. She was wonderful to show. She heard the announcer even before her rider did and did just what he said."

National Winners

Of Fadjur's 18 national winners, several stand out, including Canadian National Champion Stallion and U.S. National Reserve Champion Stallion Ibn Fadjur (x Saki); Canadian National Champion Mare Sakifa (x Saki); U.S. National Futurity Cutting Champion Surafad (x Suralee); U.S. National Champion Gelding Fadalan (x Fellany); U.S. National Stock Champion Fadloren (x Maaroudana); and multiple national title-holders Antonette (x Farzanah), Bint Fer Natta (x Fer Natta), Bint Saki (x Saki), Fad-Amir (x Bint Jeseyna), Khemosabi's dam Jurneeka (x Fadneeka), Marjanazem (x Suranazem), My Fadjurl (x Mis Saudi Arabia), and Zanntara (x Jureem).

Fadjur's better daughters include, of course, the famous Jurneeka, and also Bay Lady (x Sarma) dam of Litigator, the Canadian Reserve National Champion Stallion, and Accomplice, Canadian Top Ten Futurity Colt; Karelia (x Surima), dam of three national winners, and Bint Fer Natta and Zanntara, both just noted as national winners and also the dams of national winners.

Among Fadjur's better sons were the top-siring Fadi and Ibn Fadjur, both previously noted. Fadi was a halter and performance champion himself, and sired 10 national winners, mostly for his owner, Heritage Hills Arabians of Lake Geneva, Wisconsin. Hence, many bear the first name "Heritage" followed by second names such as Quite, Agneau, Aiglon, Eclat, Elegant, Nezblanc, and Paques.

Ibn Fadjur, although only 7 when he died, still managed to win five national titles for himself and sire another five national winners. A beautiful gray, Ibn Fadjur, like his father, was shown by Paul Polk.

Today, the Tones proudly stand Fadjurs

Fadjurs Hana (Fadjur x Mehanazem, by Fadjur) was the first mare Marge Tone produced by crossing Fadjur on his own daughters. She is one of Marge's favorite mares, and the reason she chose to continue an inbreeding program using Fadjur blood to perpetuate the "Look of Fadjur," as the Tone Ranch likes to say. Photo by M. Pope

Prize (Fadjur x Marjianazemtu, by Fadjur), as they continue their program of linebreeding Fadjur's bloodlines. They consider Prize to be Fadjur's most look-alike, act-alike son. He was 2 years old when Fadjur died.

"At first, no horse was allowed in Fadjur's corral," said Kathleen. "Marge said

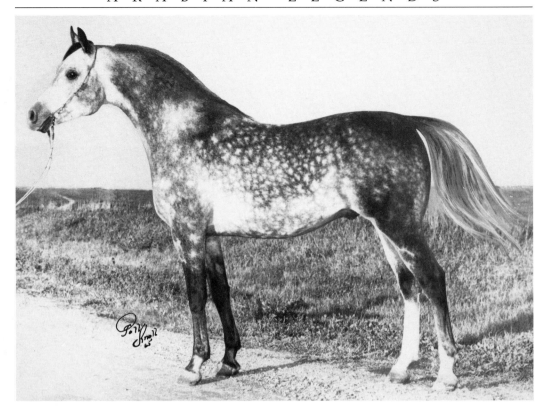

A 1965 photo of Fadi, Fadjur's top-siring son out of Saki. A halter and performance champion himself, he sired national winners, mainly for his owner, Heritage Hills Arabians of Lake Geneva, Wisconsin.

Photo by Polly Knoll

she couldn't stand it. Then, a month later, she said she couldn't stand to see it empty, and so Fadjurs Prize went there to live.

"We don't know if it is really possible, but it seems that, over time, he has picked up many of Fadjur's habits and characteristics just from living in that corral! We aren't saying he is Fadjur, but amazing things happen when he is presented. We've had people who knew Fadjur cry because they thought they'd never see him again, but, in Prize, they do. And we've had people start crying who say they never saw Fadjur, but now, through Prize, they have a chance to do so," concluded Kathleen.

Personal Favorites

Marge Tone's personal favorites among Fadjur's offspring are difficult to pinpoint. "I loved every single one of them," she stated emphatically. "For many years, I did all the foaling at the ranch. . . . I'm still present for every birth. In 1997, I even did one by myself, when everyone was gone. It was wonderful. For a few minutes, I forgot all the old aches and pains and just did what had to be done."

Still, when pressed, Marge will admit to special feelings for two Fadjur daughters,

Ibn Fadjur (Fadjur x Saki), here with Paul Polk, was the 1964 Canadian National Champion stallion, twice a Reserve National Champion Stallion (U.S. 1963, Canadian 1962), and twice U.S. National Top Ten Stallion (1964, 1965). He sired five national winners.

**Courtesy of
Jack Tone Ranch**

the in-bred Fadjurs Hana (x Bint Mehanazem, by Fadjur) and Frolik (x Saki). "If I had to do it over again, I would have started sooner breeding Fadjur back on his daughters," admitted Marge. She didn't begin that program until he was 18.

Fadjur managed to pluck the heartstrings of Arabian horse lovers both at home and around the world. Many were inspired to own Arabians because of him, while others were moved to strive for even greater accomplishments in their own programs.

Kathleen described the World Arabian Horse Organization convention held in San Francisco in 1976. "When the delegates were asked where they wanted to go and what they wanted to see while here in this country, they voted to see Fadjur. Six

busloads came to the farm. One breeder from Egypt, Dani Barbieri, said to my mother, 'I thought I bred the most beautiful Arabians in the world, but now I know that you do.'

"Also, one of Poland's breeding directors, Edward Skorkowski, who was here as a guest of Dr. Eugene LaCroix, asked to see Fadjur. Of course, we presented him and some of his offspring. Mr. Skorkowski

Fadjurs Prize (Fadjur x Marjianazemutu, by Fadjur) is considered by the Tone family to be Fadjur's most look-alike, act-alike, sire-alike son. Pictured here with Kathleen Tone Hammer at one of the ranch's regular horse management clinics-open barn parties, Fadjurs Prize lives in Fadjur's old corral.
Photo by. T. Sayles

stated that Fadjur didn't follow the rules of genetics, that he was amazed, because Fadjur's 'look' came through in every type: Kuhailan, Saklawi, etc.

"Another time a group of Russian breeders visited a ranch in Canada," Kathleen continued. "When Bint Saki was

brought out, they stood and took off their hats. The interpreter said they did so to show their respect to Fadjur and Saki. It was quite moving."

One Brazilian man, who attended another WAHO conference at which Marge also was present, wept when he realized he had just met "Mrs. Tone, who knew Fadjur so intimately."

When Lady Ann Lytton, daughter of the famous Lady Wentworth of Crabbet Stud in England, toured America, she asked specifically to visit Fadjur, and declared, "He is my favorite pin-up boy!"

Soon after the Prince of Morocco purchased a Fadjur daughter for his stables, he invited the Tones to spend a week in his country as his guests. They did so with great pleasure.

Kathleen chuckled as she related that one year at the Tones' regular open barn-clinic event, Don Ulmer, a top stock horse trainer, and a leading racing trainer stood together looking at Fadjur and marveling over his muscling, conformation, bone, hoofs, etc. Said the race horse trainer, "You know, if Fadjur was 10 years younger, I could make him race horse of the year."

"Oh, no," responded Ulmer. "If he were 10 years younger, he would be in my barn and he would be the national champion stock horse!"

Despite such international acclaim, Fadjur remained, in essence, the epitome of the family horse. One of Marge Tone's many grandchildren, Peggy Hammer Morrissey, fondly said, "My favorite memory is of Grannie serving Fadjur a dish of cut up carrots and apples with a giant candle in the middle on his birthday. We would take pictures and movies—Grannie treated him just like a human.

"One year, when I was 9 or 10, on Easter all 15 grandchildren were dressed in matching outfits for church and our egg hunt. We have treasured photos of all of us in our matching clothes with Fadjur on Easter Sunday.

"Through Fadjur," she continued, "our

The Tone family's life is centered on good Arabian horses. Here Jack and Marge Tone's granddaughter, Peggy Hammer Morrissey, wins a sidesaddle championship on the Fadjur son Sa-Fadjur, out of Saki.

Photo by Rick Osteen

family formed a special bond; he brought us closer together. So much of our lives revolved around him. Now, as an adult, I realize what an unusually wonderful childhood we all had, because of this horse."

But Fadjur meant the most to Marge Tone. "He was a gift," she said. "He was as human as any person. His personality and attitude were wonderful. I was so happy to go out and just do things with him. . . ."

". . . My father used to tell me stories about these wonderful horses when I was 5 years old, back in 1920. That was my first Arabian experience. Each night, some of my favorite stories were of the Arabian horses he had read about and seen in photos. He described to me how beautiful and special they were, told me they were very rare, and hoped I would be lucky enough to see one some day. I never imagined how that dream would come so true. And that a special Arabian horse would become one of the great loves of my life."

Fadjur is buried in a corner of his special corral.

He is the most beloved Arabian horse of his generation, and was a show ring superstar.

KHEMOSABI is a horse of the people, a star-spangled banner of the Arabian breed. Bright bay, with a distinctive blaze face and four snowy stockings, he is as flashy as a sequined drum major marching and twirling in an Independence Day parade.

When presented to an audience—and gracious sakes, how he loves a crowd—everyone from toddlers and teenagers to parents and grandparents whistle and shout and clap their hands as he arches his neck and dances to their ovation.

In his younger years, he was wonderful to ride, powerful, animated, feisty. Yet in his later years he lovingly tolerated school children swarming about his knees and face. Virtually every person who has ever met Khemosabi—and there have been thousands—has a heart-warming story to tell about the experience. Simply put, Khemosabi is the most beloved Arabian horse of his generation.

Khemosabi (pronounced Key-mo-sah-be) was a show ring superstar, winning U.S. national championships in both stallion halter (1973) and western pleasure (1976). He won the same two top awards in Canada (in 1976), the only stallion to date ever to win both a halter and a performance national championship in the same year (and, further, at the same national show). With a long list of other wins, as well, Khemosabi earned the highest IAHA lifetime achievement award offered, the Legion of Masters, which allows four "+" marks to follow his name. Only a handful of horses have done so.

Even more impressively, Khemosabi has passed on his show ring panache and his sweet disposition to an amazingly high percentage of his offspring. In all, he sired more than 1,200 registered purebred Arabians, of whom over 300 have won Arabian show ring championships in every event imaginable. Others excel in open competition in reining, dressage, jumping, cutting, and other cattle events. His descendants also were—and are—successful out-

The bright, flashy, charismatic Khemosabi was always a crowd favorite.   **Photo by Jerry Sparagowski**

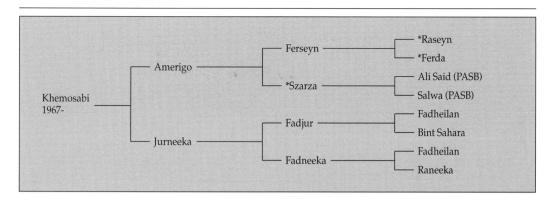

side the show ring in racing, endurance riding, and competitive trail riding.

For much of his adult life, Khemosabi has been the leading living sire of champions in the breed and remains the all-time leading sire of purebred offspring.

Although it somehow seems unlikely, one could argue that Khemosabi might have missed the train to fame if not for the belief and efforts of a gregarious California woman named Ruth Husband and her warm-hearted spouse and companion, Dr. Bert Husband. Khemo and the Husbands formed a bond, which has lasted throughout his lifetime of 30-plus years. Indeed, Ruth claims to have seen the stallion even before he was born.

On May 13, 1967, Ruth was having dinner after a horse show in Stockton, Calif., with 10 other well-known Arabian enthusiasts, including Sheila Varian, Jeff Wonnell, and Red and Bobbie Beyer. Suddenly, she recalled, "I saw a vision of what our mare Jurneeka's baby was going to look like. I saw him exactly: a mahogany bay horse with four high stockings and a broad blaze."

Ruth mentioned it to her companions, "and they all looked at me like I was crazy, but that was not unusual—I often do crazy things," she laughed. Her companions calmly continued their dinners.

Just a few hours later, at 2 a.m. on May 14, the phone rang in Ruth's hotel room. "It was way across the room, and I stumbled to it in the pitch dark and picked it up—my heart was racing," she said.

Dr. Bert was on the line and excitedly told Ruth that Jurneeka (the Husband family's multiple national award-winning mare) had just foaled—a birth witnessed by a small crowd of neighbors and the Husbands' three sons. "As he described the new little colt, shivers ran up my spine," Ruth recalled. "It was eerie. He was exactly as I had envisioned him hours

before—a bay with four high stockings and a blaze. It scared even me."

Right from the start Khemo loved an audience, and he seemed to prefer people to horses. "He was born loving people," said Ruth. "When we tried to take pictures of him, all we ever got was a nostril. He was right in your face, a tiny baby who just wanted to be loved."

Khemosabi grew healthy and strong at the Husbands' small ranch in Whittier, Calif., and soon it was time to make his show ring debut as a yearling. Oldest son Paul showed him first, in May 1968, and garnered a respectable third-place ribbon.

Then Dr. Bert took the yearling to the Santa Barbara show where they won Khemo's first blue ribbon. Ruth remembers the day well. "When the crowd started

Halter and Performance Record: Legion of Masters Award winner; 1973 U.S. National Champion Stallion; 1976 U.S. National Western Pleasure Champion; 1976 Canadian National Champion; 1976 Canadian National Western Pleasure Champion.

Progeny Record:

Purebred Foal Crops: 28
Purebred Foals Registered: 1,238
U.S./Canadian National Winners: 75
Class A Champions: 308
IAHA Legion of Honor Award Winners: 33
IAHA Legion of Supreme Honor Award Winners: 18
IAHA Legion of Excellence Award Winners: 5
IAHA Legion of Merit Award Winners: 18
IAHA Legion of Supreme Honor/Merit Award Winners: 4
IAHA Legion of Merit/Excellence Award Winners: 1
IAHA Legion of Supreme Merit Award Winners: 4
IAHA Legion of Masters Award Winners: 1
Race Starters: 3
Race Money Earned: $10,217

"It's as if Khemosabi's eyes are telling you, 'I like you ... let's be friends.' But a photo just doesn't capture what it's like to be with him," says Ruth Husband.   Photo by Javan

cheering, I thought they were cheering for Bert. He and Khemo were all over each other, as Khemo had not been trained to stand up properly at all. And I thought Bert was very brave and very cute. I still do. It never occurred to me that they were cheering for the horse. After all, he was just our backyard boy at the time. I was shocked when they won."

Dr. Bert wasn't. He believed in Khemosabi right from the start. "After we won, I rushed him into the trailer to get home because so many people wanted to buy him, and I was afraid I might just sell him," confessed Dr. Bert. That experience proved to be a mere trickle in the waters that would become a deluge of show ring ribbons and worldwide acclaim.

Why was he so good? While Khemosabi's pedigree is excellent, it is difficult to point to any single ancestor as the significant progenitor. Khemosabi was a product of the best of several bloodlines, a hybrid whose background was as all-American as many of its citizens. He seemed to have taken the genes of his parents and molded them into an animal better than both and somehow, uniquely, an entirely different being.

His sire, the gray Amerigo, was by the English Crabbet-bred Ferseyn. Through both his sire, *Raseyn, and dam, *Ferda, Ferseyn traced to the famous stocking-legged chestnut Mesaoud. Amerigo's

Amerigo, the sire of Khemosabi, was of English Crabbet and Polish breeding.

Photo by
Johnny Johnston

Khemosabi was a product of the best of several bloodlines.

dam, *Szarza, on the other hand, was pure Polish, with two lines to Kuhailan Said.

Trainer Jeff Wonnell showed Amerigo, and the pair won the 1967 U.S. National Stallion reserve championship. It was also Wonnell who handled the breeding of Jurneeka to Amerigo. One June day in 1966, while competing at the Oregon All-Arabian Show, Wonnell noticed that Jurneeka, who was in his show string along with Amerigo, was back in heat although she had earlier been bred to Amerigo. So that night, under cover of darkness on the fairgrounds' deserted racetrack, Wonnell bred the two horses.

"I remember looking around and wondering, 'Where on earth is Jurneeka? She's the love of my husband's life, and she's missing!'" Ruth recalled of that night. "Just then, into the show barn from out of the dark walks Jurneeka, with Jeff right behind leading Amerigo. I realized right away what was going on, and I said, 'No daughter of mine is get-

ting married without flowers!' So, I gave her some hay. The next morning, someone had stapled a rose to her door." This time Jurneeka stayed in foal.

Jurneeka, with U.S. National reserve championships in 1964 in both western and English pleasure, was the result of crossing a half-brother and half-sister, Fadjur and Fadneeka, who were both by the stallion Fadheilan. Fadheilan was by the "old Egyptian" sire *Fadl and out of the Polish mare *Kasztelanka. Fadjur's dam was the legendary mare Bint Sahara, who produced a dynasty for owner Frank McCoy.

Among the spectators when Khemosabi won that first blue ribbon at the Santa Barbara show were horse trainer Mo Morris and well-known breeder Sheila Varian. Morris would become Khemosabi's first professional handler, and Varian would launch his breeding career.

263

The Fadjur daughter Jurneeka was the dam of Khemosabi. She's shown here in a 1966 photo with Paul Husband in the saddle after winning an English pleasure class at a Spokane show. Jurneeka was a U.S. and Canadian Top Ten mare in halter and a U.S. reserve national champion in both English and western pleasure.

Curry-Cornett
Photography

Dr. Bert and Ruth Husband have always been Khemo's biggest fans. Ruth also managed the Khemosabi syndicate, and answered all of the horse's fan mail. Photo by Johnny Johnston

"We leased Khemosabi as a 2-year-old, feeling he was going to be a major sire," Varian said. The Husbands also took their mare Carinosa to be bred to Khemosabi at Varian's ranch.

A year later, by Khemo and out of the Bay-Abi daughters Bayanka, Bay Cinda, and Baychatka, were foaled Kaiyoum, Bay Sabha, and Moska. The latter two are Khemosabi's top-producing daughters. Moska continues to influence the Varian breeding program, now in its seventh generation. The Husbands' Carinosa that year produced the national-winning halter stallion Khari. Khemosabi was off to a flying start.

Show Career

Mo Morris was Khemosabi's first professional trainer. He started driving the colt at age 2 (but showed him at halter), and showed him again, in both performance and halter, when the stallion was 4 and 5 years old.

Gene LaCroix showed Khemosabi to his U.S. and Canadian national championships in western pleasure.

Photo by
Jerry Sparagowski

"He was one of those horses who learned his lessons the first time through, and you never had to teach him that skill again."

"The first time I showed him was in 1968 at a show in Salem, Ore.," Morris recalled. "The night before, he managed to wriggle out of his stall and went visiting—but no harm was done. The next day he was junior champion at halter, and then stood reserve show champion to the stallion Tornado, shown by Howie Kale.

"Khemosabi has been perfect since he was a baby," offered Morris. "He never went through an ugly growthy stage; he stayed proportionate and muscular throughout his life. And he still looks wonderful. I think you could hitch him up today and drive him off. He'd love it," Morris said in a 1997 interview.

"He was one of those horses who learned his lessons the first time through, and you never had to teach him that skill again. He had a good brain, he was a good student," added Morris. "He was a won-

derful halter horse—bright and animated, a real showoff. Later, we also won some fine harness. He could move very well, with power and flash. Khemo loved that, too, and was very good at it."

Ruth, who would become Khemosabi's biggest fan, continued to remain skeptical of Khemosabi's abilities for quite some time. "I guess I thought we were just lucky," she said. "Once early in Khemosabi's show career, at the Daffodil show in Washington, I had my faith tested. All day, the judge had been lining up in the middle those horses who won and placed, and had been excusing those left on the rail. In Khemosabi's class, he lined up his horses, turned in his card, and left Khemo on the rail! I thought, 'Oh, well, he probably isn't as good as we think.'

A 1994 photograph of Khemo when he was 27 years old.

Photo by Stuart Vesty

"Suddenly, a very large man came crashing down those rickety, noisy old bleachers and started yelling to the judge that he had 'left out the best horse!' and pointed at Khemo. Just then, the announcer started reading the judge's card and said, 'In first place, Khemosabi . . . .' The judge had just been playing with the crowd. The man was so embarrassed, but even he, a total stranger, was a believer. And I finally started to see Khemosabi's magic."

In 1969, horse trainer and commercial airline pilot Tom Bason, a friend of Ruth and Dr. Bert, was on leave from his flying job in Africa and stopped in at a horse show at San Francisco's Cow Palace to watch a few classes. Mo Morris spotted him and came up to say that Ruth was looking for Bason, and, in fact, wanted to offer him a job.

"You know it always amazes me," mused Bason, 30 years later, "that the most insignificant moments later turn out to be so very significant. I had a contract to fly in Africa for 2 more years, but I went down to the Husbands' place anyway to talk with Ruth and Bert. That's when I saw Khemosabi for the first time. I thought he was a really beautiful 2-year-old colt— and I wanted to show him—but I never dreamed that he would have the impact on my life that he had."

Bason went back to Africa and settled up with the airline company. Upon his

The Khemosabi son Khari (out of Carinosa) was named Canadian National Champion Stallion the same year, 1973, that Khemo won the U.S. national stallion championship.

Photo by Johnny Johnston

return, the Husbands leased a barn in Solvang and Bason became the full-time trainer for an illustrious show string that included Khemo.

"I gave Tom Bason the first few English lessons he ever had," said Paul Husband, chuckling. Paul, along with his parents, has always been deeply involved in Khemosabi's life. "Tom was a great cutting horse and western trainer, but not an English one.

"Khemosabi had a whole lot of trot and speed and power, and so he was shown quite a bit in English (by Bason) and fine harness (by Morris)," Paul continued. "He was a very good riding horse, and I rode him quite a few times myself. Gene LaCroix, who showed him western, had to work hard to get him to slow down for those classes."

The Solvang barn holds Bason's fondest memories of Khemosabi. "It's not the great things that happened with Khemosabi that I remember as being the best," Bason recalled, "but it was the quiet little moments I spent with him. I had fashioned an extra large stall for him, and kept a little red light on him at night so I could see him in the dark. Every night about 10 p.m. I checked the barn. I'd stand by his stall and just watch him. Slowly he would turn and walk over to me and nuzzle my face and neck and we'd just stand there for a long time. Those are my best memories."

In 1971, Dr. Bert became ill and the Husbands' horses were leased out. Bason went back to Africa, and Mo Morris started showing Khemosabi again. Eventually the stallion was leased to Dr. Dean Tolbert of Driftwood Arabian Horse Farm, Huntington, West Virginia.

The incredible Khemo son Khemanche, a gelding, has won three national halter championships, Top Ten in performance, 60 show championships, and a Legion of Masters award.

**Photo by
Jerry Sparagowski**

In 1972, Dr. Bert had recovered enough to attend a medical conference in Nairobi. Ruth joined him and tracked down Bason. "She asked if I'd please come home and start over," said Bason. "You know, I love the Husbands—all of them. I really do. So I came back."

With Khemosabi at Tolbert's place, Bason and Khemosabi mainly traveled the eastern show circuit, picking up championships in English pleasure and halter. "Khemosabi would get so high sometimes in halter," said Bason, "that when he stood there snorting, the air would just whistle, and even with his head way up, he would blow the arena dust right up around us."

One judge offered to give Bason time to calm down the horse before actually judging him, but, after many long minutes, finally gave up and awarded him the blue anyway.

"I'll never forget the 1972 Ohio Buckeye Show," said Bason. The Buckeye is one of the largest Arabian shows held each year. "The judge had been placing tall, lean Arabians—the opposite of Khemosabi. I went into the stallion class last, thinking we didn't have much of a shot, and that's when it happened. I still get choked up thinking about it. The audience started to scream and they all began to stand up— like a wave. I looked over at the judge, and he was standing there with his arm crossed and his hand on his chin, with this big smile on his face. And I knew we were okay."

Ruth recalled it, too. "The fans were screaming and cheering for Khemosabi like it was an appearance of the Beatles or something. It was really amazing. Yes, he did win, but you know, even when Khemo was young, even when no one knew who he was, audiences went nuts over him. He just had that certain, indescribable something— a presence. And he loved to show off."

Khemo's sons and daughters have excelled in a variety of events. This is Khemander Kody, U.S. National Champion Cutting Horse, shown here with owner Diane Dampsey.
Photo by Jeff Janson

For most of his life, in terms of conformation, Khemosabi was right on the money. He stood nearly 15 hands, and had a short back, strong, powerful hips, and a naturally high tail carriage. His neck was beautifully arched and his head featured wide-set eyes, a slightly dished profile, and a chiseled muzzle. Khemosabi's legs were straight, with perfectly sloped pasterns and plenty of muscle. He was built for both beauty and service, and despite the fact that he was shown heavily in several different divisions, Khemosabi remained perfectly sound throughout his career.

The bay stallion was soon ready for the big time, and, in the fall of 1972, was named U.S. Reserve National Champion Stallion. He then took the top spot in 1973.

"Khemosabi was showing wonderfully," Bason said as he recalled the 1973 U.S. National Show. "As I walked up to Don Burt (one of the stallion halter judges), he said, 'Just stand him up here. If he doesn't fall over dead, he's got it made.' I laughed. I couldn't believe he'd say that."

As an added bonus, that year Khemosabi's son Khari (out of the Husbands' mare Carinosa) was named Canadian National Champion Stallion.

Khemosabi was in big demand as a sire, but 1976 found him back on the national show track. The Canadian Nationals that

The 1997 Canadian National Champion Reining Horse was Khasino Royale, by Khemosabi. He was shown by Lee Mancini.

Photo by Ferrara

year was a huge show, with several eliminations before the finals. Explained Ruth, "Gene LaCroix would take Khemo and show him in western pleasure and work him and work him, and then he would hand him over to Tom to show in stallion halter. And then Tom would hand him back to Gene for another round in western pleasure.

"This went on for several days. Through it all, Khemo was full of sparkle and shine and that Khemo charisma. He never let down. Now, how many horses do you know who could win the top award that way in two different divisions?" (Author's note: None. Khemosabi is the only Arabian stallion ever to do it at one national show in one year.)

Bason added, "Gene (LaCroix) was showing a different horse in stallion halter, and was actually competing against me there. But both he and Ray (LaCroix's brother) helped me out in so many ways. When Khemosabi was named national champion stallion, Gene walked right over in the ring, right there in the class, and shook my hand. He said, 'Tom, this is the way it should be.' I'll never forget that."

In 1977, Khemosabi was retired to stud at the Pereira Ranch in Santa Ynez, California. "Those were the fun years," offered Ruth. "We've never enjoyed life like we did when Khemosabi was up there. On the weekends, we would drive up—Bert loved it so—and all the way up he would be debating with himself: 'Should I ride him first or drive him?' You know, Khemosabi was a very good driving horse. Bert would hitch him up and they would drive everywhere—and I mean everywhere. Then, they would come back and Bert would saddle him up and they would just disappear. It really was Bert's happiest time."

Mike Villasenor also had Khemosabi at his Nabers-Villasenor ranch in southern California for several years. There, as everywhere, the stallion continued to spread his magic.

The Husbands have always had fun with Khemosabi. As part of his promotional campaign, son Paul came up with the idea for a comic strip based on the popular "The Lone Ranger" television series. Illustrated by Karen Haus Grandpre, an artist for Hanna-Barbera Productions, the storyline featured the brave young stallion fighting evil with the help of "Ruth, his faithful red-haired companion." It played to rave reviews and many laughs in the major Arabian magazines of the 1970s and 1980s.

During public presentations, the well-known *William Tell Overture* became Khemosabi's theme. As the first few notes came blasting over the loudspeakers, the stallion invariably raised his tail and began dancing in place, playing the crowd for all he was worth. He was the star, and he knew it.

Horse trainer Doug Dahmen found that out the hard way one February night in 1985. Khemosabi, who had been kept close to home for several years, was nevertheless invited to that year's Star World Show in Scottsdale, as part of a parade of great stallions. Dahmen, positioned out in the warm-up ring, tried to hold back Khemo as the opening bars of the famous music thundered through the big-top tent. A freight train could not have stopped the 18-year-old stallion, and Khemosabi bounded into the ring with Dahmen hanging on for dear life. The spectators, who numbered in the thousands, were, after all, his people and he—Khemosabi—was the star of the show!

Khemosabi settled into life as one of the breed's most popular sires as if he knew that this was the reason for which he was born. At the height of his career, he bred 200 mares in one year, and, through 1997, at age 30, he continued to enthusiastically go about his business.

Khat, another Khemo son, has six national titles in halter, English pleasure, and driving divisions. He was ridden and shown by Stanley White. Photo by Rob Hess

Offspring

At the national level, 75 sons and daughters have national awards. Further, 55 of his daughters and 22 of his sons have gone on to produce and sire national winners (through 1997).

Khemosabi is best known for passing on his distinctive color and markings,

Another of Khemo's offspring, Ka-Li-Ga, ridden by owner Debra Johnson, has 71 championships and 20 national titles in English sidesaddle, country English pleasure AOTR, and show hack.

Photo by Rob Hess

soundness and athleticism, and a sweet, kind disposition. Although space limits preclude a complete list of superior individuals he has sired, among his best offspring are: Khari, his first-born son mentioned earlier; GS Khochise, who has won more national titles (36) than any other horse in history; Khemanche, who shares with his sire a rare Legion of Masters achievement award and "made people groan when we took him in the arena, we won so much," laughed Ruth; Khara Mia and Kharinosa; Rho Keem and Rho Sabee; Khemander Kody, a national champion cutting horse; Kaiyoum, bred by Varian; Kharino, a champion field hunter; the lovely halter mare GA Honisuckl Rose; and the list goes on and on.

Over the years, as one might imagine, the Husbands were offered a king's ransom for Khemosabi. But as Dr. Bert often said, "Anybody can have a million dollars. Only we have Khemosabi." In 1981, however, the family did decide to syndicate him, and sold 126 shares to 76 owners.

Ruth, of course, has always been the syndicate manager. In addition to overseeing Khemosabi's care, communicating with shareholders, promoting and marketing his offspring, and various financial matters, Ruth has become the stallion's personal social secretary as well.

"Sometimes I think I've spent my life answering fan mail," she said with a broad smile. "I answer every single one we receive. I always have." Then she continued, tongue firmly in cheek, "It is my sworn duty; I am his handmaiden."

As the most popular Arabian stallion in America, Khemosabi has received thousands of letters and visitors over the years. "We get letters now from parents who want pictures and a letter from Khemo for their kids because they had a letter and picture tacked up on their bedroom walls when they were kids—it meant so much to them," said Ruth. "Others write to request a visit as a birthday or anniversary gift. They just want to see him and touch him. One man, a groom on the East Coast, saved his money for years in order to come and see Khemo. He finally flew in, and we took him to the ranch. He stayed

272

Kharino, a full brother to the Khemosabi son Khari, is an exceptional hunter. Among other awards he has won the Field Master's Plate, a perpetual trophy of the Los Altos (Calif.) Hounds Hunter Trials. He's shown here with owner Susan Gerber up.

with Khemosabi, literally, for 2 full days. Then he flew back to his wife and family. It was his dream come true."

Both paupers and princes have loved Khemosabi. Ruth Husband recalled a visit from Princess Alia of Jordan. "She just stood and scratched him out in the pasture for a long, long time. Then she sat right down in the grass, and he ate all around her and nuzzled her. She just sat there. I was having a heart attack and was so worried, but Khemosabi really liked her and they had a wonderful time."

Among his other royal fans have been the Earl and Countess of Pembroke; the Countess of Rutland; the King of Morocco, who owns a Khemosabi daughter; and the chairman of South Korea, who also has a Khemo daughter—to name just a few.

World-famous artist LeRoy Neiman did two pages of Khemosabi sketches and paintings in his famous book—"unheard of, for him, as you know," added Ruth. "And speaking of all over, there are Khemosabi paintings and artwork everywhere! On dishes and pins, purses and

briefcases, tack trunks, and all sorts of memorabilia. It's astounding. We were driving along one day and a van passed us that had Khemosabi painted on its spare-tire cover! His image has become so popular with so many different people."

Still, many stallions are beautiful, sire wonderful offspring, and even love to ham it up for an audience. So, what is it, exactly, that makes Khemosabi so extraordinary?

"It is his eyes," answered Ruth. "He talks to you with his eyes. He tells you he likes you, very much, with his eyes. When you make that connection with him, it is a special moment in time. You know, I have experienced it many times, but later I can't remember it exactly. Isn't that weird? I can't describe it and photographs have never captured it. Yet many people have experienced it and have told us so."

In February 1997, during the annual Scottsdale Arabian Horse Show, Khemosabi at age 30 was inducted into the very

GA Hunisuckl Rose, a Khemo daughter who is a Canadian National Champion Mare and a U.S. Reserve National Champion Mare.

Photo by Diana Duer

first Arabian Horse Trust Hall of Fame. He was the only living horse to be so honored.

As Khemosabi entered the ring the final night of that show, with Paul Husband gripping the lead line and grinning ear-to-ear, there wasn't a dry eye in the place. Some of the thousands in attendance had flown into Scottsdale for this moment alone. Then, as he always has, Khemosabi pranced and danced for his cheering fans as the strains of the *William Tell Overture* filled the desert night air. He continued to preen as those people who had been a significant part of his life were introduced by veteran show announcer Harry Cooper. When he and Paul finally exited the ring, to a thunderous standing ovation, those present knew they had witnessed one of the greatest moments—and greatest stallions—in Arabian horse history.

As this book went to press, Khemosabi had celebrated his 32nd birthday and was living happily at Rancho Valle Del Sol,

GS Khochise, a Khemo son, has more national titles—36 through mid-1997—than any other Arabian horse in history. He is owned and shown by Betty Chapman, Puyallup, Washington.

Photo by Jeff Little

Bonsall, Calif., with Laura Cronk, the ranch manager and another of his great friends. His stall overlooks Cronk's office, and, as she says, "He loves to stand there and listen to me talking on the phone—and he's laughing at me. I know it!

"In fact, if he were a human being, he would be like George Burns, sitting on the couch, surrounded by beautiful women, telling stories and making people laugh. I think the main reason for his longevity is that by giving love, he is loved in return—surrounded by the love of so many people—and he thrives on that love," added Cronk.

Perhaps Ruth Husband summed it up best. "I believe the Lord sent Khemosabi to us, all of us," she stated, with firm conviction. "He has meant so much to so many people, and has brought great joy to this world."

AUTHOR PROFILE

MARIAN KAYE STUDER CARPENTER mounted—and often abruptly dismounted—her first ponies at age 4 on her grandfather's farm in southern Minnesota. There, too, she read Marguerite Henry's *King of the Wind* and galloped bareback across alfalfa fields on an assortment of Half-Arabian horses. The first horse she actually owned was York, a big-hearted chestnut three-quarter-Arabian gelding who was a gift from her grandfather. As a teenager, Marian often rode Quarter Horses with her uncle, Bill Orthel, and developed a life-long interest in cutting and other working western horse activities.

After graduating summa cum laude with a bachelor's degree in mass communications, Marian worked as a daily newspaper reporter. In early 1984, she joined the *Arabian Horse Times* magazine staff, eventually serving as its editor. Nearly 5 years later she became promotional director for The Pyramid Society, an Egyptian Arabian horse breeders group, and moved to Kentucky.

For the past several years, she has been a freelance writer who carves computer time from days jam-packed with the responsibilities of a small farm owner, 4-H horse club leader, and—most importantly—family member, with husband Gary Carpenter and four young daughters: Rachel, Abigail, Blair, and Emily. The Carpenter family lives near Carlisle, Kentucky.

*Marian with the Arabian mare Saava (#284800, better known as Sahara), who is owned and loved by Marian's friend Anne Wolff. Sahara's distinctive pedigree includes direct lines to the Egyptian stallion Nazeer, the English Crabbet horses *Raseyn and *Raffles, the Polish mare *Chloe, and, incredibly, the first horse registered in the Arabian Horse Registry of America, the mare *Nedjme #1.*

Photo by Dennis Hinckle Photography

REFERENCES

The following materials were among those used for reference for this book:

*And Miles to Go, The Biography of a Great Arabian Horse, *Witez II*, by Linell Smith. (See Arabian Horse Trust, publisher.)

Ansata Ibn Halima—The Gift, by Judith Forbis. (All Forbis books available through The Pyramid Society or Arabian Horse Trust.)

Arabian Finish Line magazine, RR 1, Box 623, Micanopy, FL 32667; 352-591-0571.

Arabian Horse Times magazine, Walter Mishek, publisher, 1050 8th St. NE, Waseca, MN 56093; 507-835-3204.

Arabian Horse World magazine, Denise Hearst, publisher, 1316 Tamson, Suite 101, Cambria, CA 93428; 805-927-6511.

Arabian Horse Journal magazine. (Out of print.)

Arabian Horse News magazine. (Out of print.)

Arabian Jockey Club, Corky Parker, executive director, 12000 Zuni St., Westminster, CO 80234; 303-450-4714.

Arabian Horse Registry of America, 12000 Zuni St., Westminster, CO 80234; 303-450-4748.

Arabian Horse Trust, 12000 Zuni St., Westminster, CO 80234; 303-450-4710.

Authentic Arabian Bloodstock, by Judith Forbis.

Crabbet Influence magazine, Georgia Cheer, publisher, Silver Monarch Publishing, Box 188, Battle Ground, WA 98604-0188; 360-687-1600.

Gainey Arabians, video and Pioneer Scrapbook, Arabian Horse Trust. (All Arabian Horse Trust videos and scrapbooks are produced by and available through the Trust.)

International Arabian Horse Association, 10805 E. Bethany Dr., Aurora, CO 80014; 303-696-4500.

Jimmy & Thelma Dean, video and Pioneer Scrapbook, Arabian Horse Trust.

Knoll, Polly—writer/photographer, Box 555, Beaver Dam, WI 53916; 920-885-4146.

Lasma In Retrospect. (Out of print.)

Magid, Arlene—writer/researcher, 2014 Cherokee Pkwy, Apt. L, Louisville, KY 40204; 502-451-7420.

McCoy's Arabians, video and Pioneer Scrapbook, Arabian Horse Trust.

Parkinson, Mary Jane—writer/researcher. (Please see *Arabian Horse World.)*

Reference Handbooks of Straight Egyptian Horses, All Volumes. (Available through The Pyramid Society.)

Results, Inc., Christy Egan, owner, 303-258-3336.

Sparagowski, Jerry—photographer/resource, 1702 Turtle Rock Court, Carrollton, TX 75007; 972-242-2599.

Tersk Heritage. (Out of print.)

The Arabian Horse: From War Horse to Show Horse, by Gladys Brown Edwards. (Available from Arabian Horse Trust.)

The Arabian Horse Through History, by Judith Forbis and Dr. Eugene LaCroix. (Available through Arabian Horse Trust.)

The Classic Arabian Horse, by Judith Forbis.

The Kellogg Arabians, by H.H. Reese. (Out of print.)

The Kellogg Arabian Horses, by Mary Jane Parkinson. (Contact *Arabian Horse World.)*

The Marshalls of Gleannloch Farms, video and Pioneer Scrapbook, Arabian Horse Trust.

The Pyramid Society, 4067 Ironworks Pike, Lexington, KY 40511; 606-231-0771.

West (Lauter), Jo—writer/reseacher, Box 773632; Steamboat Springs, CO 80477; 970-879-7106.

W.K. Kellogg Arabian Horse Library, Cal-Poly University, 3801 W. Temple Ave., Pomona, CA 91768-4080; 909-869-3081.

W.K. Kellogg, video and Pioneer Scrapbook, Arabian Horse Trust.

PHOTO INDEX

The *Western Horseman*, established in 1936, is the world's leading horse publication. For subscription information: 800-877-5278. To order other *Western Horseman* books: 800-874-6774. *Western Horseman*, Box 7980, Colorado Springs, CO 80933-7980. Web-site: **www.westernhorseman.com**.

Books Published by Western Horseman Inc.

ARABIAN LEGENDS by Marian K. Carpenter
280 pages and 319 photographs. Abu Farwa, *Aladdinn, *Ansata Ibn Halima, *Bask, Bay-Abi, Bay El Bey, Bint Sahara, Fadjur, Ferzon, Indraff, Khemosabi, *Morafic, *Muscat, *Naborr, *Padron, *Raffles, *Raseyn, *Sakr, Samtyr, *Sanacht, *Serafix, Skorage, *Witez II, Xenophonn.

BACON & BEANS by Stella Hughes
144 pages and 200-plus recipes for delicious western chow.

BARREL RACING, Completely Revised by Sharon Camarillo
128 pages, 158 photographs, and 17 illustrations. Teaches foundation horsemanship and barrel racing skills for horse and rider, with additional tips on feeding, hauling, and winning.

CALF ROPING by Roy Cooper
144 pages and 280 photographs covering roping and tying.

CUTTING by Leon Harrel
144 pages and 200 photographs. Complete guide on this popular sport.

FIRST HORSE by Fran Devereux Smith
176 pages, 160 black-and-white photos, about 40 illustrations. Step-by-step information for the first-time horse owner and/or novice rider.

HORSEMAN'S SCRAPBOOK by Randy Steffen
144 pages and 250 illustrations. A collection of handy hints.

IMPRINT TRAINING by Robert M. Miller, D.V.M.
144 pages and 250 photographs. Learn to "program" newborn foals.

LEGENDS by Diane C. Simmons
168 pages and 214 photographs. Barbra B, Bert, Chicaro Bill, Cowboy P-12, Depth Charge (TB), Doc Bar, Go Man Go, Hard Twist, Hollywood Gold, Joe Hancock, Joe Reed P-3, Joe Reed II, King P-234, King Fritz, Leo, Peppy, Plaudit, Poco Bueno, Poco Tivio, Queenie, Quick M Silver, Shue Fly, Star Duster, Three Bars (TB), Top Deck (TB), and Wimpy P-1.

LEGENDS 2 by Jim Goodhue, Frank Holmes, Phil Livingston, Diane C. Simmons
192 pages and 224 photographs. Clabber, Driftwood, Easy Jet, Grey Badger II, Jessie James, Jet Deck, Joe Bailey P-4 (Gonzales), Joe Bailey (Weatherford), King's Pistol, Lena's Bar, Lightning Bar, Lucky Blanton, Midnight, Midnight Jr, Moon Deck, My Texas Dandy, Oklahoma Star, Oklahoma Star Jr., Peter McCue, Rocket Bar (TB), Skipper W, Sugar Bars, and Traveler.

LEGENDS 3 by Jim Goodhue, Frank Holmes, Diane Ciarloni, Kim Guenther, Larry Thornton, Betsy Lynch
208 pages and 196 photographs. Flying Bob, Hollywood Jac 86, Jackstraw (TB), Maddon's Bright Eyes, Mr Gun Smoke, Old Sorrel, Piggin String (TB), Poco Lena, Poco Pine, Poco Dell, Question Mark, Quo Vadis, Royal King, Showdown, Steel Dust, and Two Eyed Jack.

LEGENDS 4
Several authors chronicle the great Quarter Horses Zantanon, Ed Echols, Zan Parr Bar, Blondy's Dude, Diamonds Sparkle, Woven Web/Miss Princess, Miss Bank, Rebel Cause, Tonto Bars Hank, Harlan, Lady Bug's Moon, Dash For Cash, Vandy, Impressive, Fillinic, Zippo Pine Bar, and Doc O' Lena.

LEGENDS 5 by Frank Holmes, Ty Wyant, Alan Gold, and Sally Harrison
The stories of Little Joe, Joe Moore, Monita, Bill Cody, Joe Cody, Topsail Cody, Pretty Buck, Pat Star Jr., Skipa Star, Hank H, Chubby, Bartender, Leo San, Custus Rastus (TB), Jaguar, Jackie Bee, Chicado V, and Mr Bar None fill 248 pages, including about 300 photographs.

PROBLEM-SOLVING by Marty Marten
248 pages and over 250 photos and illustrations. How to develop a willing partnership between horse and human to handle trailer-loading, hard-to-catch, barn-sour, spooking, water-crossing, herd-bound and pull-back problems.

NATURAL HORSE-MAN-SHIP by Pat Parelli
224 pages and 275 photographs. Parelli's six keys to a natural horse-human relationship.

REINING, Completely Revised by Al Dunning
216 pages and over 300 photographs showing how to train horses for this exciting event.

RODEO LEGENDS by Gavin Ehringer
Photos and life stories fill 216 pages. Included are: Joe Alexander, Jake Barnes & Clay O'Brien Cooper, Joe Beaver, Leo Camarillo, Roy Cooper, Tom Ferguson, Bruce Ford, Marvin Garrett, Don Gay, Tuff Hedeman, Charmayne James, Bill Linderman, Larry Mahan, Ty Murray, Dean Oliver, Jim Shoulders, Casey Tibbs, Harry Tompkins, and Fred Whitfield.

ROOFS AND RAILS by Gavin Ehringer
144 pages, 128 black-and-white photographs plus drawings, charts, and floor plans. How to plan and build your ideal horse facility.

STARTING COLTS by Mike Kevil
168 pages and 400 photographs. Step-by-step process in starting colts.

THE HANK WIESCAMP STORY by Frank Holmes
208 pages and over 260 photographs. The biography of the legendary breeder of Quarter Horses, Appaloosas, and Paints.

TEAM PENNING by Phil Livingston
144 pages and 200 photographs. How to compete in this popular family sport.

TEAM ROPING WITH JAKE AND CLAY by Fran Devereux Smith
224 pages and over 200 photographs and illustrations. Learn about fast times from champions Jake Barnes and Clay O'Brien Cooper. Solid information about handling a rope, roping dummies, and heading and heeling for practice and in competition. Also sound advice about rope horses, roping steers, gear, and horsemanship.

WELL-SHOD by Don Baskins
160 pages, 300 black-and-white photos and illustrations. A horse-shoeing guide for owners and farriers. The easy-to-read text, illustrations, and photos show step-by-step how to trim and shoe a horse for a variety of uses. Special attention is paid to corrective shoeing techniques for horses with various foot and leg problems.

WESTERN HORSEMANSHIP by Richard Shrake
144 pages and 150 photographs. Complete guide to riding western horse

WESTERN TRAINING by Jack Brainard
With Peter Phinny. 136 pages. Stresses the foundation for western training.

WIN WITH BOB AVILA by Juli S. Thorson
This 128-page, hardbound, full-color book discusses traits that separate horse-world achievers from also-rans. World champion horseman Bob Avila shares his philosophies on succeeding as a competitor, breeder, and trainer.